CS

OF

MARITIME TRANSPORT

THEORY AND PRACTICE

Books in the same series:

Port Agency
Shipbroking and Chartering Practice

British Library Cataloguing in Publication Data
McConville, James
Economics of Maritime Transport, Theory and Practice
1. Title.
ISBN 1 85609 162 7

ECONOMICS

OF

MARITIME TRANSPORT

Theory and Practice

by

JAMES McCONVILLE

London School of Foreign Trade Professor, and Director
of Centre for International Transport Management
London Guildhall University

LONDON
WITHERBY & CO LTD
32-36 Aylesbury Street
London EC1R 0ET

Published for the Institute of Chartered Shipbrokers

First Published 1999

WITHERBY

PUBLISHERS

© James McConville
1999

ISBN 1 85609 162 7

Published and Printed by:
Witherby & Co. Ltd
32-36 Aylesbury Street
London EC1R 0ET

Tel: 0171 251 5341
Fax: 0171 251 1296
International Tel: +44 171 251 5341
International Fax: +44 171 251 1296

FOREWORD

The Institute of Chartered Shipbrokers is charged under its Royal Charter with the dissemination of knowledge, the maintenance of standards, and the provision of a professional qualification. In the dynamic field of international trade and shipping business this is a challenging task.

The Institute has members and students in some 70 countries involved in all aspects of shipping, and its professional qualification is recognised worldwide.

The professional needs to have an understanding of the business environment in which he or she operates. It is also essential to have the ability to analyse the commercial implications of their and others actions as well as the capacity to cope with change.

It is in this context that The Institute made the decision to publish a series of shipping business text books. These combine both theory and practice, and intend to serve the practitioners within the mainstream of shipping business as well as students at college and university and those studying for professional examinations.

The authors contributing to the series are all experienced practitioners in their specific area of shipping business. Therefore in the increasingly pressured sphere of international seaborne trade this series of text books on the major disciplines within maritime commerce make a wide range of expertise accessible to those whose business is, or will be, shipping.

ACKNOWLEDGEMENTS

No book can be the product of any individual, a truism especially apt in the present case. Therefore, it is with particular pleasure, on completing this volume, to be able to acknowledge numerous and substantial institutional and personal debts. Generally, may I express here my gratitude to past and present students, university colleagues, and friends for their many suggestions and constructive criticisms for improving the contents and structure of this volume. In particular for the assistance in preparing the apparently endless drafts. Thanks are due to D. Quinlan, who brought order out of chaos, and prepared all the tables and figures, R. Greenhill for his unstinting support throughout the long gestation period, J. Crilley for supplying extremely useful information, J. Lipczynski, D. Glen and H. Leggate who appraised the entire manuscript and made a wealth of corrections and suggestions largely incorporated into the text. The latter also made a number of useful criticisms of the earlier drafts. Their influence is evident in many places. Finally, to express gratitude for the generous support of B. Fletcher who encouraged the author to write this work. For all the above kindness, my sincere thanks. However, I did not always heed the good advice offered. As will be discovered, the adventure of such writing has lead not only to inelegance of expression, but to errors and omissions. The responsibility for these is claimed in the time honoured fashion to be entirely mine.

J. McConville
London Guildhall University
January 1999.

THE PREFACE

The contemporary development of the international maritime transport industry has been accompanied by the emergence of maritime economics as a major area of analysis, both in terms of theory and empirical research. The primary purpose of this book is to demonstrate how this analysis can be applied to the complex problems of the industry.

The objective of writing this book is to fulfil a long-felt need for a book which is relevant to the problems and the institutional setting of the maritime industry. There exists a conspicuous dearth of books on this subject. The writing stems originally from working within the industry, and subsequent lectures and seminars to undergraduates, graduates and students on professional courses. While rigorously shaping the book's design to meet the need of the prospective reader, a comprehensive structure has been opted for and it is virtually self-contained in that it presents all the basic definitions, concepts, principles and theories which are generally associated with maritime economics. The proposal here is twofold. First, to distil from the concepts of economic theory those elements which are of importance for understanding the functioning and economic problems of the maritime industry. This is achieved by presenting most of the theoretical material within a basic analytical framework, supported by simple graphs and numerical and mathematical examples. Secondly, theory is perceived as an attempt to explain how particular observations or events are relevant to one another. Without theory, what is left is a complex mass of meaningless facts. It follows, logically, that observations and sound theory are linked together. In this text, an attempt has been made to relate research and theory to what is happening within the industry that is, in the real world.

Questions are often posed by students as to whether or not maritime economics is worthy of study, for most would agree that it is a subject not without difficulties, requiring, as it does, considerable energy and thought. This question can be responded to in a number of ways. Firstly, for individuals at a stage on the road to a successful career within the industry, are sitting undergraduate and professional exams, particularly those of the Institute of Chartered Shipbrokers, which include papers on the subject. Secondly, any responsible person working within the industry should be aware and be able to understand and interpret the contemporary economic problems and relate them to the maritime industry. For example, the growth over time, of seaborne trade in certain geographic regions, or the impact of a sudden event like a major disaster, such as an earthquake. In other words, it is a useful method of interpreting, and, perhaps solving some of the numerous problems which the industry is continually confronted. Thirdly, and some would say the primary reason, is that economics, and specifically maritime economics, is a 'technique of thinking.' This is to argue that this subject is one which has its own particular intellectual reward. It is a method of thinking in a logical and analytical way in expressing the outcome simply and precisely. Having said all that, perhaps the best reason for toiling in the fields of Maritime Economics, is that it is interesting, exciting and stimulating to study.

The main task for maritime economics is to provide an understanding on the basis of international seaborne trade, in which shipping is a crucial factor. In analysing these activities, maritime economics has to concern itself with the use of scarce resources in three ways. Firstly, the way in which these resources have been allocated; secondly, the degree of utilisation; and, finally, their growth over time. This has been done within the basic framework of the industry's operational and institutional structure. It is around the resource allocation problem that the present volume has been organised, all of which involves the examination of the analytical characteristics of the industry. The volume is structured in three parts. Firstly, a broad introduction. Secondly, the basic economic concepts which determines the construction of various sectors and markets and the method used to allocate resources in them. These are used, in the third section, in the process of analysing the economic, physical and structural characteristics of the industrial sectors, their conduct and purpose. This is largely done on the basis of their development, and the evaluation of the market conditions under which they function. That is to say, applying economics to the way in which the complex maritime system works.

CONTENTS

Part I INTRODUCTION

Chapter One

INTRODUCTION

"But yet the 'transport' industries, which undertake nothing more than the mere movement of persons and things from one place to another, have constituted one of the most important activities of men in every stage of advanced civilisation."[1] There is a temptation here to modify Marshall's quote, to 'maritime transport' for there can be little doubt that it does constitute 'one of the most important activities of man' for it creates economic value in conveying goods and people from one port to another. In an international economy, no country is self-sufficient in the commodities that its population needs and expects. Consequently small coasters, huge tankers and liners every day move millions of tons of cargo, ranging from coffee, fruit juice and tea to the latest computer or cars. These are some of the realities of the industry and the purpose of this volume is to apply basic economic analysis to these realities.

The aim here is to answer questions of maritime economics about such things as freight rates, market structures and international sea-borne trade. Since there are no specific economic tools for the Maritime Industry, traditional economic theory and analysis has been applied to shipping and maritime problems. These basic economic tools can assist in attempting to solve a wide range of problems which an industry as large and complex as shipping generate.

The industry is engaged in the production of water-borne transport of goods and people. This is a service, an intangible non-material economic good, produced for the benefit of industry and consumers. Such economic goods satisfy some human want, and are scarce in relation to the use to which they are put. These characteristics give them value.

The shipping industry can be defined as a group of individual industries or sectors operating within different markets and reacting to different economic conditions. Some sectors are capable of operating at the margin of others, as for example, the role of a conventional cargo liner being taken by dry cargo tramp tonnage. At the other extreme, sectors have nothing in common for example, cruise liners and the bulk crude oil tanker. The Rochdale Committee defined the industry thus: 'Shipping is a complex industry and the conditions which govern its operations in one sector do not necessarily apply in another; it might even, for some purposes, be better regarded as a group of related industries. Its main assets, the ships themselves, vary widely in size and type. They provide the whole range of services which are needed to transport passengers and a great variety of goods, whether over shorter or longer distances. Although one can, for analytical purposes, usefully isolate sectors of the industry providing particular types of service, there is usually some interchange at the margin which cannot be ignored'.[2] In this text, the shipping industry will be seen as a diverse group of industries or sectors and, together with the equally complex port industry, will be termed Maritime Transport.

The primary economic function of maritime transport services is, like all transport, to bridge the gap which exists between producer and consumer. Producers are the individuals or organisations which supply goods or perform services. The consumers are those seeking satisfaction from such goods or services and have the financial ability to pay for it. Consumers can either demand goods or services for their own personal satisfaction, for example, cruise passengers, or consumers demanding goods and services as part of the production process, creating other goods or services. The vast majority of ships' cargoes falls into the latter category. The producer consumer gap has two interacting aspects, that of geographical space and time. Space, in this context, refers to the physical distance; the size of the gap. Time indicates how long it takes to cross the gap. There are, therefore, two obvious measures of this gap, that is, the distance in terms of nautical miles, and that of time in terms of months, weeks, days or hours. From an economic point of view, such measures are of little relevance, as they can be combined in a single concept of cost or resource cost per unit of time. The concept of cost not only unites and submerges the measures of distance and travel time, but introduces the additional criteria, of efficiency. Economic efficiency relates to the value of output per unit of time at minimum cost of resources employed. Such criteria can be related to the size of the gap. If the gap is small or decreasing, costs are small and decreasing and it is, therefore, being bridged efficiently. If the gap is wide, costs will be high and it will be bridged less efficiently, all things being equal.

This book studies the economic criteria in conveying goods across the maritime transport gap, the sea, using the most efficient methods available to do so. The method of achieving this is to analyse the economic criteria which motivates the behaviour of the supplier of the ship and the port services owners and operators and their interaction with the demands of consumers that is, charterers, shippers and passengers. Those interested in maritime economics will be pre-occupied with the massive amount of scarce resources which the industry consumes in its provision of services to satisfy human wants. They will also be interested in any decision or change having an effect on the volume of resource allocation to the industry and the wider economy.

Wants and Resources

The maritime economic system can be seen as a set of institutional arrangements. Its function is to employ productive resources most efficiently to satisfy the process of seaborne trade in all its aspects. It follows that the basic concern of maritime economics is the vast amount of scarce resources used in the provision of shipping services to satisfy human wants. Here, within the maritime context, is what many see as the central economic problem, that of aggregate human activity in relation to scarce resources that is, that economics is a study of human effort to satisfy wants with severe limited resources. Human wants are the mainspring of all economic activities. Such wants have two characteristics, they are diverse and appear to be insatiable. They further can be seen at two levels of increasing need; the biological requirement of food, shelter and clothing, and the desire arising from the culture in which people live. It can be seen simply in the desire to possess consumer goods, like smaller radios or disc players. The process of possession of such things is often combined with the gaining of consumer status, as with the ownership of a large car. The desire to possess such, it could be argued, non-essential objects derives from the realisation of the lack of these things and, is therefore, highly suggestive. A simple and obvious statement covering all the above criteria is that human needs and wants are unlimited and to satisfy them are the ends to which economic activity is directed.

The provision of maritime services requires the co-operation of what are called **factors of production**, or resources. According to A. Marshall these are 'the things required for making a commodity' and are included in the following categories. In the present case, they are 'Land', 'Labour', 'Capital' and 'Entrepreneurship'. All these factors possess three essential characteristics. Firstly, they are scarce, that is, limited in quantity. Such a resource can be defined as one, the desire and amount of which would exceed the supply if they were available free, the price was nil. Secondly, they are versatile, capable of being put to different uses. Thirdly, they can be combined in varying proportions to produce a given service or commodity.

To classify these factors of production individually **'Labour'**, refers to human skills and ingenuity, which combine in the production process. This resource consists of the capacity for human effort or labour power, both of muscle and mind. It is the principle and the active factor without which nothing can be accomplished, for it provides the skills necessary for economic production.

'**Land**' refers to all natural resources. Its physical attributes, the 'gifts of nature', include fertile land and everything beneath and above it, water, minerals etc., the supply of which is strictly limited. These are resources used either as raw materials in production or in the provision of food.

'**Capital**', real capital are physical goods, such as tools, machinery and equipment, to extract and process raw materials into finished commodities. Strictly speaking, capital refers to man-made goods used in production of other goods and services. It is things like buildings, port facilities, ships and other materials, which are the product of past investment decisions and are used in the production process. It should be noted that, here, capital is used in the sense of physical equipment, not financial capital such as, securities in the form of stocks and shares. The essential characteristic of capital is its use in economic production. It is a stock of wealth used productively.

'**Entrepreneurship**' is the managerial organisational factor, its function is to combine the other factors of production. As this does not occur spontaneously, it requires the other factors to be employed, regulated, and co-ordinated. It is the individual or group who plays the key role in co-ordinating resources, innovating, and often bearing the risk, their aims being to produce the maximum amount of economic wealth with the minimum amount of effort and resources. Traditionally, entrepreneurs are included as a factor, but many contemporary economists simply include it as part of labour and therefore reject it as a full factor. Some go so far as to classify resources into two broad categories, concentrated around labour. These are labour as all human resource and, secondly, capital as all non-human resource.

The delineation of factors of production into different categories must not be seen as creating rigidity, for being versatile and having alternative uses is of cardinal importance. Substitution is always possible, where, for example increased capital can be used and the amount of labour reduced. This can occur even when there is a high level of resource specialisation. Take for example ports before containerisation. There were highly specialised dockers and stevedoring labourers but, with time, they were substituted with considerable amounts of capital in the form of gantry cranes and container vessels. With time considerations, few, if any, productive processes require specific levels of particular resources because of the versatility of all resources. They can be put to alternative use. It therefore follows that any use they are put to at a particular time involves a sacrifice, for they can only be used in a specific way to produce a particular product or service.

Opportunity or Alternative Costs

The above argument is one of the general themes running through this chapter and the whole volume. Limited resources which can be used in alternative ways but, once employed in a specific way, involve some sacrifice. Such a sacrifice can be thought of as a 'cost'. The cost of producing a particular product or service can be defined as the value foregone, which is the measure of the value of resources used in the next best alternative process. This concept has a number of titles. **'Opportunity costs'**, **'Substitution cost'** and **'Alternative cost'**, all of which are indicative of its meaning. To construct a hypothetical example of Opportunity Cost, the production of an additional unit (X), a car ferry, costs the same amount as (Y), a new break-water, this reflects the value which must be given up, sacrificed, or foregone for the alternative, the ferry. This is due directly to the factor of production involved in the proposed building of (Y) being transferred to the production of (X). Such an example rests on the highly simplified assumption that choices are limited to two goods, the ferry and the break-water. In the reality of production, individuals or firms have to choose between a multiplicity of goods and services to be created from scarce resources. From this, the impression should not be given that the concept 'usefulness' is limited to hypothetical examples, indeed the concept of 'opportunity or alternative cost' is a tool used extensively by many in the maritime industry when analysing any problems involving the use of scarce resources.

Production and Utility

'Utility' is an economic concept defined as satisfaction, pleasure or need fulfilment derived from consuming goods or services. If, the everyday definition of the production process is used, it is, of a purely technical relationship combing the factors of production, land, labour, capital and entrepreneurship in the physical transformation of manufacturing or creating things. Difficulties arise using this form of definition for service industries, not least maritime transport. Only in very exceptional cases do they engage in physically changing material. If, on the other hand, this purely technical definition is replaced by one which defines production as an activity which serves directly or indirectly to satisfy human wants through exchange, the semantic ambiguities are removed.All activities, either manufacturing or services, can yield positive economic results from being produced or being part of the production process. Taking this argument a step further, production, be it goods or a service, is simply the creation of what the economists call utility. This, as argued, is defined as the power or ability of a commodity or service in their consumption to satisfy wants directly or indirectly, by maximising subject to budget constraints, an ultimate psychological product termed utility. It should be noted that, in this context, no enquiry is made into the ethical or moral consideration. For example, a ship breaking a United Nations Boycott is a moral, not an economic, question and must be answered on moral, and not economic, grounds. In this way production and consumption can be seen as the creation, or diminution, of utility.

Maritime transport creates a number of particular types of utility which are elements in the general increase in utility. In some sectors of the industry, such as cruising, the voyage itself presents the consumer, the holiday maker, with immediate and direct utility. Ferry services create utility for the passenger, but a pleasant crossing is usually considered as a bonus, as the gain in utility is achieved at the passenger's destination. This can be seen as the concept of **place utility** and is generally referred to as the movement of freight to a destination where it will be more useful, the movement of a commodity from a place where it has a relatively low level of utility to where utility is increased. This movement of a commodity will usually include exchange or **possession utility**, the process of transferring the commodity from one individual or firm to another, increasing its relative utility. There is, in addition, **time utility**, the availability of certain commodities at particular times, for example, pilgrims travelling by sea to Medina to be in Mecca for the annual religious festival the Haj . It is clear that maritime transport has no part in the physical form utility, as with manufacturing industries, but, during the production process, the necessary movement of commodities across either national or international waters necessitates maritime transport. Therefore, it is an essential element in the process. It would be interlinked with all forms of increases in levels of utility. Take, for example, iron ore, rubber or any material used as a component in a new car. Its production includes maritime movements and will be part of its numerous interwoven stages of production until the final product reaches the consumer. It follows from this that, in the creation of utility through production, shipping freight rates are, in reality, part of the cost or resource cost of the production process.

Freight Markets

The primary method by which allocation discussions are made in the maritime industry is by a system of markets, for goods, services and resources. Buyers, that is charterers or shippers and sellers, that is shipowners, meet or communicate in a market. As with all markets there are two aspects, organisational and structural. Market organisation refers to the technical means by which shippers and shipowners come into contact. Market structures refer to the features of the market that determines the form of relationship between shippers and shipowners. These aspects in varying combinations yield different results within the maritime context, and much of the volume will be concerned with analysing them. That is the functioning of the freight market and the price (freight) mechanisms, in order to illustrate how decisions about allocation of resource in the industry are made and what the outcome of such decisions are.

Arguably one of the most important characteristics of maritime transport is that it is not demanded for itself. There are consumers, passengers who find sea transport itself pleasurable, but these are the minority. The majority of individual passengers wish simply to arrive at their final destination. Given the opportunity, they will choose the voyage where the absolute and relative cost of the trip is minimised. The demand is therefore derived from their objective, to arrive at their final destination. In the movement of cargoes, the derived nature of demand is more explicit. Here the **derived demand** for cargo space is related directly to the demand for the commodity which is to be shipped. This commodity would be a material part of a productive process. The derived demand for shipping space, therefore, relates directly to the demand for the commodity requiring shipping or port facilities, not for their own sake, but for the contribution they make to the production of the final consumer good. For example, the consumer is not interested in a crude oil tanker, when all that is demanded is a gallon of petrol or a quantity of heating oil. Maritime demand is determined by the demand of the final consumers for the product. The greater this demand, the greater will be the demand for the factors producing it, e.g. shipping. The converse will also apply, as the fall in demand for the final consumer product will cause a contraction in the demand for all factors contributing to its production. Such a market situation, which is by no means unique to the maritime industry, means that suppliers of shipping services will, in general, be unable to influence the demand for their product. Some sectors, at certain times, could, perhaps, have minimal influence on the demand through modifications in the freight rates or tariff, but this must be seen as an unusual occurrence, on a small number of operations. Such exceptions serve to emphasise the general vulnerability of the maritime industry to vagaries of demand which are wholly outside the industry's sphere of influence.

9

The supply may be defined as the varied quantity of commodities or service, which the producers are willing and able to place on the market at a particular price and time. In shipping, the supply of tonnage or services is the amount of available capacity and its average speed in relation to the conveying of cargo or people from one port to another. The freight rate qualifications are important, because it is generally assumed that, the higher the freight rate offered, the larger will be the capacity supplied. In maritime economics there are three levels of supply; active, available and potential. These relate clearly to two of the time periods or runs used; the immediate and the short, but not the long-run. The immediate run refers to the stock of ships operating at the time. It constitutes the active supply. The short-run is a period in which the quantity of plant and equipment cannot be changed. In such a period, the available supply consists of active supply, plus vessels under repair or delayed for some reason, and tonnage laid up for lack of employment, due to the disposition of the freight market. There is also what is assumed to be a small quantity of tonnage not operating on the commercial freight market which, should circumstances change, would easily become active. This is termed potential supply. Should the freight market boom, all the available and potential supplies could quickly become active supply in the short-run.

In the third period, the long-run, everything can be changed. The equipment, number of and character of firms within the industry can be completely re-organised. In shipping, a **new building** programme can be undertaken and a similar programme of scrapping or demolishing can be completed. In this way, the carrying capacity, speed and the general level of productivity of tonnage within the industry, the supply, can be substantially altered.

In the following text, costs for supplies of maritime services will be clarified under specific headings. Prices or tariffs paid by consumers will be designated as the **freight rate** or simply freights. This can be defined as the quantity of money a shipper or consumer will exchange for a unit of shipping services. These are payments for the transportation of cargoes, they are the price of shipping a specific cargo on a particular voyage. Strictly speaking, for all general cargo, freight rates are quoted on the basis of one ton or one cubic metre, passengers of course pay carriage.

There is a multiplicity of factors influencing the consumers decision to ship a consignment or take passengers to travel, not simply the freight or tariff, for example, time spent and qualitative developments, such as safety reliability, comfort etc. Both price and time costs, and occasionally other qualitative factors, will be combined in the concept of **'Generalised Cost'**.[3] This can be deferred as the totality of cost of any voyage or journey. It is a method whereby time, quality of services, and many other costs are combined in a single cost function.. For the present, the study of freight rates serves to introduce the concept of a **Freight Rate Market**, an institution in which buyers and sellers are brought together for the purpose of making transactions. This market creates an interactive situation for freights will tend to move to the level at which demand for the shipper equates to the supply from the shipowner. In the freight market, shippers express a preference for what they want by the level of rates they are prepared to pay. This market can be defined according to the structure and characteristic of the industry or the sector of the industry in other words, the type and group of firms supplying the freight service to the market, for example the tanker market. In economics, two main criteria are usually used in classifying the market. The number of suppliers or sellers in the industrial sector and, the extent to which the product of one supplier can be substituted for that of another supplier by the buyer. In this way, different freight market structures are being delineated in what follows. Much of the present volume will concentrate on explaining and analysing the process of different industrial and international markets and the mechanism of the freight rate. This is in order to be able to illustrate how decisions about the allocation of the resources within the maritime industry are made and the outcome of these decisions. In the maritime industry, increased emphasis is being placed on the predictive, that is, the forecasting ability of economic analysis. This is particularly important in producing the various international economic trends influencing the patterns of resource allocations within the industry and its markets. The predictive power of the analysis has implications for policies designed to intervene in, or influence, the freight market mechanism, the mechanism central to the allocation of factors of and production within the industry. Such freight mechanisms or systems are essential concepts in maritime economic theory.

The main task of this book is to provide an understanding of the basis of international seaborne trade, and the way shipping costs affect the progress of that trade. In analysing these activities Maritime Economics has to concern itself with the use of scarce productive resources in three ways. Firstly the way in which these resources have been allocated, secondly the degree of utilisation and finally the growth over time of these resources. This has been done within the basic framework of the industry's operational and institutional structure. It is around the resource allocation problem that the present volume has been organised. All which involves the examination of the analytical characteristics of the industry. This has been accomplished within the limits of a book designed specifically for readers with no previous knowledge of maritime economics either on a theoretical or applied basis. The elements of the subject have been laid out systematically in three parts. Firstly, this broad introduction followed by some tools of theoretical analysis. Secondly, the economic concepts which determines the construction of various sector and markets and the method used in resource allocation. In the third and largest section these concepts are applied to the process of analysing the economic, physical and structural characteristics of the industrial sectors, that is the dry and wet bulk, liner trades and ports concentrating on deep sea activities. Largely on the basis of their development and the evaluation of the market conditions under which they function. That is to say applying economic criteria to the way in which the complex maritime system works.

Summary

Maritime Economics is a field of study concerned with the manner in which scarce productive resources are used to bridge the spatial separation of international trading countries most effectively. That is to say the function of maritime economic theory is to describe and analyse maritime economic phenomena. It consists therefore of a body of concepts and principles, based on economic theory, which assist in the understanding, explaining and occasionally making predictions about the maritime industry. This is an industry consisting of individual shipping sectors and ports, which interact to varying degrees. It is an industry or group of industries whose services generally are not demanded in their own right but as part of an often long and complex process of production. These industrial sectors are not entirely disparate, despite their operating to satisfy discrete markets and industrial demands. Hence this book studies the economic criteria in conveying goods across the maritime transport gap, the sea, using the most efficient methods available to do so. The method of achieving this is to analyse the economic criteria which motivates the behaviour of the supplier of the ship and the port service owners and operators and their interaction with the derived demands of consumers that is, charterers, shippers and passengers.

FURTHER READING

While this volume aims to be a comprehensive text, should the reader wish to widen the area of study analysis the following Economic, Transport Economics and other texts are suggested.

Economic Text Books:

Sloman J. 'Economics'
3rd Edition Prentice Hall, London 1997.

Parkin M. *et al* Economics
Addison-Wesley Longman, London 1997.

Transport Economics:

Button K.J. Transport Economics
2nd Edition Heineman, London 1993.

Stubbs P.C. *et al* Transport Economics
Revised Edition Charles Allen Unwin, London 1984.

Maritime Economics Bibliographies and Journals:

McConville J. and Rickaby G. Shipping Business and Maritime
Economics: An Annotated International Bibliography
Mansell London 1995.

Maritime Policy and Management. An International Journal of
Shipping and Port Research.
Taylor and Francis (Quarterly).

Lloyds Shipping Economist (Monthly).

----

[1] Marshall, *A Industry and Trade* (Fourth Edition), London Macmillan & Co.,
1923, p.423.
[2] Committee of Inquiry into Shipping (Rochdale Report) May 1970. H.M.S.O.
Par.2.
[3] This is an important idea, of which the reader should be aware, but which
will not be considered in what follows, as only limited research has yet been
done relating the generalised cost concepts to the maritime industry.

Chapter Two

TOOLS OF ANALYSIS: ESSENTIAL TECHNIQUES

Introduction

Maritime economics is a discipline or field of study connected with the manner in which existing material and human resources are used in the industry and how they change and develop over time. Maritime economic theory consists of a body of concepts and principles which assist in the explanation of the industry's progress. The industry's function in the real world is richly complex. Such an overwhelming number of factors relating to any maritime economic question necessitates the development of theories and models. Such theories function both as a method of reasoning and as the accumulation of such reasoning about specific phenomenon to do with the production of maritime services. They are concerned with analysing rather than describing, the question is 'why' not of 'how'. Initially students are often prejudicial, or apprehensive about these techniques of economic analysis. Claiming they can be dispensed with, for they are out of date and fail to relate to contemporary facts. When questioned the response is invariably a jumble of unrelated facts interwoven with some long disposed of economic theories. As Alan Fox points out 'Your self-styled 'practical' man is apt to deride theory. This usually means simply that he has never been

15

required to examine the curious jackdaw's nest of unrelated assumptions, generalisations and hypotheses (i.e. theory) upon which his behaviour is based. Keynes, the economist, made a characteristically waspish comment on the subject. "Practical men, who believe themselves to be quite exempt from any intellectual influences, are usually slaves of some defunct economist.'[1] What is obviously missed is that if theories include thousands of detailed variations and exceptions in an attempt to make them more 'realistic' in the descriptive sense, they cease to be theories. What these theories and models achieve is to bring the questions down to manageable proportions and make it possible to see the wood despite all the trees.

Unlike the physical sciences, economists are only rarely able to perform controlled experiments to test how their theories operate in practice. In chemistry, for example, the formula for a chemical reaction such as $Z_N + H_2SO_4 \Rightarrow Z_NSO_4 + H_2$ can be written. It states when zinc is placed in sulphuric acid, zinc sulphate will be formed and hydrogen will be released as a gas. Because chemistry is a much more exact science, there is no question that this will occur. Maritime economics, on the other hand, is not an exact science. There are no absolutes. Responses will be circumspect; what is the likely or unlikely result following from certain economic decisions or activities. Frontiers between the social sciences are not rigid and the extension of maritime economics to transport, welfare and traditional economics is not unusual. To make any analysis possible, vast simplifications are required, as with other social sciences, to create hypothetical situations. This is achieved by models containing a number of assumptions that aim to highlight the essential features or the key variables of a problem being examined, in an attempt to understand it. Occasionally it is argued that such a process of abstraction is unrealistic but in other areas of activities such abstractions are an unquestionable everyday occurrence. For example, an atlas of the world, a menu, or navigational charts. The latter is an essential piece of navigational equipment onboard ship; it outlines the coast and primary points of lights, buoys and underwater obstructions which are always changing necessitating the information be kept up-to-date. Such charts are essential tools precisely because they ignore irrelevant information such as the type of weed or crustacean which grow in it, fish which swim in it, the colour of the sea and the sort of vessel which trades over it, etc., etc. The chart presents the ship's officer only with information which is relevant and pertinent to the needs of the vessel's safe passage from one point to another. As one author points out in economics "never do we come to real life, however closely we may approach it, for reality is always more complex than the economist's picture of it. This fact frequently makes students feel that economic analysis is unrealistic, because the world with which it deals seems to be so much simpler than the real world. To think this, however, is to misunderstand the whole nature of economics. Economic analysis is not a perfect picture of economic life; it is a map of it. Just as we do not expect a map to show every tree, every house, and every blade of grass in a landscape, so we should not expect economic analysis to take into account every detail and quirk of real economic behaviour. A map that is too detailed is not much use as a map".[2] Similarly, maritime economic models are abstracts concentrating on what is perceived as the relevant information from a welter of real world detail.

Such simple economic models as used here clearly cannot simultaneously include a large number of economic variables, hence constructive models for economic discussion introduce the assumption of **'Ceteris Paribus'**. This Latin phrase means 'all other things being equal' or 'remaining unchanged'. If the object is to examine the change by a variation in one single variable, for example the impact of a price fall on the demand for a product, everything else is held constant (ceteris paribus). This simplification is essential in producing a model or theory consistent with the complex field of economic activity as in the maritime industry.

Another essential element in economic modelling is the **hypothesis** that all participants seek the maximisation of something. A shipping company will operate so as to achieve the highest level of profit or the lowest level of cost possible. Alternatively they may forsake profit maximisation goals for example maximising the utilisation of their vessels. Individuals are assumed to maximise their level of consumption that is utility. This hypothesis of maximisation is obviously an abstraction for it can take no account of any irrational behaviour. For example, when an ageing vessel continues operating despite all economic and commercial indicators pointing to the need for the tonnage to be scrapped. This course of action would be contrary to the economist's definition of rationality, a presumption is made of 'self interest' behaviour being perceived as rational. Firms or individuals will never deliberately make a decision or take a course of action knowing in advance it is against their self-interest. In this way rational economic activity implies that they are consciously seeking to achieve the highest level of utility, or as much profit as possible. The use of this maximisation hypothesis has two clear advantages. First objectives ensures precision and second, and combined with the latter it allows the widespread application of mathematical techniques. The hypothesis of rational maximisation behaviour has been the subject of considerable and continuous controversy over the years, particularly in the area of profit maximisation. Here, because of its usefulness in analysing the variety of real world phenomenon it will be regarded as a method rather than some universal truth.

The models use an extensive technical vocabulary. Fortunately, only some of this jargon is necessary in this volume. Certain words may already be known, but in maritime economics they take on a more precise meaning. Words like conference, capital, utility and port. Others will be unfamiliar, for example, elasticity, oligopoly, bunker costs. These and other terms are introduced in the text and will re-appear throughout the volume. In a similar way to other social sciences, maritime economics is concerned with the behaviour of variables. These are things which may take different values over time as conditions change - the supply of tonnage, the freight rate, the second hand price of tonnage are all examples of industrial variables. Occasionally relationships between variables are expressed as functions of one another. The tonnage of tankers passing through the Suez Canal is a function of the demand for oil and oil products within Europe.

In the example, the tonnage of tankers is **dependent** on the demand for oil and oil products and therefore described as the **dependent variable**. The demand for oil and oil products **explain** the demand for tanker tonnage and is therefore called the **explanatory** or **independent variable.**

Those studying maritime economics are fortunate in being able to use quantifiable relationships. Economics, more than any other of the social sciences makes use of quantifiable dimensions. There is amongst some individuals, an anxiety about working with lines, curves, diagrams and elementary mathematical

Table 2.1   World Merchant Shipping Laid Up 1975-1985

Year	Dead Weight Tons (Millions)	% of World Tonnage (DWT)	Alphabetical Denomination (See Figure 2.4)
1975*	46	9	A
1976	38	6	B
1977	43	7	C
1978	30	5	D
1979	11	2	E
1980	9	1	F
1981	27	4	G
1982	84	12	H
1983	80	12	I
1984	62	9	J
1985*	64	10	K

Total World Fleet (Million D.W.T.) 1975; 544.2 and 1985 - 665.8
Source: General Trends in Shipping No.3 1981 and No.8 1985, London H.M.S.O.

formulae because it will be difficult and confusing. However, they are often the best, quickest and easiest method of understanding concepts and to see relationships among variables.

It is to overcome this initial apprehension that the following examples have been designed. To begin, historical data showing the movement in variables over time are illustrated in a diagram or graph. Table 2.1 shows the world merchant fleet tonnage in **Dead Weight Tonnes** (DWT) **'laid up'** or inactive, that is unemployed over the period 1975-1985. There are also percentage and alphabetical columns which will be used later.

Graphs and Charts

The information from the above schedule or table can now be transferred to a simple bar chart or graph. In a similar vein to most diagrams it begins with a zero point of origin. Two lines go straight out from the origin, perpendicular to one another. One is the vertical axis, referred to as the 'y' axis, the other is the horizontal axis, referred to as the 'x' axis. These axis are marked with numbers or scales. These indicate the amount of the variable being measured along each axis. In this case the vertical axis, (y) describes dead weight tonnage in million tonnes from zero to seventy million tonnes (DWT). The horizontal axis (x) measures the time period 1975 to 1985. In figure 2.1 two years have been selected at the beginning and end of the period, namely, 1975 and 1985

As can be seen from the above, in the year 1975 some 46 million dead weight tonnes were laid up. A decade later this had increased to some 64 million tons, an increase of 18 million tonnes. The tonnage is indicated by the dotted line at 46 and 64 million D.W.T. respectively on the 'y' axis and the year by the bar on the 'x' axis. What is also clear is that the difference in the amount laid up was 18 million dead weight tonnes; that is 46 million in 1975 taken from 64 million in 1985.

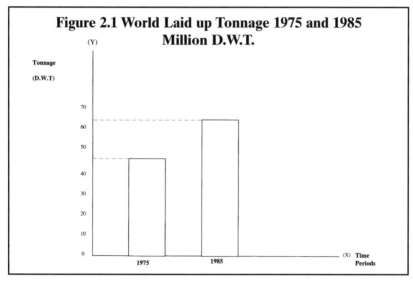

The bar chart, derived as it is from the schedule is clear and consistent, but if it is assumed that there is a desire to mislead the reader or to create a different impression, the graph can be manipulated to serve this end. One method is to change the base line, and not begin at zero, for example, 30 million dead weight tonnes as in figure 2.2.

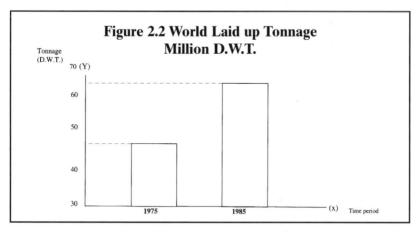

Here, the visual impression is of a situation where the tonnage appears to be nearly double between the two periods of 1975 and 1985. Confusion may also arise if, for example, a percentage rather than the actual tonnage is used as in figure 2.3.

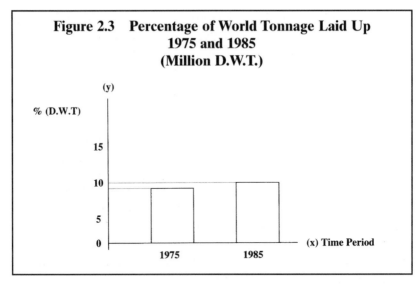

Figure 2.3   Percentage of World Tonnage Laid Up
1975 and 1985
(Million D.W.T.)

In this case, little difference is perceived between 1975 and 1985, and a different impression is given. This is because the size of the Total World fleet changed radically between the two dates. In 1975 it stood at 544.2 million d.w.t by 1985 it had increased to 665.8 million d.w.t, an increase making the comparative percentages in real terms very different. Hence, care must be taken as to the origin scales and type of measure used in graphs in order to ensure the correct interpretation.

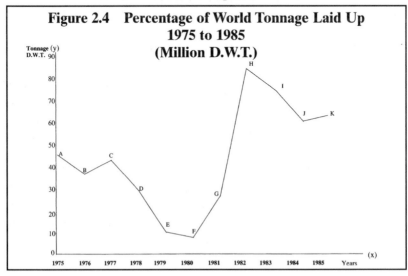

Figure 2.4   Percentage of World Tonnage Laid Up
1975 to 1985
(Million D.W.T.)

To examine in more detail movements in total laid up tonnage over the whole period, this is demonstrated in the above figure 2.4. Here the vertical axis (y) indicates the amount of tonnage (million d.w.t) and each year of the period on the horizontal (x) axis. These movements are made explicit with the use of alphabetical denominations.

Over the period the amount of tonnage laid up rose as already argued, A to K. When considered in detail, the situation is more complex. There is a fairly steady decline during the first half of the decade A to F, followed by an extremely rapid increase of some seventy million dwt F to H. The period ends H to K with some twenty million dwt, leaving the lay-up total. Presumably returning to commercial activity or being scrapped. Hence this type of figure shows clearly the movement of some criteria in this case laid up tonnage over time.

Production Possibility Curves

It is useful here to point out a basic economic lesson that ship and port owners have a fixed amount of resources and a given technology at any one time, with which to produce maritime services. By production is meant the creation of utility that is to say, in the present context that the creation of maritime services. This was one of the underlying themes in the previous chapter. A shipowner, entrepreneur will not only have to make choices about which resources to use in the production process but will also have to decide how these are to be allocated between alternative outputs. In reality such choices will be made simultaneously for shipowners to decide the level of resource need at the same time as the level of service output. If the two decisions are for convenience separated here, it will be assumed that first the shipowning company has in the short-run a limited amount of factors of production, termed here resources. Secondly that they produce two shipping products, a ferry service and a bulk crude oil or tanker service. Thirdly to assume an arbitrary numerical term unit of service, a method of representing the situation in the table or schedule and figure that follows:

Table 2.2   Service Production Possibility

SERVICE OPTIONS	FERRY UNITS	TANKER UNITS	OPPORTUNITY COST OF TANKER FOREGONE TO PRODUCT A UNIT OF FERRY	PRODUCTION CHANGES ①.
A	0	30		
			2	A G B
B	1	28		
			3	B H C
C	2	25		
			5	C I D
D	3	20		
			8	D J E
E	4	12		
			12	E K F
F	5	0		

① See Figure 2.5

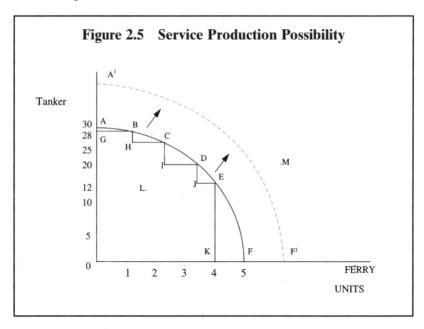

Figure 2.5   Service Production Possibility

Service Production Possibilities

The table and production possibility curve sometimes referred to as a transformation curve, show the alternative maximum combinations of units of ferry and tanker services which have to be produced with a fixed quantity of resources per unit of time.

24

The slope of the curve represents the rate at which tanker services have to be sacrificed to increase ferry service output. The curve is concave to the origin because in order to obtain an additional unit, an increasing number of units of tanker service must be forgone. It is unlikely that resources employed in one service will be equally efficient in producing the other. In the extreme case all resources are dedicated to the production of thirty units of tanker service (A) or at the other extreme five units of ferry service (F). To move away from these extremes A to point B, increases in the ferry service two units of tanker service are sacrificed for one unit rise in ferry services. These rises in the figure are indicated by the horizontal (x) axis, increasing the G to B, from H to C, from I to D, from J to E, and from K to F. This causes reductions in the production of units in tanker service measured on the vertical (y) axis A to G, B to H, C to I, D to J, E to K. The movement becomes larger and larger and the curve increasingly steep. A situation of increasing cost, the concave curve indicates that in order to obtain an additional unit of ferry service more units of tanker service must be sacrificed. The reduction in tanker service production gets larger and larger, in order to obtain an extra unit of ferry service. Initially a unit of ferry service can be produced with resources that specialise in ferries and are of little use in tanker services. As ferry service production increases the shipowner must direct to it resources which are increasingly more useful in terms of tankers. It therefore becomes increasingly more expensive in terms of tanker services forgone.

These increasing opportunity costs of ferry services represent the specialist characteristics of resources that is to say all resources are not equally efficient in all activities. There are another two points to discuss, firstly L within the production possibility boundary or frontier. This point will not be considered by the shipowner as it does not fulfil the rational maximisation hypothesis, since a higher production is possible. The other point M then cannot be obtained because it is situated well outside the resource limitation of the production possibility curve.

The second production possibility curve A^1 to F^1 have been added to the figure, this indicates with a technological advance or productivity improvement in the industry both sectors could benefit. The curve moving outwards, a similar movement could also indicate, of course, that the resources available to the shipowner have increased allowing a combined level of production to increase.

Analysis of the Distribution: Mean and Standard Deviation

Statistical methods are applied regularly to maritime transport. This analysis fulfils two roles, firstly it can be used to test out theories against the observation of maritime industrial activity. Secondly these observations can be used as measures in terms of quantitative relationships between various, both dependent and explanatory or independent functions. The basic reason for classifying data and constructing graphs is to determine the type and level of distribution.

Although graphs and charts are useful tools for illustrating distribution and trends, further analysis requires the calculation of key statistics. Among the most important of these are the **mean** and **standard deviation**. The arithmetic mean or for brevity, the mean is the average value and is calculated by dividing the sum of the observations by the number of observations:

Equation 2.1

$$\text{Mean} = \frac{\text{Sum of the observations}}{\text{Number of observations}}$$

Using the data in table 2.1, the mean or average tonnage of ships laid up per year over the period 1975-1985 is:

Mean number of tons per year   =

$$\frac{46+38+43+30+11+9+27+84+80+62+64}{11}$$

$$= 44.91 \text{ tons}$$

(To make it clearer the million D.W.T has been left out)

The number of observations is usually denoted by n and each observation can be expressed as $x_1, x_2, x_3, ...etc.$ until the last observation x_n. The mean itself is written as

Thus equation 2.1 above can be written as:

Equation 2.1

$$\bar{x} = \frac{x_1 + x_2 + x_3 + ...+x_n}{n}$$

or the preceding formulas can be written in a much shorter form

if the summation symbol (Greek Sigma) Σ is used.

It is a symbol indicating the sum of all values of the quantity written

after the symbol. This equation 2.1 is written:

$$\bar{x} = \frac{\sum_{i=1}^{n} x_i}{n} \qquad where$$

$$\sum_{i=1}^{n} x_i \text{ is the sum of observations } 1 \text{ to } n$$

Having calculated the mean, it is useful to examine the dispersion of the data around this value in order to establish the volatility or fluctuation of the tonnage over the period. The standard measure of dispersion is called the **standard deviation**. The standard deviation looks at the difference between the actual and mean value. The deviations are then squared to ensure that all numbers are positive. If this squaring process did not take place, then negative deviations would cancel out the positive deviations and the measure of dispersion would be meaningless. The 'n' squared observations are then summed and divided by 'n' to give the **variance**. The standard deviation can then be calculated as the square root of the variance. Equation 2.2 shows the expression for the standard deviation:

Equation 2.2

$$\text{Standard deviation} = \sqrt{\frac{(x_1 - \bar{x})^2 + (x_2 - \bar{x})^2 + (x_3 - \bar{x})^2 + \ldots + (x_n - \bar{x})^2}{n-1}}$$

Using the summation sign described in equation 1.1, this can be simplified to:

$$\sigma = \sqrt{\frac{\sum_{i=1}^{n}(x_i - \bar{x})^2}{n-1}}$$

where σ is the standard deviation

Returning to the example in table 2.1, the variance and standard deviation may be calculated as follows:

World Merchant Shipping Laid up 1975-1985

D.W.T. Millions	Squared Deviations		
46	$(46\text{-}44.91)^2$	=	1.1881
38	$(38\text{-}44.91)^2$	=	47.7481
43	$(43\text{-}44.91)^2$	=	3.6481
30	$(30\text{-}44.91)^2$	=	222.3081
11	$(11\text{-}44.91)^2$	=	1149.8881
9	$(9\text{-}44.91)^2$	=	1289.5281
27	$(27\text{-}44.91)^2$	=	320.7681
84	$(84\text{-}44.91)^2$	=	1528.0281
80	$(80\text{-}44.91)^2$	=	1231.3081
62	$(62\text{-}44.91)^2$	=	292.0681
64	$(46\text{-}44.91)^2$	=	364.428
	Sum Of Squared Deviations		_____ 6450.9091

$$\text{Standard deviation} = \sqrt{\frac{\sum_{i=1}^{n}(x_i - \bar{x})^2}{n-1}}$$

$$= 25.40 \text{ million dwt}$$

The standard deviation around the mean is 24 tons - more than half the mean itself. Thus the annual tonnage can be seen as volatile.

Correlation

The statistical methods presented thus far have been concerned with a single variable x and its dispersion. It is also important to examine the relationship between two or more variables. For simplicity, the following discussion will focus on linear relationships.

The extent of any linear relationship may be formalised by calculating the correlation coefficient. This coefficient can have a value between +1 and -1, with +1 representing perfect positive correlation and -1 representing perfect negative correlation. Graphically this may be illustrated as follows:

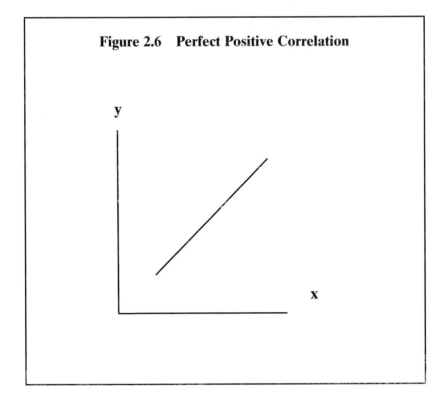

Figure 2.6   Perfect Positive Correlation

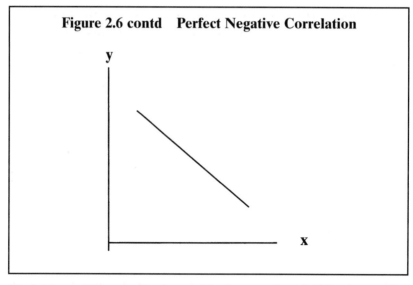

Figure 2.6 contd Perfect Negative Correlation

Variables will be perfectly positively correlated if both x and y move in the same direction, up or down along a straight line. Perfect negative correlation occurs when both move in opposite directions along a straight line. In practice, the correlation will not be perfect, but will lie somewhere between -1 and +1. This situation is illustrated in figure 2.7.

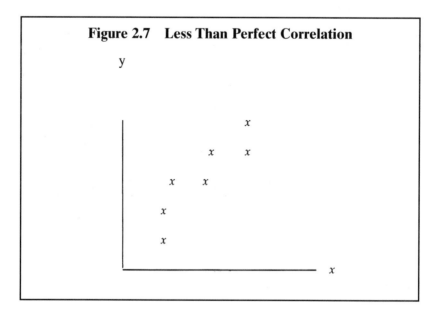

Figure 2.7   Less Than Perfect Correlation

In this case, a formula can be used to determine the degree of correlation between variables x and y. This formula is based on the covariance between x and y and the individual standard deviations of x and y as follows:

Equation 2.3

Correlation coefficient = $\dfrac{\text{Covariance between } x \text{ and } y}{\text{Standard deviation of } x \times \text{Standard deviation of } y}$

or in symbol form:

$$\rho = \frac{1}{n-1} \frac{\sum\limits_{i=1}^{n}(x_i - \bar{x})(y_i - \bar{y})}{\sigma_x \sigma_y}$$

Table 2.3 shows data on world seaborne trade 1985-1995 for iron ore and coal. The example that follows uses this data to explore the relationship between the variables.

Table 2.3   World Seaborne Trade 1985-1995 For Iron Ore And Coal (Billions of Ton-Miles)

Year	Iron ore	Coal
1985	1675	1479
1986	1671	1586
1987	1728	1653
1988	1919	1719
1989	1983	1798
1990	1978	1849
1991	2008	1999
1992	1896	2001
1993	2001	1949
1994	2165	2014
1995	2280	2090

Source: Fearnleys (Oslo), Review 1995.

For the purposes of calculation, let iron ore be variable x and coal variable y.

Year	Iron ore x	Coal y	$(x-\bar{x})^2$	$(y-\bar{y})^2$	$(x-\bar{x})(y-\bar{y})$
1985	1675	1479	68502.59	123650.69	92034.74
1986	1671	1586	70612.43	59848..73	65.008.19
1987	1728	1653	43568.21	31555.97	37978.80
1988	1919	1719	314.35	12463.49	1979.38
1989	1983	1798	2140.91	1065.37	-1510.25
1990	1978	1849	1703.21	337.09	757.72
1991	2008	1999	5079.41	28345.09	119999.02
1992	1896	2001	1658.93	29022.53	-6938.76
1993	2001	1949	4130.63	14009.09	7607.00
1994	2165	2014	52107.19	66320.89	41855.59
1995	2280	2090	117834.29	67267.61	89030.51
TOTAL	21304	20137	367652.18	401186.55	338901.91

Mean of x	$=$	$\dfrac{21304}{11}$	$=$	1936.73
Standard deviation of x (iron ore)	$=$	$\dfrac{367653}{10}$	$=$	191.74
Mean of y	$=$	$\dfrac{20137}{11}$	$=$	1830.64
Standard deviation of y (coal)	$=$	$\dfrac{401188}{10}$	$=$	200.30
Correlation coefficient between iron ore and coal	$=$ $=$	$\dfrac{1}{10}$ 0.88	$\times$	$\dfrac{338901.91}{191.74 \times 200.30}$

The purpose of this exercise was to illustrate the procedure for studying the relationships between two variables. That is to say the degree of a real relationship between a variable x iron ore, and y coal. The outcome is that there is a high degree of correlation between them. This is not an unexpected result, since both are key elements in the production of steel.

Summary

Maritime economics seeks to understand the behaviour of various economic elements; It is not a precise science and, as such, is open to interpretation. At the simplest level, this can be a graphical representation of data in order to highlight trends. The analysis may be extended to a consideration of averages and volatility by the calculation of mean and standard deviation. Relationships between variables can further be explored by examining the extent of correlation. These tools of analysis are by no means exhaustive, but introduce the basic concepts of data analysis which are referenced later in this book.

Further Reading

Goodwin E.M. and Kemp J.F.
Marine Statistics - Theory and Practice
Stanford Maritime Ltd, London 1979.

Evans J.J. and Marlow P.B.
Quantitative Methods in Maritime Economics (2nd Edition)
Fairplay Publications, London 1990.

---

[1] Fox A. Managerial Ideology and Labour Relations. British Journal of Industrial and Labour Relations Vol. 4 1966 Page 366. Quoting from Keynes. J. M. General Theory of Employment, Interest and Money. London Macmillan (1935) and 1967 p383
[2] Boulding K.E. Economic Analysis 4th Edition (Vol. 1) New York. Harper & Row, 1955 p 13

Part II
ECONOMIC THEORY OF SHIPPING

Chapter 3

DEMAND

Introduction

The demand for shipping services is a **derived demand**, arising as a direct result of the demand for commodities which require to be hauled by sea. Shipping is, therefore demanded not for itself, but because it is part of the production process of other goods. Oil tanker demand derives from the demand for crude oil products such as heating and fuel oil, petroleum, etc. Like all productive factors, shipping shares the common property that the demand for its service derives from the consumers ultimate want of goods and services. The level of seaborne trade determine the number of shipping and cargo space required. The aim here is to concentrate on demand for tonnage; to move commodities whose future consumption necessitates some seaborne transportation.

There are two other forms of demand in the industry. Speculative demand for tonnage is based on the expectation of financial advantage in purchasing a vessel or vessels for resale in the short-run. Here, such tonnage is basically perceived as a speculative property to be bought and sold rather than operating in seaborne trading.[1] There is also now a much diminished demand for passengers wishing to take voyages, particularly over long distances. The discussion here will however, concentrate on seaborne cargo trade.

Statistics and Trends

It has been calculated that between 80 and 85% of world trade in terms of weight is transported by sea. In terms of ton miles or kilometres[2], this figure increases to between 90 and 95% of international trade. In value terms, the percentage remains high, if not quite so overwhelming as that of weight or ton miles. These estimates indicate that, despite the rapid development of other modes of transport, (for example the growth of overland movement, particularly within Europe, and also air-freight), by far the greatest movement by weight in international transport is by sea. Hence much of the short distance, and almost all the long distance inter-regional trade involving inter-commodity exchange is seaborne.

An indication of a long term trend in this trade since 1965 is shown in table 3.1

Table 3.1   Development of International Seaborne Trade
1965-1995
(Million Tons)

Year	Tanker Cargo	Dry Cargo	Total	Total (Billion Ton Miles)
1965	862	812	1,674	5,849
1970	1,440	1,165	2,605	10,654
1975	1,742	1,433	3,175	15,225
1980	1,871	1,833	3,704	16,777
1985	1,459	1,923	3,382	13,065
1990	1,794	2,246	4,040	17,035
1995	2,050	2,601	4,651	20,190

Source: UNCTAD Review of Maritime Transport (Annual)

The central point presented here is that the use of international seaborne trade between 1965 and 1995 increased by more than two-fold. A substantial amount of this enormous expansion is concentrated in the first decade 1965-1975. Since then, growth has been slower, with an absolute decline in the mid-1980s. To look at the tonnage first, total cargo has as virtually doubled within the first ten years and expanded at a slower pace since with a decline in the mid 1980s. Tanker cargoes are of importance to this examination of long-term trends, as their changes are most dramatic. Following a very rapid rise, they more than doubled in ten years. But there has only been slow growth since, with a serious contraction in the mid-1980s, and by 1990s, the earlier peak has just been surpassed. Dry cargo tonnage, on the other hand, did not increase quite so dramatically in the earlier period, but continued to grow at different rates throughout the period of the time covered, surpassing tanker cargoes during the 1980s. The demand for tonnage depends critically not only on the simple cargo or tonnage ships, i.e. the volume of trade, but also on the length of voyage. It thus reflects patterns of trade and routes of vessels. The best indication of this is ton miles or kilometres of transport performance. This ton mileage is calculated by multiplying the tonnage by the shipping distance.

Equation   3.1

Ton mileage = Tonnage x Shipping distance
(with cargo)

For example, ten tons of cargo loaded over a distance of 250 nautical miles equals 2,500 ton miles of shipping movement. This is a useful indicator, not only of the quantity shipped, but of the distance transported. In ton mileage terms, the emphasis of the expansion between 1965 and 1975 is highlighted, an increase well in excess of two-fold being achieved. There only a comparatively marginal increase in the recent period. a contraction in the mid-1980s is particularly marked.

There are numerous sources where contemporary and historical calculations of shipping demand can be found apart from the UNCTAD Review of Maritime Transport, the source used in the above table. Perhaps the most convenient is found in 'Maritime Transport' - an annual review published by the OECD. This is used in the following table which looks at a somewhat longer period in terms of percentage growth.

Table 3.2   Average Annual Percentage Variation in Total Seaborne Trade 1950-1990

Period	Tonnage Shipment (Tons)	Ton Mile Transport Performance
1950-1955	8.7	-
1955-1960	6.2	-
1960-1965	8.6	-
1965-1973	8.4	12.9
1973-1980	2.2	1.2
1980-1990	1.0	0.0

Source: Maritime Transport OECD Annual Reports

What the above table illustrates is the expansion in total seaborne trade in the decades following the Second World War. This expansion was remarkable by any standard in the period up to the first oil and shipping crisis of 1973. This initial crisis removed the presumption of a consistent and underlying level trade expansion. The second crisis in 1979 confirmed this and undermined the notion of a gradual return to pre-crisis levels of growth. In terms of tonnage shipped, prior to 1973 the average growth was virtually always in excess of 8%. Since then, there has been a substantial contraction. In the more detailed annual change table, over a number of years this has been negative - a situation which only arose during one occasion between 1950 and 1975. The ton mileage requirement and the percentage increase may engender a global analysis based on the best measurement of shipping demand available at present, despite it being of a crude and generalised type. The figures are not available until 1965 and show a remarkable growth increase during the period 1965 - 1973. While this is an indicator of the expanding conditions of the period, particularly for dry cargo where shipping distances increase steadily, the more important factor is the closure of the Suez Canal. The ton mile performance in oil had been steadily declining until the closure in 1967. This caused a sudden and substantial increase of 2% in ton miles in one year. Prior to the canal closure some 8.1% of dry cargo and 18.3% of all international oil shipments used the canal. North bound oil made up some 86% of total shipments through the canal. At the time of the closure, the Canal was capable of accommodating a fully-laden tanker of up to 65,000 DWT and was prepared to receive vessels up to 200,000 DWT in late 1967. It has been calculated that on the three major Persian (Arabian) Gulf routes, that is the Mediterranean, Northern Europe and the East Coast of North America, if all vessels of 65,000 DWT used the canal in both directions, and up to 200,000 DWT on the ballast leg (south-bound), the transport performance would require approximately 3,000,000 ton miles. With the closure, this was set at 4,800,000 ton miles. The closure of the Suez Canal thus had an enormous impact on transport distance and hence ton mile performance. The re-opening of the canal on the other hand has only a minimal impact, for during its closure the world fleet had undergone a massive re-organisation and technological development, particularly in relation to larger tankers.

Demand and Economic Growth

The close connection between international levels of economic growth, or the lack of it, and the level of seaborne trade is at first sight obvious but, as will be argued, it is not as unproblematic as it seems. Industrial economic development is the central factor in the volume of international seaborne trade, but the volume can also be influenced by technological development[3] as well as political factors. The latter can have an important impact on seaborne trade, not only in terms of political crises of one form or another, but in a nation's long-term objectives. These can be achieved using political, social and economic instruments, for example, quota traffic or levels of international equity; (elements which will be examined in detail later). Despite this there has been no disagreement about the importance of long-term factors. The central long-term factor being economic. The demand for shipping is related primarily to the level of national and international economic activity. Put simply, international seaborne trade is dependent on economic growth which, when that growth is rapid, expands in a similar way, as does the demand for tonnage. This link seems obvious, but there is no direct or functional relationship that exists between the international economic situation and the level of seaborne trade. Studies which have been done on the level of Gross National Product (GNP) and the relationship to the level of international seaborne trade have concentrated on OECD countries performance. These are Europe, North America, Japan and Australasia. Changes in shipping demand are significant, where there are modifications in the level of activity among the industrial developed countries. This is hardly surprising as the OECD accounts for 80% of the world's international product production and approximately 70% of world exports in terms of value. In recent years, in tonnage terms, they have made up some 40% of loaded cargo and 67% of unloaded cargo. Hence an economic boom and recession amongst these countries will have a marked effect amongst seaborne trade.

To take the argument a step further, the demand for shipping can be seen as coming from two sources, the commodities for industrial utilisation and those for final consumption. Industrial consumption may be closely related to shipping demand. The level of international stocks will also be an important element here. High levels would suggest time-lag repercussions and uneven demand reactions. Such industrial demand will be relatively inelastic in aggregate. That is to say that large changes in freight rates will only have a marginal effect on quantity demanded. The expansion of demand for OECD countries raises a different question. In the period between 1950 and the early 1970s there appears to have been a broad correlation between the expansion in the world economy and the growth in the demand for shipping, shipping demand being in excess of economic growth. It can be argued that trade liberalisation and the removal of tariff barriers is of importance in this explanation. World production for much of the period was in the region of 5.5% per annum, compared with seaborne trade at a growth of 8%. The first and second oil crises of 1973/74 and 1979/80 changed this relationship. The collapse of the OECD demand during this period was due not only to economic down-turn, but to fuel conservation. Demand for shipping was more responsive to this added fuel factor than other parts of the economy and as such, the fall in demand for shipping was greater than that general economic down-turn. Although there is an obvious relationship between economic growth and seaborne trade, the correlation is less than perfect. This is due to specific technological factors, and crises that have made a greater impact on seaborne trade than on other aspects of the economic activity

Demand Theory

It has been argued that the demand for shipping is closely but not perfectly related to the level of international economic activity. To look now, in more detail, at the concept of demand. Demand is much more than a simple expression of desire; it must be backed by the charterer's willingness and ability to pay the freight rate. The relevant concept here is that of **effective demand.** This is not the same as need or desire as it essentially signifies the ability to pay. Defining economic demand at the level of the individual consumer can be done in this way. Demand is the quantity of an economic good or a service which can be brought at each and every possible price during a given time period. One author made an analogy with physics, "in physics, the volume and pressure of a gas are related by Boyle's law, which states that the volume of a gas varies inversely with pressure, if all conditions remain constant. In economics the relationship, between quantity purchased and price is expressed by the law of demand, which holds that the quantity purchased of goods varies inversely with its price, if all other conditions remain constant."[4] Such a basic definition of demand concentrates solely on the negative relationship between demand and price, but demand, in addition, has a number of other variables, consumer's income, taste and preference, the price of other

41

goods, the expectation of consumer, financial and socio-economic factors. These will be gradually included in this analysis which follows.

Utility

In one form or another, as with all economics, the assumptions underpinning demand is that consumers either as individuals, or aggregate of individuals or a firm, will consistently act in a logical manner; their behaviour will be rational. Given this rationality, the consumer will aim always to maximise their utility within their budget constraints. Utility means the amount of satisfaction or need fulfilment derived directly or indirectly from the consumption of some economic good or service. It should be made clear that no enquiry into the ethics or the morality of such wants is made. As one authority put it, for utility power to give satisfaction it must be desired; it need not be desirable.[5] Recently, smoking has increasingly become an example of this. All economic production is a process of increasing utility, as Bonavia states, "Matter is more desirable or useful in one form than another; and accordingly mankind is busy stimulating or assisting nature to change the seed to the fruit, the ore to the metal. Matter is more desirable at one place than another, at one time than another; and thus transport and distribution, and the whole merchanting mechanisms are evolved. The function of transport is to carry commodities from points where their marginal utility, the significance of a little more or a little less, is relatively low to where it is relatively high. This process is interleaved, as it were, with the process of physical change, so that the final utility of any commodity can be visualised as composed of "layers" of different utilities, of form, of place, and of time."[6] Hence the shipping of commodities creates utility because it creates user value in a number of ways.

1. *The Utility of Place and Location.* The availability of goods in a certain place where they are wanted. Shipping cargoes are obviously a part of this function. For example, bananas shipped to consumers in northern countries.

2. *The Utility of Time.* The availability of goods at the time which they are required. Christmas trees just before the holiday, but not a day later, or heating oil during the winter; both markets involving shipping.

3. *The Utility of Form.* The change in the material or physical form of a good in such a way as to increase its ability to satisfy wants. For example, Middle East crude oil converted to gas or petroleum in refineries adjacent to consumer markets. This requires the use of shipping services.

4. *Intangibles.* Most services are, of course, intangible in that they do not result in the physical production of a commodity .

A theory has been developed using, in part, the above criteria to explain the inverse relationship between price and quantity. This is known as the utility theory. Cardinal utility uses the assumptions already mentioned of consumer rationality tied to the aims of planning their spending as to achieve the highest possible levels of satisfaction; that is utility, within the limitations of income and the market prices of commodities. Total utility for the consumer will be the entire amount of satisfaction which is obtained by the consumption of various amounts of commodities in a given time period. The theory of consumer behaviour has defined the problems confronting the consumer as that of maximising utility derived from consuming goods or services within the constraints of their income or budget and the prices of various goods or services which can be bought. This can be achieved by arranging all expenses so that no readjustment of the pattern of consumption at the margin will yield additional utility. Utility for the last unit, or next one considered worth buying is known as marginal utility. For the consumer, if the marginal utility is less than the price, then less will be purchased, but if marginal utility is greater than price then more will be purchased. This analysis can be extended to the case where the consumer buys many commodities. Maximum satisfaction will occur when the ratio of marginal utility to price between all goods remains equal.

Equation 3.2

$$\frac{\text{Marginal Utility of Good A}}{\text{Price of Good A}} = \frac{\text{Marginal Utility of Good B}}{\text{Price of Good B}} = ... \frac{\text{Marginal Utility of Good N}}{\text{Price of Good N}}$$

or

$$\frac{MU_A}{P_A} = \frac{MU_B}{P_B} = \quad........ \quad \frac{MU_N}{P_N}$$

Although there are two commodities expressed here, Good A and Good B, the analysis can be extended to any number of goods represented by Good N. When this equality holds, the consumer can be said to be maximising utility.

If this does not occur, then improvements may be made by adjusting the budget in such a way as to increase utility by changing from one good which yields lower utility to another yielding a higher utility, a process of substitution which must continue until the maximisation of utilities is gained.

The above equation did not take into consideration the income or budget constraint under which the consumer operates. The total expenditure of the consumer cannot exceed income, here denoted as I. The total expenditure on commodity A is equal to the price of A multiplied by the quantity purchased. The same holds for all the other commodities purchased. The income constraint can be expressed by the following equation:

Equation 3.3

$$Q_A.P_A + Q_B.P_B + ...Q_N.P_N = I$$

Where Q is quantity purchased

P is the price of the commodity

The equation is a statement of the consumer's budget problem when considering a number of commodities. The marginal utility of a commodity is the increase in satisfaction that an individual receives from consuming an additional unit of that good or service.

As the amount of consumption of a particular good increases, so does its total utility, after the initial unit , however, each additional unit consumed gives increasingly less satisfaction and therefore less utility is obtained. Thus whilst total utility increases with increased consumption, marginal utility diminishes per unit of time. This is known as **the law of diminishing marginal utility**. This states that as the amount of a product brought increases the marginal utility to the individual consumer tends to decrease. It will therefore be less highly valued and will only be bought at a lower price. It should be noted that the economic law is not to be confused with statute law or regulation. It is best considered as a 'general tendency.' Some economic textbooks, rather than referring to this law, use the term **'hypothesis of diminishing marginal utility.'**

The consumer, it is observed, gains utility from the consumption of some good or service, but it is necessary to distinguish between total utility (TU) and marginal utility (MU) obtained from consuming various quantities of a commodity. Total utility refers to the entire amount of satisfaction obtained from consuming various quantities of a commodity or service per given time period. **Marginal utility** is the extra utility received from consuming one additional unit of a commodity or service in a given time period. Economic textbooks provide simple examples of the concept of a utility, for example a bar of chocolate or a carton of orange juice. Assuming that a consumer had not eaten a bar of chocolate for some time, the first that he or she eats would be very enjoyable, providing a high level of satisfaction, that is utility for the consumer. The second bar will increase total utility, but not at the same rate as the first; marginal utility will decline. A lower value is placed on the second and subsequent bars from the first. This will continue until the consumer has reached saturation point; this means that he or she is completely full and places no value or a negative value on obtaining an additional bar. This example has been translated into table 3.3

Table 3.3   Total and Marginal Utility of Chocolate Bars (Per Unit of Time)

Quantity	T.U.	M U
0	0	-
1	10	10
2	16	6
3	20	4
4	22	2
5	22	0
6	20	-2

The table, for reasons of interpretation, will treat utility as though it can be measured. There is some controversy in the literature as to whether or not utility can be measured. An important point is that the theory does not require the measurement of utility. All that is required is that the consumers are capable of distinguishing between larger and smaller amounts of utility. The table above indicates that total utility continues to increase, but at a decreasing rate, until between four and five bars have been consumed, and this stands at 22 units. This is the maximum point and is known as the saturation point. Consuming beyond this point leads to a decline in total utility. The final column of the table indicates the marginal utility of the consumer's consumption of each extra bar. This serves to highlight the fact that marginal utility rises, reaches a maximum, and then falls continuously, indicating declining satisfaction. The table data is illustrated in figure 3.1 and 3.2.

In figure 3.1 the total utility increases in declining amounts indicated by the curve, until it reaches saturation point at 22 units. Beyond this it contracts. This is confirmed by the diminishing marginal utility in figure 3.2 which eventually reaches a negative value. For example, the first bar gives the consumer 10 units of utility, whereas the fourth bar only adds a further 2 units to the total utility. A demand curve can thus be derived directly from the marginal utility curve and concept of

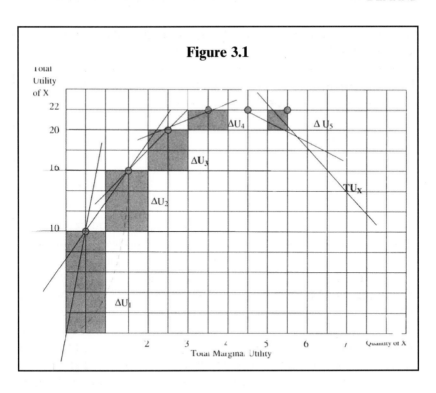

Figure 3.1

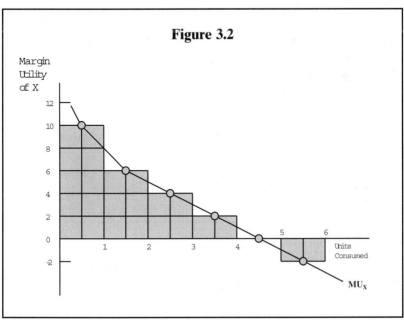

Figure 3.2

utility. In order to do this, it is necessary to consider what happens when there is a change in the price of chocolate, assuming that prices of all other goods are held constant. If the price of chocolate rises, then the equilibrium position established by equation 3.2 is disturbed such that:

$$\frac{\text{MU Chocolate}}{\text{MU Other goods}} \quad < \quad \frac{\text{Price of Chocolate}}{\text{Price Other goods}}$$

To restore the equilibrium, the consumer must buy less chocolate, which will then raise its marginal utility. Thus, as the price of a good increases, the quantity demanded decreases, and the demand curve slopes downward. This inverse relationship between price and quantity is referred to as the **law of demand.**

The logic of the proposition of utility theory was generally accepted by economists up until 1930 and here it has been used to give a general background to the problems of demand. The utility theory, as has been stated, has been criticised because of its subjective nature causing an inability to measure or give any precise value to utility. The lack of any statistical data brought into question the concept of the law of diminishing marginal utility. These criticisms about the difficulty of measurement can be summarised as follows. Firstly, the assumption that money has a constant value utility; it is argued that this will be dependent on the amount of money which the consumer possesses. Secondly, there is the problem of divisibility, that consumers have a choice of a little of each commodity and can change this at the margin in order to maximise utility. The difficulty emerges when there are no margins; either the whole commodity is consumed or none at all. This is usually the case when an individual is travelling. Take, for example, a sea-voyage. A traveller must take the whole voyage and cannot, under normal circumstances, decide to leave the vessel in mid-ocean, even if diminishing marginal utility is great, the voyage remains indivisible. Thirdly, it is impossible to compare different individual utility. To continue with the sea voyage example, one individual may still be gaining utility long after another individual's total utility has declined sharply.

Finally, the main criticism made by transport economists is that with both the movement of freight and people there is a considerable amount of spatially scattered choice all of which will require an outlay as time. Such particular problems present difficulties for utility of a generalised theory. It is due largely to these theorems that the classical utility explanation of consumers' behaviour and of an individual's consumer demand, the indifference curve theory, was developed and accepted. Whilst this is often considered to be an alternative theory, it is an important complementary theory to the classical approach and again it gives a clear understanding of consumers' behaviour than will exclusive use of either theory.

Indifference Curves

So far the discussion has been based on the concept of cardinal utility. This means that each consumer attaches a specific value to each good or service, or quantity of goods or services. This method often uses a mystical unit of measure known as utils. There are, of course, inherent difficulties in using such units. Indifference curve analysis changes the emphasis of utility from cardinal to ordinal. The latter idea requires the consumer to be able to rank the preferences for substitutable commodities in bundles rather than attach quantifiable units of satisfaction to them. The theory is of consumer behaviour based on the assumption that utility for different bundles of commodities can be ranked by the consumer in order of preference. It is also assumed that income and prices of all goods remain constant and that they are all what is termed 'normal' goods. The consumer is assumed to be a rational maximiser of satisfaction, and on these assumptions, indifference schedules can be constructed. These consists of various combinations of two goods, or two bundles of goods which will yield a consumer with the same amount of utility over a given time period. The idea is of indifference to any combination as illustrated by table 3.5. For the purposes of the example, only two goods are available, food and clothing.

Table 3.5   Bundles of Food (y) and Bundles of Clothing (x)

Bundles of Food	Bundles of Clothing
1	25
2	15
3	10
4	6
5	2

The above schedule indicates that a consumer is indifferent between 5 bundles of food and 2 bundles of clothing, or 1 bundle of food and 25 bundles of clothing, and so on. The schedule can be converted into indifference curves showing the various combination of two bundles of goods which will yield to the consumer consistent equal amounts of utility per unit of time (Figure 3.3).

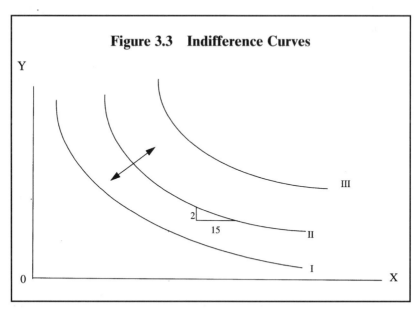

Figure 3.3   Indifference Curves

The indifference curve represents a series of bundles of two goods, clothing (x) and food (y) between which the consumer is indifferent. The curve is convex to the origin and thus negative sloping. This shape shows that as one good becomes more plentiful, relative to the other, its subjective growth becomes smaller in terms of other goods. This reflects the **'law of substitution,'** which simply means that as food becomes scarce, there is an increase in the relative substitution value in relation to other goods (2 bundles of food = 15 bundles of clothing). The rate at which one bundle of goods is substituted for another as it moves along the indifference curve is known as the **marginal rate of substitution.** The curve, of course, will give a consistent level of utility. hence, whilst the consumer has less and less food, there is a gain of more and more clothing. An individual's indifference curve represents a particular level of satisfaction utility. An indifference map can be drawn to represent different levels of satisfaction. A higher indifference curve represents a higher level of satisfaction. Curve III therefore indicates a higher level of utility than curves I and II. The consumer aims to reach the highest possible indifference curve. Such advancement is constrained by the consumer's income and the price of the goods. This may be illustrated diagramatically by the budget line in figure 3.4.

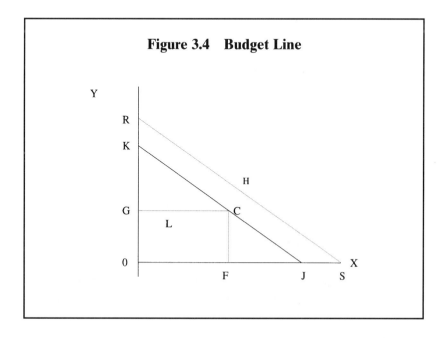

Figure 3.4   Budget Line

Line KJ is known under a number of titles, all broadly conveying the same meaning, e.g. Budget Constraint Line, **Budget Line**, Money Price Line, Line of Attainable Combination and Consumption Possibility Line. Here it will be referred to as the budget line. This line is merely a graphical representation of the constraints placed on a consumer by the given level of income. The consumer has a fixed amount of money. At this fixed level of income, the prices of goods x and y are such that consumption can be 0J of x, 0K of y, or a combination of the two. Hence, the budget line is indicated by KJ. The consumer cannot, because of the budget line, go beyond this, say at point H, since limits on income will not allow this. Nor will the consumer purchase goods within the limits of the budget line, say at point L, as this will not be rational in that it does not fit within the maximisation aim. The consumer may choose bundles of x and y anywhere along the budget line. At point C, for example, an individual would be choosing 0F of x and 0G of y. The dotted line RS illustrates the movement of the budget line should the consumer's income

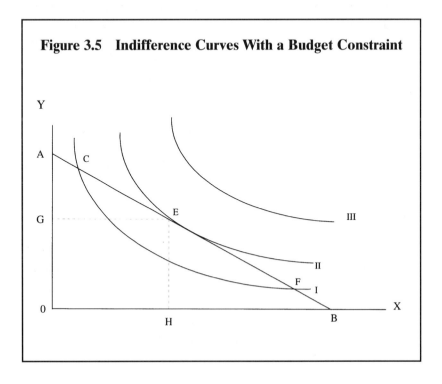

Figure 3.5   Indifference Curves With a Budget Constraint

increase. This is known as the income effect. So far the discussion has concentrated separately on indifference curves and maps as indicated by consumers preference and the budget line as constraints on realising those preferences. How does the consumer allocate his limited budget between the purchases of goods x and other goods indicated by y? This question is answered by combining the two concepts of the indifference curves of the budget lines together in figure 3.5.

The main assumption is emphasised when constructing such a model that the consumer aims always to obtain the greatest satisfaction; that is to obtain the highest possible indifference curve. The consumer in the above model gains maximum satisfaction at point E, purchasing 0H of x and 0G of y, leaving GA for other purchases. E is the point of tangency of the budget line through the highest possible indifference curve II which represents the highest level of satisfaction obtainable within the budget limitations. There are other points where indifference curves intercept the budget line in the model Figure 3.5, namely C and F. Both of these are on indifference curve I; a lower curve giving therefore a lower level of satisfaction. Whilst the indifference curve III is beyond the limit set by the budget line AB. It is therefore unattainable unless there is some change in the position of the budget line or its slope.

Relaxing the earlier assumption of constant consumption, consumer income and price stability of all goods, it is possible to examine the effects of all three on demand. These are the Price Effects, Substitution Effects. and Income Effects.

Price Effects

Figure 3.6 shows the change in the price of good X. This will alter the consumer's purchasing power. Consider an initial budget of K2. If the price of good X is increased, then less of good X can be brought. The budget line will shift towards the origin to K1. Should the price, on the other hand, contract, then the budget line will shift out away from the origin to K3.

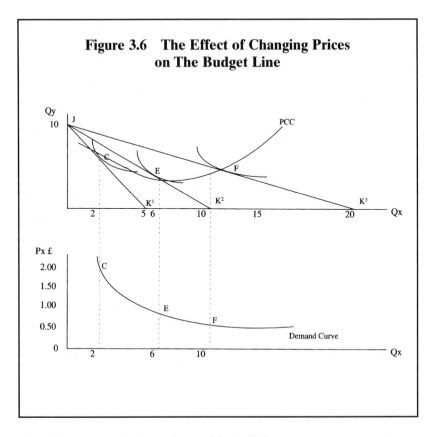

**Figure 3.6   The Effect of Changing Prices
on The Budget Line**

Combining the budget line with indifference curves creates a price consumption curve (PCC). This is a curve on an indifference map indicating the level of demand of a consumer for a given commodity at different prices. Here it is assumed that the price of good Y remains constant, whilst the price of X commodity changes. The budget line shift displays a decline in the price, beginning at K1 and moving in stages to K2 and K3. The equilibrium position of each price change is at the point where the indifference curves are tangential to the new budget line at C, E, and F along the PCC line. The PCC shows that successively larger quantities are brought as price falls.

On the budget line JK1, the consumer maximises utility at point C, purchasing 2X and 6Y. Assuming that income remains constant at £10, and the price of Y remains constant at £1 per unit, a reduction in the price of X from £2 to £1 would cause the budget line to flatten to JK2. The new equilibrium could be established at E, with the purchase of 6X and 4Y. A further reduction in the price of X to £0.50, creates a new budget line JK3, and optimum point F, representing 10X and 5Y.

The PCC can then be used to derive the individual's demand curve. The quantity of X remains on the horizontal axis, whilst the vertical axis becomes the price of X. At a price of £2, 2X (C) are purchased. A fall in price to £1 increases the quantity purchased to 6X. (E) Finally, at £0.50 (F) per unit, 10X will be bought.

Substitution and Income Effects

The fall in the price of X has two effects. Firstly, it changes the relative prices of the goods X and Y, and secondly, it reduces the expenditure required to achieve the initial level of satisfaction.

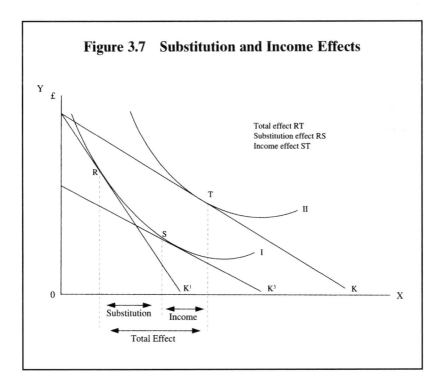

Figure 3.7   Substitution and Income Effects

In other words there is a substitution effect and an income effect. The substitution effect is the result of the change in relative prices, with real income constant. It is represented by a movement along the indifference curve. The income effect is the change resulting from the change in real purchasing power, with relative prices held constant. This effect is represented by a shift to another indifference curve All changes in price may be decomposed into both income and substitution effect. These may be represented graphically in Figure 3.7.

Points R and S represent the optimal quantities of X and Y before and after the fall in the price of X, with K1 and K2, the corresponding budget lines. RS is the total price effect. In order to isolate the substitution and income effects, line K3 is introduced. This is the line which represents the same level of real purchasing power and satisfaction before the change, but the relative prices after the change. Thus the line is parallel to K2 but tangential to indifference curve I. The substitution effect is represented by the movement along the original indifference curve I at the new relative prices - RS. The income effect is represented by the movement to the higher indifference curve solely due to the greater purchasing power - ST. Thus indifference curve analysis can be used to show how the consumer decides between goods within budget constraints and changing prices. The income effect is such that at lower prices the consumer has greater purchasing power and can therefore buy more goods and services. If the price of the product they are buying increases, then the consumer will look for substitutes, and thus reduce the quantity demanded. This analysis further explains the law of demand.

The derivation of the individual demand curve can be used to determine the market demand for a commodity. The market demand curve is derived from the horizontal summation of all the individual demand curves in the market. This is illustrated in the following example of the UK demand for Egyptian potatoes.

The individual consumer schedules are shown in the table below

**Table 3.4   UK Demand Schedule for Egyptian Potatoes
Quantity demanded per unit of time)**

Price Per Unit	Consumer I	Consumer II	Consumer III	Total Quantity Demanded
70	1	3	0	4
60	3	6	3	12
50	6	9	5	20
40	8	12	10	30
30	11	14	13	38

This can be converted into individual demand curves in Figure 3.8:

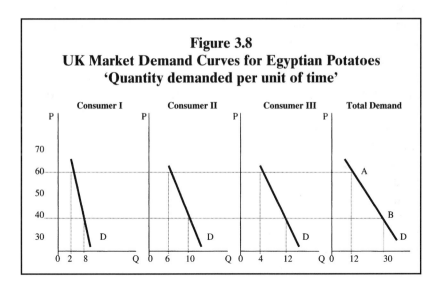

Each consumer at different levels of price will purchase a certain amount of potatoes as given by their individual demand curves (D). Consider a price of 60. The horizontal summation of all consumers denoted by point A shows the total market demand for quantity 12. At a lower price, at say 40, the horizontal summation of all consumer demand curves is shown at point B. Here the law applies and has increased total market demand to 30. This is the aggregated demand of all consumers and has been calculated for simplicity on the basis of three consumers or purchasers. It could, of course, be based on a greater number to the nth degree. In this way the total market or industrial demand can be constructed. At its foundation is the concept of individual utility, in particular marginal utility.

Summary

This chapter has examined the growth and trends in the demand for seaborne trade over the last thirty years. The demand for shipping is a derived demand in that it depends on the demand for the final product. There is also a positive relationship between the demand for shipping and economic growth. Shipping is 'normal good' in that a price fall increases the quantity demanded. Demand theory explains this phenomenon in terms of diminishing marginal utility. Additional units of the product will be valued less highly, and will therefore be bought at a lower price. Indifference curves can be used to rank bundles of different goods in order to obtain higher levels of satisfaction. Such preferences are affected by budgets, income and changing prices. For a normal good, a fall in the price will result in a higher quantity purchased. Hence the demand curve is downward sloping.

Further Reading

Gwilliam K. M. and P.J. Mackie, 'Economics and Transport Policy', London George Allan and Unwin Ltd, 1975.

O' Loughlin C., 'The Economics of Sea Transport', Oxford, Pergamon Press, 1967.

Stubbs P.C., W.J. Tyson and M.O. Dalvi, 'Transport Economics', London George Allan and Unwin Ltd, 1980.

Wohli M. and C Hendrickson, 'Transportation, Investment and Pricing Principles', Chichester, John Wiley and Son, 1984.

[1] See Chapter 4 for a detailed discussion
[2] explained below
[3] NB: This can be supply as well as demand driven
[4] Garb G., Microeconomics: Theory, Applications, Innovations, London Macmillan 1981, p.30.
[5] Bonavia M.R., The Economics of Transport, Cambridge, Cambridge University Press, 1954
[6] op.cit. Bonavia M.R., p.2.

Chapter Four

SUPPLY

Introduction

The object of economic theory is to construct a model which analyses the economic behaviour of individual units and their interaction within an economic system. The consumers; the shipper of cargo and passengers, that is the demand side examined in chapter 3. It is the supply element which will be examined here, the supply of tonnage offered by the shipowners.

The supply of any commodity or service can be defined as the amount producers are willing and able to offer for sale at a particular price at a certain time. The ability indicates that it is effective supply. At different prices, producers are likely to offer different amounts. Supply can be seen as a two-dimensional relationship between quantity of goods or services the suppliers will sell at all possible prices, in a particular period of time, *ceteris paribus*. Normally, the supply curve will be upward sloping to the right, since a higher price will induce producers to place more goods or services on the market. It may also induce additional producers to enter the market. At a lower price many producers will hold back their supplies, especially if they think an increase in price is imminent.

61

Shipping supply can be defined simply as the quantity of shipping services offered on the market at a particular freight rate over a given period of time. The freight rate and the time qualification are necessary because under normal conditions, the higher the freight rate, the larger will be the quantity of shipping services supplied and the longer the period of time, the more the shipowner will be able to adjust the amount of tonnage offered to take advantage of any change in freight rate. This relates to one of the basic laws of economics; the relationship between price; that is freight rate, and the quantity supplied, *ceteris paribus* - that is all other things being equal. The higher the freight rate, the larger the quantity supplied. Conversely, the lower the freight rate, the smaller the quantity supplied. There is therefore, under normal conditions, a positive or direct relationship between freight rate and the quantity of tonnage shipowners offer on the market. There are a number of underlying assumptions here. The discussion is based on a competitive market where there is no serious interference with the functioning of the price mechanism. Further, the discussion does not consider costs which underpin all supply. These will be examined in some detail later.

There are three shipping market supply situations. Firstly, the market engaged solely in the buying and selling of vessels themselves, usually referred to as the second-hand or sale and purchase market, dealing with vessels which continue to trade. Secondly, there is the market dealing with shipping services where the supply of tonnage is of central importance for its transport function. Thirdly, the market for scrapping and demolishing ships.

The supply of tonnage consists of all vessels in the world fleet and is shown in the table below. Here the assumption is made that supply is simply synonymous with total tonnage. This is not to argue that the statistics are precise, but they are a convenient way of broadly indicating the annual amount of tonnage and its change over a considerable period of time.

**Table 4.1   The Supply of Tonnage 1970 -1996
(100 GRT+)**

Year	Number	Tons (GRT '000s)	% change over previous year (GRT)
1970	52444	227490	7.5
1971	55041	247203	8.7
1972	57391	268340	8.6.
1973	59606	289927	8.0
1974	61194	311323	7.4
1975	63724	342162	9.9
1976	65887	372000	8.7
1977	67945	393678	5.8
1978	69020	406002	3.1
1979	71129	413021	1.7
1980	73832	419911	1.7
1981	73864	420835	0.2
1982	75151	424742	0.9
1983	76106	422590	-0.5
1984	76068	418682	-0.9
1985	76395	416269	-0.6
1986	75266	404910	-2.7
1987	75240	403498	-0.3
1988	75680	403406	0.0
1989	76100	410481	1.8
1990	78336	423627	3.2
1991	80030	436027	2.9
1992	79845	444305	1.9
1993	80493	453109	2.0
1994	80048	466199	2.9
1995	81084	482842	3.6
1996	84011	503406	4.3

Source: Lloyd's Register of Shipping, Statistical Tables

The table gives a long-term statistical record of the change in the global supply based on tonnage (Gross Registered Tons). Over the period 1970 - 1996, the world fleet increased in tonnage GRT by 121 %. The 1970s saw the greatest appreciation of fleet size of 85%, representing a huge increase in supply. In the 1980s (1983 - 1987) the fleet began to decline. This followed the peak in 1982. In this year the constant expansion in the world fleet had experienced for three decades ground to a halt. Throughout the remainder of the decade, there has been a virtual balance between newly built vessels being delivered and the scrapping of uneconomic tonnage and vessels lost for other reasons. During the final year of the decade 1989 experienced the first increase in tonnage since 1982. The 1990s experienced a gradual expansion to a new peak in 1996.

The discussion so far has considered the total tonnage of the world merchant fleet at a particular time. This can be referred to as total supply; that is all vessels which are capable of trading within a given time period. The condition of the shipping freight markets will have a considerable influence on this total over time. In the short-run it will be of central importance to the percentage of total supply engaged in trading. This trading of operating tonnage is known as **active supply.** The remaining surplus tonnage is known as **available supply.** This is made up of vessels laid up for lack of any suitable commercial employment, tonnage undergoing repair or detained for some other reason. There is, in addition to these, two major categories that can be termed **potential supply.** This is made up of newly built vessels and vessels entering operations from some other area of activity. The above can be defined simply in equation 4.1:

Equation 4.1

Total Supply = Active Supply + Available Supply + Potential Supply

---

The movement of tonnage between active and available or potential supply will be sensitive to the freight rate because of the positive relationship between price and supply. The volume of available supply that is laid up and the amount of tonnage scrapped or broken up will, with time lags, vary inversely with the level of freight rates. A contraction in freight rates increases the amount of tonnage laid up. This is often the initial shipowners response to low rates because vessels are costly to operate. Should the freight rate remain depressed for some considerable time, there will be an increased amount of tonnage broken up or scrapped. A further influence here will be the price of scrap per ton. The process is reversed when freight rates improve. Tonnage is reactivated; that is brought out of lay-up. Such favourable freight rates may move previously uneconomic tonnage into operational profitability creating a reluctance to scrap. As already suggested, time lags must be included in any analysis, particularly during periods of depressed freight rates. Shipowners often take time to react to such market conditions for a number of reasons such as the existence of charter commitments or the expectation that the depressed market is short-term. This means that the tonnage will remain part of the active supply at low freight rates in the short-run.

These are the central factors in the supply which will now be examined in more detail. The basic argument here is that there is a limit in the short-run to the total capacity; that is total supply is finite in the short-run. Further, the time it takes to build new vessels has only a marginal effect on total capacity in such a short-run. The supply curve illustrates the relationship between the quantity supplied and the freight rate. No matter how high freight rates may be there is a limit to the supply of capacity that can be offered on the market. At a low level of freight rates, some vessels can be laid up. Logically, at any freight rate less than shipowners costs, there will be some withdrawal of vessels from active supply.

Supply Constituents

There are four main methods of changing the level of shipping supply. New construction, scrapping, changes in speed and laying up. There is also within supply the second hand market often referred to as the sale and purchase market. This market facilitates the transfer of ownership within the industry. New construction creates additions to total supply, scrapping deletions from that supply. They cause significant variables in the level of the industry's tonnage. The function of changing speed and laying up or reactivating laid up tonnage is to adjust supply levels in the short-run. Lay-up is often referred to as a barometer indicating the level of general and sectional market activities. Each of these supply elements will be dealt with individually in the following section.

Shipbuilding

Shipbuilding is the primary method of increasing the supply of tonnage within the shipping industry. It generally increases not only in the number and tonnage of vessels but the quality of that tonnage. This assertion is based on the simple premise that tonnage improves through increased productivity; vessels built in the late 1990s will be much improved on the vessels built say, in the late 1970s. Hence supply is increased on two levels, the number and tonnage of vessels and the improvement in what can be termed their economic or commercial performance. The demand for new building, the decision by shipowners to invest, will differ according to the economic climates in which they operate. The prime demand comes from companies requiring new tonnage to fulfil their actual transport requirements. These requirements can be those of a production process, as with oil companies or firms operating a regular service, the liner trade being an obvious example. Such investment activities are often related to long-run programmes of capacity development. The second group are speculators, who invest in new ships at a particular time when they perceive the price to be low, in the expectation of selling the vessel on later, at a higher price. This speculative aspect is based on the time that elapses between the placing of the contract, building the vessel and its delivery. Unlike other capital investment, the price of newbuildings can and often does fluctuate rapidly. Such speculations are seldom concerned with the production process of maritime transport, except occasionally in the very short-run. They are 'risk takers' with the ability to interpret price moves often based on considerable statistical and other information. Demand for newbuilding constitutes a minor element in their activity, for these are concentrated on the second hand shipping market. Shipbuilding companies themselves often engage in speculative activity. This occurs when contracts for new tonnage are at a low price they will embark on new building projects, such investment being based on the expectation of selling the vessel at a later date hopefully before it is completed.

Shipbuilding was until the 1950s an assembly industry concentrated almost wholly in Europe, in particular the United Kingdom and in North America as it had been for the previous century. In the next two decades the whole climate in which the industry operated underwent a radical change. First the dramatic development of the industry in Japan and in the other Asian countries, combined with the growth of the flags of convenience fleets with no attachment to a particular nationally based building industry. Secondly, in the years immediately following the second world war there was a buyers' market for the shipbuilding industry, shipowners experienced little difficulty in negotiating the necessary finance to invest in new tonnage from financial and banking centres, particularly those in the United States. During the late 1950's order books were depressingly thin. There was apprehension of the close down of some capacity with all the economic and social ramifications; this necessitated substantial government intervention. A trend interwoven with the third factor the closing of the Suez Canal in 1956 and again in 1967. An important influence in the demand for larger vessels, very large crude carriers (VLCC) and later ultra large crude carriers (ULCC). Such tonnage represented far larger levels of investment than previously. Both these latter factors combined to fundamentally change the shipbuilding industry. This involved the institution of a new financial credit system which shifted the financial burden from what had previously been the function of the shipowner to the function of the shipbuilder. These and other changes are reflected in the regional reorganisation of the industry as shown in the following table:

Table 4.2   % MERCHANT SHIPS COMPLETED BY REGION 1960 TO 1995 (100 GRT+)

	UK %	Europe %	Japan %	Korea %	Others %	Total (GRT Million)	Index 1960=100
(1950)	(42.7)					(3)	
1960	15.5	56 1	21.9	—-	7	8	100
1965	10.9	43.1	41.5	—-	4.5	11	140
1970	6.3	39.8	48.1	0.0	5.8	20	250
1975	3.4	40.2	49.7	1.2	5.5	34	408
1980	3.3	21.2	46 5	4.0	14 8	13	156
1985	0.9	23.6	52.3	14.4	8.8	18	216
1990	0.8	21.6	43 0	21.8	12.8	20	189
1995	1.5	18.8	41.5	27.7	10.5	22	265

Source ISL. Shipping Statistics Year Book 1996 page 305

The above traces a number of developments in the industry in terms of gross registered tonnage built. These trends are closely related and react to others in the shipping market, the most important being that of the freight rates, the market for second hand tonnage and scrapping. Both the index and the total tonnage columns give some indication of the cyclical pattern within the industry. The market or demand swings are highlighted in the decade of the 1970's when a long-run peak in production occurred. It was a period in which the world fleet grew from 329 million (DWT) to 546 million (DWT) in 1975, despite the 1973 oil crisis, and continued to increase to 682 million (DWT) by 1980. The restructuring and reorganising can be seen in the changing regional percentages, against a general growth in total tonnage. The 1950 figures are simply included to highlight the supremacy of the United Kingdom at this time and the speed at which it declined, and Japan later joined by Korea expanded. The wider European industry faired marginally better than that of the United Kingdom but in the two decades 1960 - 1980 its percentage share more than halved. In broad terms the index shows the industry is characterised by large changes in levels of output. The table also illustrates a movement from concentration in Europe through some balance between the regions to a similar concentration in Asia. An underlying element in these changes have been the technological development of the shipping industry. The developments have caused the shipbuilding markets to become dependent on three main ship types tankers, bulkers and container vessels. A concentration serving to emphasis the cyclical market patterns; if for any reason one of the three major types experiences a substantial change in demand it will be rapidly transmitted to the industry creating a boom or a slump in the orders for new tonnage.

Investment

An investment decision in new building, is one to purchase additional capital. Such capital investment will take two forms, the purchase of new vessels to replace ones which are worn out or secondly additional new building enlarging the stock of vessels. The replacement of worn out capital is known as **'Replacement Investment'.** The amount of investment which takes place over and above such replacement investment is known as **'Net Investment'**, it is the addition to the stock of capital after the requirements for replacement have been achieved. A shipowners total or gross investment will be as follows:

GROSS INVESTMENT = REPLACEMENT INVESTMENT + NET INVESTMENT

The shipowner will invest in the new vessels (capital goods) either to prevent the productivity capacity of the tonnage owned falling, as existing vessels wear out, or expand tonnage capacity. Such primary investment decisions seek to optimise capital from the view point of the shipowner, that is the private individual or the shipping group. The basic aim being that the revenue or other benefits of the capital investment should more than compensate for its cost. The issue is the choice a shipowner makes in allocating scarce resources. Further such a decision to invest is made in the knowledge that a capital is particularly durable, that the vessel will operate over a considerable period of time[1]. There is a general lack of alternative uses for the vessel. When making the decision to invest not only must the opportunity cost be considered but once that decision has been made calculations of the amount of revenue, freight the vessel will earn over the time period of ownership and what will be her second hand or scrap value at the end of this period when the tonnage is dispensed with.

Scrapping

To scrap, break up, demolish or what is occasionally referred to as dismantle the vessel it is to remove it permanently from the total supply of tonnage. Thus scrapping is the only guaranteed method of removing a vessel totally from the industries supply. The decision to scrap is based on the appraisal of the long-run market situation in relation to a particular vessel. It is an assessment of the vessel's earning capacity as against its total cost. The decision to scrap, will relate to a situation, where, shipowners expectations about the future trading prospects and profitability for the vessel are negative. There are usually other options open to owners to lay-up or to sell the vessel on the second hand market. These will be denied to owners if the vessel is physically and economically obsolete that is to say that its scrap value is greater than its potential trading value. The decision can be dependent on unforeseen decline in the value of the capital asset due to one or the combination of factors for example technological, economic, political, and regulatory changes. Despite these and other factors, the primary one is the freight market and its prospects both in general, and in the particular market sector in which the vessel operates.

A simple analysis sees an unambiguous relationship between freight markets and tonnage of scrap offered and by implication the price of that tonnage to the ship breakers. A depressed freight rate means an increase in the supply of tonnage offered for demolition and a lowering of the scrap price. An improvement in the freight rate market causes a withdrawal of tonnage on offer and a corresponding increase in the scrap price. This relationship means an inverted movement in supply of tonnage for scrap and its price. In such an analysis the demand side must not be overlooked, in other words the demand emanating from the user of scrap metal material in the steel and construction industries. Their interest is not in the vessel carrying capacity but in the weight, what is known as its Light Displacement Tonnage (LDT). This is the weight of the whole vessel including machinery, equipment and spares. The amount of steel from a vessel varies considerably and is dependent on the vessel type. An important point here is the amount of non-ferrous metal in the vessel such as manganese, bronze and copper which commands considerably higher prices than steel. In addition to this the value of resaleable items, for example pumps, generators, anchors and chains and so on, will be of importance. The value of an individual vessel will be dependent on its type, age and general condition; hence discussing price in terms of LDT will only give a broad indicator of trends.

The price of scrap tends to follow the movement of the freight market in all sectors of the industry. A depressed freight market engenders low expectations of future revenue earnings amongst shipowners and increased amount of tonnage is sold to breakers. This process is reversed in periods of buoyant freight markets when expectations of future revenue raised among shipowners creates a reluctance on their part to sell tonnage for scrap. There will be a consequential reduction in the suppliers scrap putting pressure on the ship breakers to increase the price per LDT. This analysis suggests that there are two levels of interrelated factors, the micro level of the shipping and the ship breaking (scrapping)

71

industry where there is a floor, a basic minimum amount that will be demanded for scrap tonnage. During periods of high freight rates there is a price ceiling which secures the minimum amount of scrap required. This is the macro level when the freight market is buoyant, it has been stimulated directly by the increased level of demand for sea borne transport. An important element in this will be a boom in the steel industry with its increased demand for coking coal and iron ore as well as scrap. Hence the activity at both the micro and macro levels serve to reinforce one another.

It is possible to summarise much of the above discussion on the criteria individual shipowners use in making the decision to sell their vessels to the breakers. The main variables included can be set out in terms of a simple formula

---

Equation 4.2

$$P_0 - P_t \rangle \sum_{t=1}^{n} \frac{(Y_t - C_t)}{(1+r)^t}$$

Where P_0 is the current sale price of the vessel

P_t is the expected value of the vessel at time t

t is the time period

Y_t is the anticipated income or earnings at time t

C_t is the anticipated costs at time t

r is the rate of interest

The equation suggests that there will be a tendency to sell a vessel to the breakers if the current sale price P_0 is greater than the expected sale price P_t. On the right hand side of the equation, income Y_t will be both current and anticipated earnings, that is current and expectations of the freight market. Cost levels are represented by C_t. (Y_t-C_t) will produce current and future profits or lack of them. These profits must be discounted back to the present day using the appropriate rate of interest. Put simply the shipowner will make the decision to sell the vessel for scrap if the price P_0 is greater than the expected price P_t as given by the present value of future profits. Hence the present and future freight markets situation and expectations of the future movements both in income and cost will be central to the amount of tonnage leaving total supply for the ship breakers.

Laying-up

The withdrawal of tonnage from active supply is to lay-up the vessel. This is seen as a temporary solution, the assumption being that laid up vessels will eventually return to active supply. Laying-up occurs during periods when there is a surplus supply of tonnage in relation to the level of demand from cargo shippers. The amount of tonnage laid up, sometimes referred to as idle tonnage, is the barometer giving a clear indication of the economic and commercial condition of the industry. There is little or no laid up tonnage in periods of shipping prosperity, when freight rates are buoyant. Conversely, increasing amounts of tonnage are laid up during periods of recession which are signalled by low freight rates and lack of adequate employment opportunity for vessels. The cardinal point here is that the laying up process is a temporary one, and the tonnage can be returned to trading operations, active supply, as soon as freight rates improve enough to make reactivation commercially possible. Thus while there are other factors influencing the timing of shipowners' decisions to lay-up or reactivate tonnage, the most important is the level of the freight rate. It follows that the trend in laying up vessels mirrors the freight rate, but with a time lag. The annual average of vessels and tonnage laid up, with the percentage of world D.W.T. is indicated by the following table.

**Table 4.3 Total Tonnage Laid up: Annual Average World
Fleets 1980 - 1996
(excluding storage vessels, 000s tons)**

WORLD				
End Year	**Number**	**G.R.T.**	**D.W.T.**	**% D.W.T.**
1980	402	5,445	9,190	1
1981	527	15,436	27,391	4
1982	1,549	45,978	83,761	12
1983	1,663	42,488	78,827	12
1984	1,302	33,303	62,350	9
1985	1,170	46,363	49,187	7
1986	953	13,933	24,104	4
1987	649	9,762	16,243	3
1988	424	4,161	6,243	1
1989	298	2,945	4,607	1
1990	310	2,885	4,473	1
1991	335	3,228	5,071	1
1992	445	7,054	12,336	2
1993	427	5,534	8,916	1
1994	360	4,415	6,967	1
1995	354	3,874	5,397	1
1996	300	2,849	3,834	1

Source: Transport Statistics Report, Merchant Fleet Statistics, London, Department of Transport, H.M.S.O. (Annual).

The relative buoyancy of freight rates during the late 1970s and early 1980s is reflected in the low level of tonnage laid up. The rapid decline in demand and hence freight rates of 1982-1984 correspond to a peak in total tonnage laid up, the highest ever recorded at one point in the period, 1726 vessels, some 99,900 D.W.T[2]. There was a gradual decline from this peak, gaining momentum towards the end of the decade. By the 1990s, only approximately 1% against some 12% of the tonnage total were laid up, again this is interrelated with the improvement in the freight markets during the same period.

The difference in size, age, ownership and flag registration of vessels will mean different lay-up rates. The assumption was that small, relatively old vessels, would be among the first to lay-up. This presumption has been increasingly questioned since the vast increase in vessel size and the oil crises of the early and late 1970s. The trend now appears to be for the larger bulk carriers, in particular tankers which are ageing assets, to lay-up first. One of the major influences here is the average size of the consignment to be shipped. This has contracted during the long period of low freight rates, explained by the unwillingness of consignees to hold large expensive stocks.

The substantial amount of tonnage laid up indicated by the table should not be used to convey the idea that shipowners are eager to lay-up their vessels. The opposite is true, shipowners are generally extremely reluctant to lay-up their tonnage. Such action means that all revenue from a vessels operations cease immediately. This point must be emphasised, for while laying up causes revenue to stop immediately, certain costs do not cease. There are fixed costs associated with vessel capital, and maintenance costs even in a laid up condition. Thus the movement from active supply will occur when the vessels freight earning potential falls below the cost of operating the vessels by more than the incurred costs while laying up, plus switching costs. The level of freight rate at which this occurs is known as the vessels lay-up rate or lay-up point. It is the freight rate at which it is more advantageous for a shipowner to lay-up a vessel than to continue trading. The most important factor influencing the choice is therefore the shipowners expectation of the freight market. The options for the shipowner can be summarised as follows:

1. To continue trading

This will be dependent on expectations of freight rates improving in the immediate or short-run. It could be combined with a voyage at loss making rates or in ballast to where the vessel is in a better location to take advantage of any freight rate improvement.

2. To wait, in fully operational condition, for example, off some port, for a favourable freight rate offer.

3 To re-classify or re-flag a vessel

The aim of this being to restructure costs, and hence lower them.

4. Lay-up the vessel

5. Sell the vessel on the second hand market, or for scrap.

These options serve to illustrate the importance of the expectations of freight rate trends in both the short and long-run. Svendsen comments *"to a greater extent than most businessmen, the shipowner must be an economic prophet and the future of his company depends on how true his prophecies turn out to be"*.[3]

To examine these options in more detail: In option 1 there is considerable reluctance to lay the vessel up. Such reluctance is often combined with the hope that other shipowners will withdraw their tonnage to lay-up, thus curtailing supply and presumably causing an improvement in the freight rate. This will allow the individual shipowner to continue trading under increasingly favourable operating conditions. The shipowner will therefore accept a loss making or distresses rate in the short-run. However, this loss making rate often serves to undercut existing rates and further depresses the market.

Option 2 is, in some respects, similar to 1. A 'wait and see' attitude prevails, combined with the ability to react rapidly because of operational readiness at any sign of improvement in the freight rates. It is similar to waiting for a bus rather than walking a short distance to a destination. The longer the wait, the increased temptation to remain simply because they have waited so long already. The underlying assumption is that a revival in freight rates is imminent and, as with the bus, the waiter will be rewarded. Various psychological factors come into play in this decision. To lay-up a vessel may be seen as a failure, a lack of business acumen on the part of the shipowner. Such factors, although difficult to quantify, nevertheless provide an explanation of general reluctance to lay-up and the haste to re-activate tonnage.

Option 3 is an attempt to solve the problem of depressed freight rates using a different method, that is lowering costs. For example, the process of re-classification or re-registering vessels under a different flag, presumably allowing the vessel to operate profitably at lower freight rates.

Option 4 will be dependent on the shipowner's view of the vessel's employment prospects and on the laying up cost calculation. A number of factors must be considered: the deterioration of the vessel's engines, machinery and hull during the lay-up period; costs of port services and insurance; finding a suitable berth.

Option 5 is the most dramatic, as it means that the shipowner has no short or long-run expectation of profitable trading opportunities for the vessel. The most advantageous course of action is to secure the vessel's scrap value.

A general calculation for these lay-up costs is put forward by P.M. Alderton.[4]

Table 4.4   Hypothetical Lay-Up Cost

Duration in Months	Incremental Cost $	Total Cost $
1	45,536	45,536
2	9,536	55,072
3	9,536	64,608
4	9,536	74,144
5	9,536	83,680
6	9,536	93,216
7	9,536	102,752
8	9,536	112,288
9	9,536	121,824
N		+(N-1 x 9,536)

The above table highlights the importance of the initial costs and the steady increase in cost related to the duration of the lay-up. This further emphasises the importance of the expectation as to time spent in lay-up. The table does not include reactivation costs it must be pointed out. Lay-up costs are thus comprised of three elements; decommissioning cost, lay-up fee and re-commissioning or reactivation costs.

The basic analysis of lay-up in the above discussions have been examined by Svendsen[5] who constructed a model encapsulating the laid up point idea. This illustrates the interaction between demand for tonnage, the costs of supplying tonnage and the freight rate during depressed market   conditions, figure 4.1. Perhaps the best way of understanding the model is to see it as containing two supply curves, T T¹ the usual freight market curve and S S¹ the depressed freight market curve, made up of a series of lay-up points.

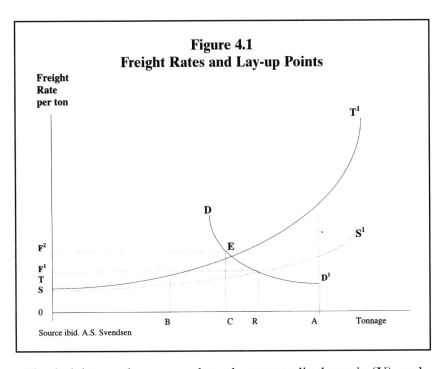

Figure 4.1
Freight Rates and Lay-up Points

Source ibid. A.S. Svendsen

The freight rate is measured on the perpendicular axis (Y), and the quantity in terms of tonnage is measured on the horizontal (X) axis. The total amount of tonnage (D.W.T.) available is represented by the distance OA (full capacity). The demand curve D D[1] shows the series of tonnage demanded at different levels of freight rate. The curve T T[1] is the supply curve, representing a series of total costs per D.W.T. for different ships. This is the cost curve of all shipowners to make an adequate return, that is a profit, up to the very last vessel. T T[1] can be seen as the supply curve of shipowners who refuse to transport cargo at a freight rate less than that of break even, or total cost of supplying the service. It is a surplus or over capacity supply curve for much of its length. The S S[1] curve represents a series of lay-up points. It is the point as already explained where-in, due to depressed freight rates conditions shipowners are willing to lift cargo at freight rates lower than the total costs of operations in the short-run. It can be argued that S S[1] performs two functions, it is a series of lay-up points, and secondly, it is the distressed freight rates at which shipowners are just willing to

79

provide transport services. In the model, if the freight rate stood at F^2, the quantity supplied would be represented by C at equilibrium point E, all vessels operating (OC) would be in profit. The remaining tonnage C to A would be withdrawn to lay-up. This is the position of the supply curve in T T^1. But if in the present position of excess capacity, or over supply, shipowners are willing to lift cargo at freight rates lower than total cost, that is at their lay-up point represented by S S^1, the interaction between the demand curve D D^1 and the depressed freight rate supply curves S S^1 means the freight rate becomes F^1. At this level of freight rate OR would be supplied. Of this quantity, OB represents a profit making situation whereby the freight rate is above the operational costs, and BR is a loss making position where the freight rate is below the cost of operation. Should the freight rate remain at F^1 for some considerable time, that is there is no increase in shippers' demand. The losses of these vessels operating between B and R would accumulate, causing owners to withdraw their vessels to lay-up, or perhaps scrap. These vessels already laid-up, represented by R to A, will reach the point where their lay-up cost and expectations about future commercial operation may make scrapping the most sensible course of action.

These examples serve to highlight the fact that shipowners do not consider lay-up simply because freight revenues have fallen below cost. Trading operations will continue until trading losses are greater than those losses due to lay-up. In other words, the total cost of supplying the vessel for trading operations will exceed the vessel's lay-up point.

The discussion in the above section has been constructed around a single shipowner, who removes tonnage from active supply but also has the implied intention of reactivating on an improved freight market. The underlying assumption here is that the individual shipowners accept the impossibility of influencing the freight market in any way. Thus these individuals are price (rate) takers, engaged in a "passive lay-up."[8]

Speed

Speed is interwoven with the concept of time and hence the level of supply. If the operating speed of any mobile unit is modified it will have an immediate impact on the output of that unit per time period. All transport investments' main product has been the reduction of journey or transit time. In the maritime industry it has served to increase supply in terms of both active and potential tonnage. The massive investment in the container revolution successfully reduced the amount of time vessels spent in port. Techniques developed of high speed ferries reduced the time vessels spend on voyage. Both serving to increase the level of tonnage offered in their particular sectors. Previously some sectors of the industry rather than aiming to increase supply wished, because of over capacity to curtail it. Lengthening voyage time had this affect in recent decades. To curtail supply by slow steaming being standard practice in some sectors, as the UNCTAD report of late 1980s commented "a relative increase in estimated surpluses on account of slow steaming. Thus, the share of slow steaming tonnage in the tanker surplus fleet increased from 47.1% in 1987 to 51.3% in 1988, and the share of slow steaming dry bulk tonnage in the dry bulk surplus fleet increased during this period from 82.2% to 85.5%"[6]. Using this type of mechanism, modifying individual or aggregate speeds of tonnage; the supply capacity of individual vessels or active supply can be varied in both directions. In this way it is possible for the freight market improvement to be responded to rapidly with an increase in active supply without any increase in the level of actual tonnage supplied. Other time mechanisms can have similar effects for example, the removal of some major congestion or port delay; similarly, a decrease in ballast or part cargo voyages, would increase the level of active supply.

Changes in speed are, in normal circumstances, only a relatively marginal element in changing the level in active or total supply. Obviously in a situation where total supply is active, that is 'laid up' tonnage is zero the only modification to supply is changes in speed within the short-run. That is assuming a given technology, active supply of freight services will be directly proportional to the amount of tonnage trading, modified by average speed. An increase or decrease in average speed will have a direct increase or decrease of level of supply particularly, as stated, when all tonnage is active.

Sale and Purchase Market

A ship functions on two levels; firstly in its operating capacity as part of the supply of sea transport; and, secondly, as an article of capital speculation. Both these are reasons for activity within the second-hand market for ships, often referred to in shipping literature as the Sale and Purchase Markets. It is a market which acts a barometer or indicator of the level of activity and expected activity within the industry and its sectors acting that is in a similar way to 'lay-up' tonnage. It serves as a method of transferring tonnage between owners and often this implies change of register. It will not therefore affect the total supply, but it can effect active supply by changing the cost structure under which the vessel, once sold operates. There are obvious economic differences between purchasing newly-built tonnage and second-hand tonnage. The former increases total supply; the latter merely transfers ownership and has no effect on supply whatsoever. The sale and purchase market exists for the simple reason that there are always some owners who want or need to sell their vessel and some wishing to purchase tonnage. Only a small minority of ships remain with the owner, who had them built, throughout their operational life. The majority are sold, perhaps several times.

The sale and purchase market is a highly competitive one, with few, if any restrictions on the level of activity. It is however, subject to pronounced cyclical fluctuations. To quote R. Kappel[7].

"In 1958 Stromme Svendsen wrote that 'about four per cent of the existing world merchant tonnage is bought and sold in the course of the year'. Since that time the volume of sale and purchase of ships has increased not only in terms of tonnage but in terms of value. In 1979 about seven per cent and 1983 about six per cent of the world tonnage had been sold and purchased.

The total number of ships being transferred on the sale and purchase (S & P) - market had been more than 1200 (1979) and 950 (1983), the total turnover increased to $7 billion (1979), and $7.8 billion (1980) and decreased to $3.55 billion (1983), due to the cyclical movement of prices, and supply and demand."

The following table and index gives some indication of just how volatile the price cycles in the second-hand tonnage market can be.

Table 4.5   Second-Hand Prices for Five Year Old Vessel 1985 - 1995 (Million US Dollars)

	TANKERS (DWT)				Bulk Carriers (D.W.T.)
YEAR	30,000		130,000		60,000
	Million $	Index	Million $	Index	Million $
1985	6.5	100	8.3	100	6.1
1986	11.0	169	13.8	166	7.8
1987	13.0	100	20.0	241	13.0
1988	16.0	246	28.0	337	17.0
1989	20.0	307	40.0	482	21.5
1990	21.5	472	37.0	446	18.5
1991	20.0	307	36.0	433	24.4*
1992	14.5	223	29.0	349	19.0
1993	18.0	277	34.5	415	19.5
1994	18.0	277	34.0	410	21.5
1995	20.0	307	35.5	428	23.0

*Category changed to 70,000 D.W.T.

Source UNCTAD Review of Maritime Transport (Annual)

A vessels value can halve or more than double in a year. The markets behaviour is governed, primarily, by variations in the levels of expectation, in particular, of the freight market. The basic consideration in all investment decisions is the net gain anticipated from any capital investment. Newly-constructed vessels are presumably more economic and efficient to operate, but, unlike older second-hand tonnage, they are not immediately available, nor are they necessarily the best investment at all times. The most important aspect in the acquisition of second-hand tonnage is the timing of its purchase. Examine three examples in relation to freight market conditions:-

Firstly, assuming the vessel is purchased during a freight market boom. This will be a period when the prices of second-hand, and, for that matter, new building will be at a premium. Such high levels of capital investment could be ruinous, should the freight market decline rapidly to levels at which shipowners were incapable of covering both the capital and operations costs.

Secondly, at the other extreme in the freight market cycle (that is, in a deep depression), second-hand tonnage will presumably be cheap, but, if it is bought at this time, it may be laid up (that is, idle for some time), creating a situation where the prospects of further profitable employment become increasingly remote.

Thirdly, to purchase tonnage cheaply just prior to the ending of a period of freight market depression, and before it becomes obvious to others active in the second-hand acquisition market. In this situation, a shipowner acquires inexpensive tonnage just prior to an upturn in freight market activity. There are two simple options open; one is to operate the tonnage commercially and, due to its low capital cost, presumably at a profit. On the other hand, the vessel can be, primarily, seen as a speculative asset, to be sold on at a premium, once the sale and purchase market improves in response to the buoyant freight market. Another advantage of low prices is, if the freight market upturn does not materialise, or is not as strong as anticipated, there is a minimum capital risk, for the vessel price is, presumably, near to its scrap value. Hence, either the vessel is purchased to engage in further trading, or as an item of capital speculation. The timing of the purchase is of paramount importance.

The sale and purchase market is highly competitive and cyclical, but price movement is usually between maximum and minimum limits. In general, the price of newly-contracted tonnage acts as a constraint on the upper limits of second-hand tonnage prices. There are exceptions to this, particularly during periods of seasoned or general freight boom, when purchasers, in order to rapidly secure tonnage, will pay in excess of the new contract prices, rather than suffer the delay necessary in building new vessels. The scrap or demolishing price acts as a minimum price, denoting the bottom of the market. While minimum scrap price functions act as a restricting influence on second-hand prices, so, in a similar way, will the maximum scrap price. To generalise, the scrap price will act as a floor to one sector and a ceiling to the other. It is, of course, a point which will be moving constantly in response to competitive market pressures.

Supply Curves

Supply is the amount of capacity shipowners will offer on the market per unit of time. The idea of capacity that is laid-up can be seen from the point of view of individual shipowners and total supply. These ideas are explored in Figures 4.1 and 4.2.

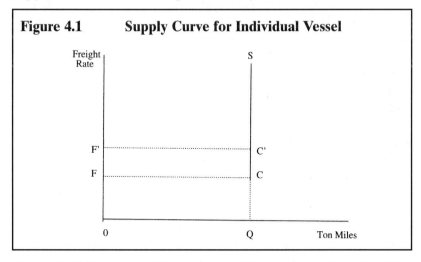

Figure 4.1   Supply Curve for Individual Vessel

For an individual vessel it can be an all or nothing situation. The supply curves (S) is seen as two straight lines, FC and CS. OF is the freight rate below which the vessel will be withdrawn from the market, its lay-up point. OQ is the tonnage or design capacity of the vessel when it is fully laden. This point on the curve illustrates that the ship owner will be more than willing to accept a higher freight rate, for example F'C', but cannot of course increase the capacity of the vessel beyond Q.

The total supply consists of all shipowners coming into the freight market. They will all have a similar cost structure, although freight levels will have a different impact on those who are in the active fleet and those available to join the active supply. This will be dependent upon the factors contributing to the individual vessel's cost structure, as for example its age, type of operation, flag, level of operation, mortgage payments, labour costs etc. On investigation it appears that the lay-up point for most vessels is a 4% deficit on gross costs or possibly 5% below the level of voyage costs. At this point, shipowners will lay the vessel up rather than let the vessel continue in service as part of the active supply. The consequence is that the series of points are created on the total supply curve see Figure 4.2.

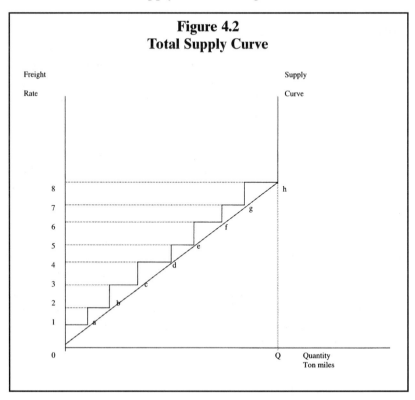

Figure 4.2
Total Supply Curve

Here is what can be termed either the individual or group vessel's distribution of lay-up points combined in a simple industrial supply curve. Further down the supply curve, the closer to the vertical (y) axis, the more economically efficient the tonnage will be. In the above figure the most efficient tonnage that which will lay-up below freight rate 1. Between 1 and 2 the tonnage is a slightly less economically efficient. Moving up the supply curve, the tonnage becomes progressively less efficient. The locus of all these freight rate quantity points a to h consist of the whole total supply curve of the vessels involved lay-up points. Freight rate level 8 and quantity h constitute full capacity; a situation in the immediate and short-run where the market can offer no more tonnage regardless of any increase in the freight rate above 8, or full capacity Q. In this way the total supply curve in the immediate and short-run is constructed. Such a tidy curve will not occur in the industry, but this serves as an illustration of the general trend.

Summary

This chapter opened with a simple definition of the industries supply; as the quantity of shipping offered at any given freight rate. This was taken an important step further, by defining the three sections which comprise total supply. Active supply, that which is involved in actual trading operations. Available supply, surplus tonnage, suitable for employment, but laid-up or detained for some reason. Thirdly, potential supply this is made up of new building, and tonnage entering operations from some other area of activity.

It was argued the supply increases and decreases consisted of two main elements, newly built tonnage and scrapping. But active supply could be modified by laying vessels up or changing their operational speed. Another modification to the structure of the fleet is the sale and purchase market, although this does not directly affect total supply. Finally, an immediate and short-run supply curve was constructed.

Further Reading

Shimojo T   'Economic Analysis of Shipping Freights'
                   Kobe Research Institute for Economic and
                   Business Administration, Kobe University.
                   1979.

A. S. Svendsen,   'Factors determining lay-up of ships'. Bergen,
                   The Institute of Economics Norwegian
                   School of Economics and Business
                   Administration, Norway, December 1957,
                   paper no. 7.

---

[1] NB when considered along side far more expensive maritime infrastructure like ports, such investment in terms of length of time is short

[2] N.B. These figures do not appear in the table because it presents only annual averages.

[3] A. S. Svendsen, 'Factors determining lay-up of ships'. Bergen, The Institute of Economics Norwegian School of Economics and Business Administration, Norway, December 1957, paper no. 7.

[4] P.M. Alderton, 'When to lay-up-the theory and practice', London, Transport Discussion Paper PDB City of London Polytechnic1988.

[5] Op. cit. A.S. Svendsen.

[6] UNCTAD review of Maritime Transport 1988 p.29.

[7] Kappel R. 'The Second- Hand Market' Breman Institute of Shipping Economics. Lectures and Contribution no39 1984. P6

[8] N.B. "active lay up" is discussed in Ch. 10.

Chapter Five

MARKET PRICE DETERMINATION

Introduction

To consider the way in an open active market, freight rates are determined. Up to this point, each side of the industry, that is demand and supply, has been individually analysed. All the relevant information concerning the shipowner, producer, supplier or seller of shipping services, is summarily embodied in supply, the function. All the information concerning the consumer, shipper or buyer of shipping services was embodied in the demand function. These established a clear relationship existing between freight rates and the quantities supplied by the shipowners, and the quantities demanded by shippers. To examine now the way in which freight rates are created. The assumption underpinning this examination is that the shipping market is perfectly competitive, thus creating a situation where all individual participants accept the freight rates as a price taker or a freight taker.[1] That is to bring both demand and supply together to determine the market price, that is market freight rate. This concept will be examined using hypothetical freight rates, demand and supply schedules (table 5.1).

89

Table 5.1   Hypothetical Demand and Supply

Freight Rates ($ per ton)	Demand (million tons)	Supply (millions tons)	Pressure on Price	
50	0	140	D<	S
45	8	124	D<	S
40	17	109	D<	S
35	30	93	D<	S
30	44	77	D<	S
25	61	61	D=	S
20	80	45	D>	S
15	105	30	D>	S
10	129	13	D>	S
5	152	0	D>	S

What the schedule confirms is that within the present parameters, the higher the freight rate, the more shipowners will offer on the market: this is the law of supply. The lower the freight rate, the more will be demanded by the shipper: this is the law of demand. Supply and demand are equal as can be seen at a freight rate of $25 dollars per ton. At this freight rate the quantity demanded and supplied is 61 million tons. With a lower freight rate, there is a shortage of tonnage, as the quantity demanded is in excess of supply. At the higher freight rate, there is an excess supply. The final column shows the pressure on freight rates, downward for excess supply, and upward for excess demand. Both pressures meet at the equilibrium freight rate of $25.   The information contained in the table is graphically illustrated in Figure 5.1.

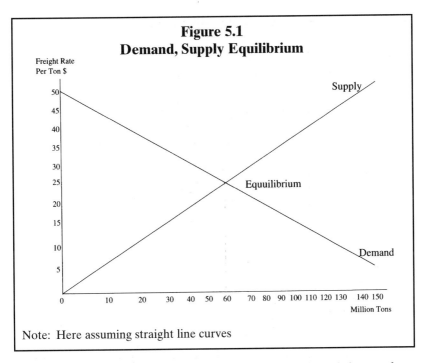

Figure 5.1
Demand, Supply Equilibrium

Note: Here assuming straight line curves

The figure highlights the basic workings of the freight market. Demand at the high level of freight rates of $50 is nil. As the freight rate decline, demand increases, for example at $35 the quantity demanded is 30 million tons, and at $10 it increases to 129 million tons. Supply shows the reverse process, at the low level of $10 only 13 million tons are offered to the markets. With an increase in freight say to $20 supply increases to 45 million tons, at the higher freight rate of $50, 190 million tons is offered to the market. The equilibrium can be clearly seen at the point where demand and supply meet.

Equilibrium is a word derived from a combination of two Latin words meaning an equal balance. Equilibrium is therefore the point of equal balance where the quantity demanded and supplied meet; a balance between two opposing forces of demand with it downward pressure and supply with it upward pressure. Equilibrium price can also be referred to A 'Market Clearing Price'. It is the point where the forces pressing in opposite directions cancel each other out; a position where there is not net tendency to move. Stability is created as long, and only as long as there are no external disturbances. This illustrates the ***laws of supply and demand*** which states that when supply is greater than demand, prices decrease, and when demand is greater than supply, prices increase. These forces drive the freight rate to an equilibrium, at which point shipowners are willing to offer the same quantity of services which shippers are willing to purchase. This is illustrated in Figure 5.2

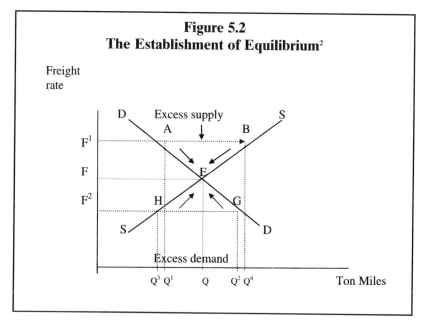

Figure 5.2
The Establishment of Equilibrium[2]

At rate F^2, there are too many buyers shippers (G) chasing too little supply, Ton miles (H), i.e. an excess demand, Q^3 to Q^2. The interaction between the buyers and sellers could push up the freight rate until F^1 is reached. At rate F^1 there is an excess supply, A to B, or Q^1 to Q^2 which forces down the rate to F. Freight rate F is the equilibrium rate at E where the quantity demanded equals the quantity supplied (Q), and there is no upward or downward pressure on the freight rate.

Changes in demand and or supply will cause these curves to shift, and thus create new equilibrium. Such shifts in demand and supply are discussed in the following section.

Changes in Demand

In cChapter 3 the demand for shipping was described as a **derived demand,** in that it is the result of demand for the products being shipped. As such, shifts in the demand for shipping will arise through shifts in the demand for internationally traded goods. An expansion (or contraction) in international trade leads to an increase (or decrease) in the volume of seaborne trade. An increase will shift the demand curve to the right, as illustrated in Figure 5.3.

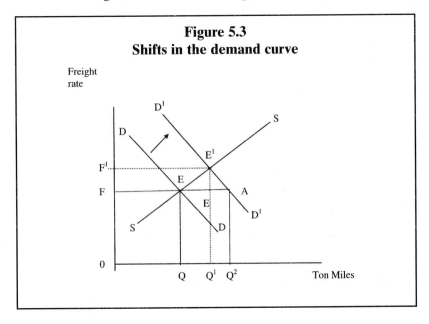

Figure 5.3
Shifts in the demand curve

Initially, the equilibrium is established at E with a freight rate of F and tonnage supplied and demanded of Q. An increase in the demand of shipping shifts the demand curve to $D^1 D^1$. With supply function fixed at SS and a freight rate F, excess demand is created, since the tonnage demanded is Q^2 (or A) and the tonnage supplied is only Q. The excess demand creates upward pressure on freight rates which 'chokes off' some of the increased demand, (Q^2 to Q^1) and encourages greater supply, and thus a new equilibrium is reached at E^1 , with a freight rate of F^1 and tonnage of Q^1.

93

Similarly a decrease in the demand curve moves to the left, combined with a supply function SS creates excess supply. The freight rate is therefore forced down which encourages greater demand and less supply. Equilibrium is then established at a lower freight rate and tonnage.

Such fluctuations in the level of international trade may be caused by a number of factors. Changes in consumer tastes and preferences may be such that greater or lesser amounts of internationally traded goods are demanded. Increasing consumer disposable income also increases the amount spent on goods and services, some of which will be internationally traded.

Changes in Supply

Shifts in the supply curve may be the result of factors such as reduced costs, technological advancements, faster turnaround in ports. Cost savings for the shipowner or shipper may arise, for example, from cheaper financing, reduced bunker fuel costs etc.[3] Their effect is to increase the amount of tonnage supplied through greater efficiencies, such as increases in the speed of ships. Increased turnaround in ports will reduce the time spent in the port and thus increase time available for voyages. Figure 5.4. shows the effect of an increase in supply of tonnage.

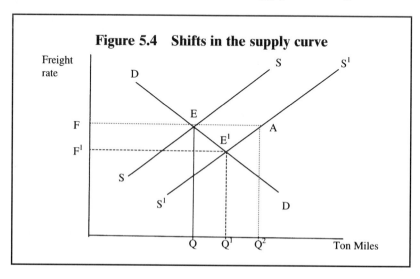

Figure 5.4   Shifts in the supply curve

The initial equilibrium is E, consistent with a freight rate of F and tonnage of Q. Reduction of shipowner's costs, *ceteris paribus*, will result in excess supply of Q to Q^2 (or E to A)at the existing freight rate. Downward pressure on the freight rate will increase demand and decrease supply (Q^2 to Q^1), until equilibrium is again established at E^1 with a freight rate of F^1 and tonnage supplied and demanded of Q^1.

Changes in Demand and Supply

So far it has been assumed that either changes is demand occur with a fixed supply, or changes in supply occur with a fixed demand. It is entirely possible, however, for both curves to shift at the same time. This may be because demand and supply curves are affected separately, or that the same factors cause shift in both demand and supply. The simplest example of such changes are a crisis for example a war, closure of a sea canal or major port, or new sources of mineral, oil, coal or iron ore are discovered.

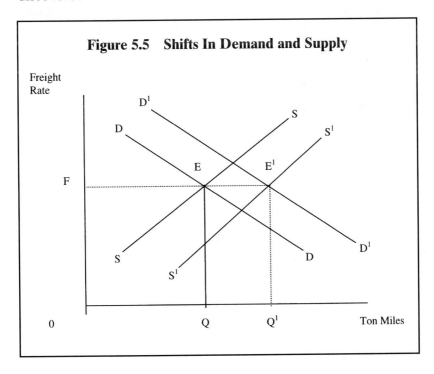

Figure 5.5   Shifts In Demand and Supply

In Figure 5.5, the original equilibrium is E at freight rate F and ton miles Q. Then both demand and supply shift in equal proportions. The freight rate remains unchanged at F, but the new equilibrium. E[1] has ton miles at the higher level of Q[1]. For example a world increase in seaborne trade volumes would shift the demand curve out to the right. Similarly if bunker fuel price fell the supply curve would also shift out to the right.

Summary

This chapter explores the determination of competitive market price, which in shipping, is the freight rate. This can be measured either in ton of cargo delivered or in the ton miles. The determinants relate to the basic principles of demand and supply from which the general shape of the curves are derived. The demand curve normally slopes downwards from left to right reflecting the inverse relationship between freight rate and the quantity of tonnage demanded. The supply curve slopes upward from left to right and reflects the relationship between freight rate and quantity of tonnage supply. The interaction of demand and supply curve establishes an equilibrium point, at which there is no net tendency to move the freight rate. Movements in supply and demand will change this equilibrium, by creating upward or downward pressure on the freight rates. This argument is taken a step further with a consideration of elasticity, which at it simplest alters the slope of the demand and supply curves. Elasticity is examined in detail in Chapter 6.

Further Reading

O'Loughlin C. *'The Economics of Sea Transport'*. Oxford Pergman Press, 1967.

Evans J. J. and Marlow P.B. London, *'Quantitative Methods in Maritime Economics'*. Fairplay Publications 1990.

----

[1] This is discussed in detail in Chapter 8
[2] There is a change here for tons to ton miles it follows the freight rate also changes
[3] See chapter 7.

Chapter 6

ELASTICITY

In the previous chapters it was seen that the derived demand for and supply of shipping was dependent upon the freight rate and other factors. The important practical question is how sensitive or responsive is shipping's demand and supply to these changes. Here, the concentration will first be upon the methods of measuring the sensitivity of demand to changes in freight rates, income, and factors of production, before examining elasticity of supply.

Elasticity of Demand

The elasticity of demand is a concept of importance which occurs frequently in maritime economic analysis. **Elasticity** is a measure of the responsiveness of a variable to a change in another variable, where the change is small. The elasticity of demand for shipping is of importance in attempting to determine the effect changes in the international economic environment will have on sea-borne trade flows. The aim here is not to look at all the variables but to concentrate on what are considered the most important, that is price or freight rate, income and factor elasticities.

Freight Rate or Price Elasticity

Price elasticity of demand is the degree of responsiveness of the quantity demanded of a good or service, to a small change in its price.   In the shipping industry, the elasticity of demand for shipping will be its responsiveness to minor changes in the freight rate.   Freight or price elasticity is normally negative.   An increase in freight rates will cause a decrease in the quantity of cargo transported.   The price elasticity of demand can be expressed as a formula, first postulated by Alfred Marshall.   It is based on defining elasticity as the percentage change in the quantity demanded divided by the percentage change in price where the price change is small.   In shipping terms, this may be expressed as follows:

Equation 6.1

Elasticity of Demand = <u>Percentage change in tonnage</u>
Percentage change in freight rate

The elasticity of demand is equal to the proportionate or percentage change in the quantity of tonnage divided by the proportionate change in freight rate.

The change is expressed as a percentage of the average price and average quantity, and so the equation becomes:

Freight rate elasticity of demand for shipping $= \dfrac{\% \Delta S\ /\ S_{average}}{\% \Delta F\ /\ F_{average}}$

where Δ is the symbol for small change

S is the quantity of shipping demanded

$S_{average}$ is the average quantity of shipping demanded

F is the freight rate

$F_{average}$ is the average freight rate

The coefficient of freight rate elasticity because of the inverse relationship between quantity and freight. This sign is usually ignored. The value of the coefficient can range from zero at one extreme to infinity at the other. Where the value is zero ($E = O$), demand is perfectly inelastic. The demand curve is a vertical straight line cutting the quantity axis. This is a situation where, regardless of price, buyers will purchase the same quantity of a commodity (Figure 6. 1). Where elasticity is infinite ($E = \infty$) the demand curve is horizontal. All output will be taken up at that price (Figure 6. 1). It is a situation related to perfect competition where there are many buyers and sellers, all relatively small and none can influence price.

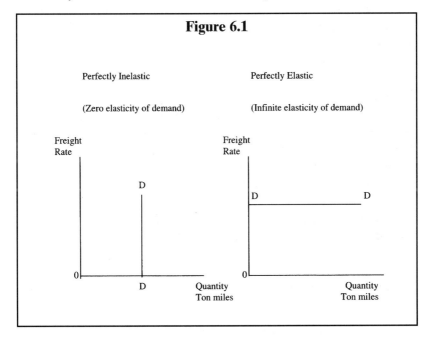

An example of infinite elasticity would be a bulk ship owner in the Northern American grain market, who finds charterers for all the tonnage available at the prevailing market freight rate. All charterers know the freight rate and therefore none will offer a higher level of freight.

There are two basic absolute measures of freight rate elasticity.

When it is greater than unity demand at a given freight rate is said to be elastic, a situation where a freight rate change of say, 1%, would elicit a change of 3% in the amount of cargo space demanded. Should the freight rate elasticity be less than unity demand for cargo space is said to be inelastic. Under these circumstances for example a freight rate change of 1% would result in a change of 0.5% in the quantity of cargo space demanded.

Table 6.1 examines three intervening conditions of elasticity between zero and infinity, using an individual shipowner who has a choice of three cargoes during a period when freight rates are contracting from an original rate. The total receipts represents the total revenue the ship owner can expect at each level of freight rate, shipping different cargoes.

Table 6.1   Three Cargo Demand Schedules

Freight Rate	Cargo A			Cargo B			Cargo C		
	Freight Rate $	No. of Tons (000)	Total Receipts ($000)	Freight Rate $	No. of Tons (000)	Total Receipts ($000)	Freight Rate $	No. of Tons (000)	Total Receipts ($000)
Original	5	2	10	5	12	60	5	10	50
	F	Q		F	Q		F	Q	
1st Decreased Rate	4	3.5	14	4	15	60	4	11	44
	F1	Q1	-	F1	Q1	-	F1	Q1	-
2nd Decreased Rate	3	5	15	3	20	60	3	12	36
	F2	Q2		F2	Q2		F2	Q2	
	Elasticity >1 Elastic			Elasticity = 1 Unitary			Elasticity <1 Inelastic		

The table illustrates how the freight rate changes in the same direction as the quantity demanded as long as the demand is elastic. It moves in the opposite direction when demand is inelastic. In the case of Cargo A the freight rate decreases from $5 to $3, cargo tonnage increases from 2000 tons to 5000 tons and total receipts from $10,000 to $15,000. Using the earlier formula, the elasticity is calculated as follows:

$$\text{Elasticity of Demand} = \left.\left(\frac{5000 - 2000}{3500}\right)x100 \middle/ \left(\frac{3-5}{4}\right)x100\right.$$

$$= \frac{86\%}{20\%}$$

$$= 4.3$$

Similarly, the elasticities for Cargoes B and C are 1 and 0.36 respectively.

Table 6.1 has now been transferred to the following figure in relating to cargo A.

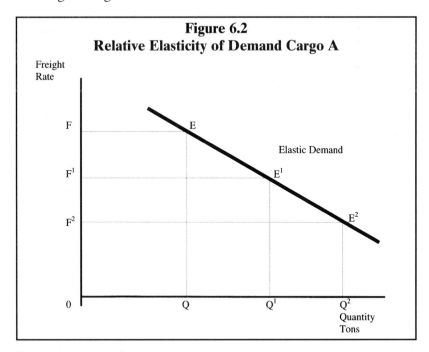

Figure 6.2
Relative Elasticity of Demand Cargo A

From the above it can be seen:

1.) Original Freight Rate = 0 F E Q

2.) 1st Decreased Freight Rate = 0 F1 E1 Q1

3.) 2nd Decreased Freight Rate = 0 F2 E2 Q2

In cargo A there is a relatively elastic demand E>1. At the original freight rate F shippers charter Q tonnage and the total amount of freight (revenue) is 0FEQ or $10,000. With the reduction in freight rate to F^1 the quantity shippers demand has increased to Q^1 and the total freight is 0F1E1Q1 or $14,000. From the figure it can be seen that $0F^1E^1Q^1$ is greater than 0FEQ e.g. the total freight receipts are greater by 4,000 at the lower level of freight rate. A further decline in rates from F^1 to F^2 means that the quantity demanded increases to Q^2. The total amount of freight increases to $0F^2E^2Q^2$ or $15,000. Hence where the demand curve is downward sloping a proportional change in freight rate will bring forth a greater than proportional change in shippers demand, because demand is elastic. That is to say, freight elasticity of demand is relatively elastic where variations in the freight rate lead to a greater proportional change in the quantity of tonnage demanded.

If a decrease of 1% in freight rate is accompanied by an increase in shippers demand of 2%, demand is elastic. This is a situation where total freight rate expenditure rises when freight rates fall, the elasticity coefficient is greater than 1.

Table 6.1 has now been transferred to the 6.3 figure in relation to Cargo B. From Figure 6.3 it can be seen that

1) Original Freight Rate = 0 F E Q

2) 1st Decreased Freight Rate = $0 F^1 E1 Q^1$

3) 2nd Decreased Freight Rate = $0 F^2 E^2 Q^2$

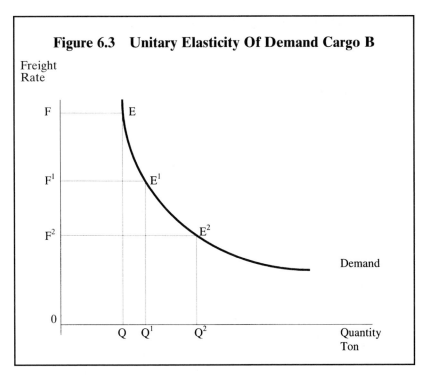

Figure 6.3   Unitary Elasticity Of Demand Cargo B

In this figure elasticity is unity $E = 1$. The rather limited case of unity elasticity occurs where all points on the demand curve are the shape of a rectangular hyperbola. A situation where an increase or decrease in freight rate will not change the total receipts. At original freight rate F shippers chartered Q tonnage and the total amount of freight expenditure is 0FEQ or $60,000. Freight rates decreased to F^1, the quantity shippers demand has decreased to Q^1 and the total freight receipts are now $0F^1E^1Q^1$ or $60.000, which is exactly the same as at the previous freight rate F. Should freight rates decrease again to F^2 the quantity shipowners demand would be Q^2 and receipts are 0F2E2Q2 $60.000 . At each level of freight rate in the table and model total freight receipts remain constant at $60,000. Hence total freight rate receipts for shipowners or expenditure for shippers will be unchanged as freight rates vary in either direction. Demand is neither elastic nor inelastic it is at the mid point between the two primary elasticities. It is unity where the coefficient is exactly 1.

Table 6.1 has now been transferred to the following figure in relation to Cargo C.

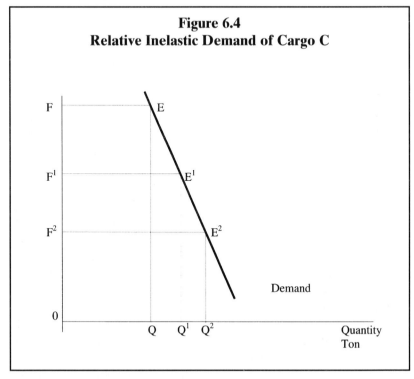

Figure 6.4
Relative Inelastic Demand of Cargo C

Cargo C in the above figure has a relatively inelastic demand. E^1 at the original freight rate F is shipper demand Q the total amount of freight receipts are 0FEQ or \$50,000. With reduction in freight rate to F^1 the quantity demanded by shippers only increased by Q^1, the total freight receipts contract to $0F^1E^1Q^1$. A further reduction in the freight rate to F^2 brings forth only a small increase in shipping demand to Q^2 and the total freight receipts contract substantially to $0F^2E^2Q^2$ or \$45,000. With reduction in freight rate there is a substantial loss in total freight receipts and only minor gains in quantity demanded. The original situation receipts are considerably greater than those following the falls in the freight rate. The demand for shipping tonnage is inelastic where the percentage change in freight rate brings forth a smaller percentage change in quantity demanded. If a decrease of 1% in freight rate is accompanied by an increase in shippers

104

demand of only 0.1% demand is inelastic, a situation where total freight expenditure falls when freight rate falls. The elasticity coefficient is less than 1.

Two further points should be made at this juncture. First all the above discussion was constructed on the basis of a reduction in freight rates. The ship owning firm contemplating changes in the freight rate will be particularly concerned with the elasticity of demand for a freight rate change. If the demand is elastic as in cargo A a decrease in freight rates would increase total receipts. Cargo C is inelastic, a fall in freight rate means a contraction in total freight receipts. The unusual case of Cargo B means constant level of freight rates. Should on the other hand freight rates be on a rising trend and a \$3 (F^2) freight rate be replaced by a \$5 (F) as the original freight rate, the shipowner's outlook changes. The elastic Cargo A becomes less attractive for a freight increase means total receipts contract. In the case of Cargo C the reverse is true, as freight rises so too do total freight receipts. As already stated Cargo B freight receipts remain constant whatever movement there is in the freight rate. Hence in this simple model if the demand is elastic a freight rate decline is more desirable than a freight rate increase in terms of total freight receipts. On the other hand if demand is inelastic a freight increase would be more desirable and the freight decline would not. The former would increase the shipowner's total receipts while at the same time it would lower tonnage chartered and total costs. Secondly, the above figures on the slope of the demand curve can only be used as an approximate indicator of relative elasticity. Models can be misleading. Simply by changing the scales of their axes, they can be constructed so as to give the demand curve virtually any slope. Hence for any reliable calculations the formula of elasticity must be used. [1]

The examination of price thus far has shown how important a concept it is for it measures the responsiveness of sensitivity of the quantity demanded to any change in its price and hence total revenue. It is, however, necessary to identify the economic and other forces which determine the elasticity values. The two prime factors are the number and availability of substitutes and time. The greater the number and the closer the substitutes available the higher the elasticity. The more difficult it is to secure substitutes the lower the elasticity. With regard to time or run, the longer time period allows for the demander, that is the consumer, to adjust to changes in price, the higher the elasticity. The shorter the period of time the lower the elasticity, all other things being equal.

Cross Elasticity

Cross elasticity of demand may be defined as the responsiveness of the quantity demanded of one good to changes in the price of another good. It may be stated as follows:-

---

Equation 6.2

$$Ei = \frac{\%\Delta Q}{\%\Delta I}$$

where Ei is the income elasticity

Q is the quantity demanded

I is the consumer's income

Elasticity will be positive if A and B are good substitutes for one another, because a change in the price of one (B) will cause a change in the demand for the other (A). For example natural gas and coal. Should the elasticity be negative they are complementary goods for example eggs and bacon, or cheese and grapes. Measuring this sensitivity or responsiveness in the quantity demanded, that is of commodity A, as a result of a change of the price of B, can be achieved by using the above formula.

Holding taste, consumer income and the number of consumers in the market constant, the numerical value of elasticity will increase the closer the relationship between the two goods. A zero valuation denotes no relationship, a negative or positive value denotes a close relationship. If Ec is greater than 0, A and B are good substitutes because an increase in the price of B leads to an increase in the quantity demanded of A, as A is substituted by consumers for B. If on the other hand Ec is less than 0, AB are complementary because an increase in the price of B has lead to a reduction in the demand for A. Should Ec be 0 or close to it AB are independent commodities like, for example, crude oil and apples.

From the point of view of the maritime transport industry where close substitutes are available increased freight rates or other costs must be treated with caution. The presence of substitutes within the maritime industry or with other modes, railways or pipelines for example, acts as effective constraints on the market power or influence a particular sector of the industry might otherwise possess.

Income Elasticity

Income elasticity of demand may be defined as the responsiveness of demand for a good to changes in the buyer's income. It may be stated as follows:

Equation 6.3

$$Ec = \frac{\% \Delta Q_A}{\% \Delta P_B}$$

where Ec is the cross elasticity

Q_A is the quantity demanded of A
P_B is the price of B

For simplicity it is generally assumed that such changes take place while holding prices and consumer taste constant. It is expected that income elasticity of a good will be positive, with an increase in income causing an increase in demand. Zero elasticity will occur where increases in income cause no increase in demand. The characteristics of income elasticity of demand for individual modes of transport, for example, cars can be important and are clearly useful in marketing and policy decisions, whereas the role of income elasticity in industrial markets, despite extensive research, is less clear cut. This is because increases and changes in income levels will have only an indirect effect on industrial goods and total services. The derived demand for freight services is an intermediate form of demand for the final product and hence difficult to include in any analysis of income elasticity. Despite these difficulties of analysis or measurement the central point is the impact the changing levels of income and economic activity will have on maritime transport.

Elasticity of Supply

Elasticity of supply is a measure of the response of supply to changes in the freight rate. This can be illustrated in Figure 6.5 which examines changes in elasticity which occur over the whole length of the supply curve.

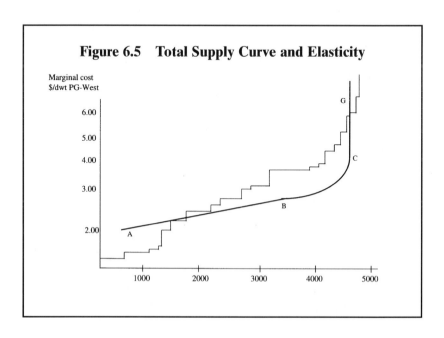

Figure 6.5   Total Supply Curve and Elasticity

Figure 6.5 takes the supply curve discussed in Chapter 4 a step further by relating it to the tanker sectors supply curve. The industrial sector supply curve was constructed by J. W. Devanney[2] with the marginal costs per d.w.t, the Persian Gulf to the west, on the vertical axis, (y) and billion ton miles on the (x) axis. It shows "the amount of capacity which will be offered by owners as a function of the [freight] rate."[3]

The curve has superimposed on it a generalised supply curve. Initially the supply curve is highly elastic (E>1). In region AB the curve is nearly horizontal; a situation where there is a considerable amount of unemployed tonnage, e.g. vessels laid up. Shippers can secure a larger increase in tonnage in response to only a marginal rise in the prevailing freight rate. At the other extreme, near full capacity employment, where the active fleet is virtually equal to the total supply, the supply curve becomes extremely inelastic, eventually perfectly inelastic. This is the region C to G where the curve is close to vertical. Here the short-run active supply of ships is inelastic and all freight rates are above the lay-up point C, elasticity is near Zero. There are two other supply situations highlighted in the figure. First, where the curve ranges vertically beyond G it is perfectly inelastic; zero elasticity, so no matter what the increase in freight rates occur, the supply remains constant. The second section of interest is that between B and C. As already stated, point C is the highest lay-up point, presumably very close to 100% capacity. Of more importance is point B. This is the point where the supply curve begins to change from elastic to inelastic. Where this point is located will be of importance to both shippers and ship-owners for any increase in the supply required, that is a movement to the right, could potentially create a freight rate boom.

Factor Demand Elasticity

If it is generally assumed that the elasticity of aggregate demand in the shipping industry over the short-run will be inelastic. In part this is due to the lack of substitutes for most shipping services. It is also argued that in most manufactured or refined products shipping or indeed total transport costs represent only a small percentage of the total cost of the final consumer product. This is combined with the inelastic industrial demand for most raw materials. Thus it is often claimed that such elasticities should be seen as a short-run phenomenon as locations of production and consumption are fixed and shipping lacks substitutes. In the long-run, however, higher levels of elasticity are expected. This is because freight costs can have an influence on trade routes and patterns and the relocation of industry.

In spite of its complexity an understanding of elasticity is vital to successful shipowning. Since shipping may be seen as a factor of production, or what is sometimes termed an input in the productive process, knowledge of the freight rate elasticity demand is an intrinsic part of making operational decisions. What then are the conditions which dictate the elasticity of demand for shipping?

This question was first answered by Alfred Marshall with some later modifications by J. Hicks. They related the elasticity of demand for any factor of production, in the original case labour, to four conditions which have since been referred to as either economic laws, propositions, rules or conditions. The discussion will first state the conditions and then examine them in detail using the shipping industry as the factor of production.

The conditions

1. *When there is the **technical possibility of substituting** other inputs for shipping in the productive process, for example, the smaller the substitution possible for maritime transport, the less elastic is the demand for its services.*
2. *The less elastic **the demand for the final output,** the less elastic the derived demand for shipping. The reverse is also true.*
3. *The smaller the **ratio of freight costs to total costs** the less elastic the demand for shipping.*
4. *The lower t**he elasticity of supply of co-operating inputs** in the production process the less elastic is the demand for shipping.[4]*

Two basic assumptions will be made in order to simplify the discussion. There is a perfectly competitive industry. The concept of perfect competition was unknown to Marshall, as this concept was developed some time later, he wrote of free industry and enterprise and free competition. This appears to have been more akin to imperfect or monopolistic competition than perfect competition. The purpose of this assumption is to remove any impediment which could interfere with the easy function of the conditions of the elasticity of derived demand. Secondly, throughout the following analysis derived demand changes will, of course, bring forth responses and implications for supply, these will by and large be ignored, assumed away. Supply will be considered in detail later. Here the aim is to concentrate solely on the derived demand for the aggregate shipping side of the equation.

The conditions will now be considered in more detail.

1. Presence of Substitutes for Shipping

The demand for anything is likely to be more elastic, the more readily substitutes for that thing can be obtained.

The derived demand for shipping will be more elastic the easier it is to obtain substitutes for shipping, and more inelastic the more difficult it is to obtain substitutes. The major element that determines the degree of elasticity is the presence or lack of adequate substitutes for shipping. The elasticity of demand for shipping is high that is more elastic the greater the opportunity for substituting another form of transport to replace it. A large proportion of international trade entails sea-borne transportation for which there is no substitute transport mode economically possible. That is to say it is technically and physically possible to move large quantities say of iron ore by aircraft, but in terms of cost and price it is totally impractical, economically not feasible. In other words there is usually no technical substitute for shipping in general.

When freight rates rise shipping becomes more expensive

relative to other forms of transport. For example if the freight rate suddenly increased substantially in the bulk trades and it was possible to transfer the trade say to railways at a lower level of freight rates e.g. there is an adequate substitute, demand for shipping would be elastic. On the other hand, if the same freight rate increase occurred on a bulk trade where there are no alternative forms of transport, no economic substitutes, here the freight rate increase would only have a minor impact on the quantity of shipping demanded.

This condition rests wholly on substitution. A measure of this is the relative change in the ratio of the quantity of shipping to the quantity to the other transport services, divided by the relative change in their freight rates.

Equation 6.4

$$E = \frac{\text{Percentage change in factor proportions}}{\text{Percentage change in the relative factor price}}$$

To repeat the condition in another form, the derived demand for shipping will tend to be inelastic when the economic and technical substitution of other forms of transport happens to be low, all other things being equal.

According to this condition derived demand for shipping will be:

a) *more elastic, the higher the elasticity of substitution for shipping,*

b) *less elastic, the lower the elasticity of substitution for shipping.*

2. Elasticity of Final Consumer Demand

The demand for anything is likely to be more elastic the more elastic is the demand for any further thing it contributes to production.

Should a particular factor in the production process say shipping, increase its freight rate then production costs and the consumer's product price may rise. This happens if consumers are unable to switch to another product then the producer will be under no compulsion to resist the demand of the ship owner for the freight increase and the price elasticity of demand will be low. The elasticity of demand for all factors in the production process, including shipping, will vary directly with the elasticity of demand for the final consumer product. That is to say the elasticity of demand for shipping is closely tied to the elasticity of demand for the final consumer product in which shipping is part of the productive process. Consider for example what would happen if there was a substantial rise in freight rates, causing a rise in production costs and the price to the final consumer. On the one hand if the increase in final price causes a substantial reduction in demand, demand is highly elastic. It would be followed by a substantial reduction in the amount of shipping demanded. On the other hand should the increase in the price to the final consumer only cause a minor reduction in demand, demand is inelastic. It follows there would only be a minor reduction in the amount of shipping required. Shipping as a factor of production is closely related to the demand for the final product.

To repeat the condition in another form. Since the demand for shipping is a derived demand it can be expected that freight elasticity of demand for shipping will be a direct function of the demand for the final product.

According to condition 2, demand for shipping will be:

a) *more elastic, the higher the elasticity of demand for the final consumer product,*

b) *less elastic, the lower the elasticity of demand for the final consumer product.*

3. Shipping as Proportion of Total Costs

The demand for anything is likely to be less elastic the less important is the part paid by the cost of that thing in the total cost of some other thing.

113

This condition relates to the share of the factor, shipping, in the cost of production. The elasticity of derived demand for shipping will be dependent on the proportion of the total cost of the final product accounted for by shipping. The condition rests on the percentage of shipping freight rate costs to the total costs of the final consumer product. It is often referred to as 'the importance of being unimportant'. If shipping freight constitutes a large percentage of total costs an increase in freight rate costs would probably cause the producing firm to charge more for the final product, prices would increase and quantity demanded would contract. Firms would curtail production and less shipping space would be demanded. In this situation shipping would be very responsive to changes in freight rates. Demand for shipping would be highly elastic. Taking the opposite case where a producer spends a small proportion of their total cost on shipping. Shipping freights are unimportant in cost terms. It follows that a considerable increase in these freights would have little effect on final consumer price. Hence the derived demand would be inelastic for the lower the proportion of total costs accounted for by shipping the lower the elasticity and the wider the scope of shipowners to gain from increased freight rates. As a general rule freight rates constitute only small percentage of the total value of the cargo and, therefore, of the final consumer product. This means that even a substantial change in freight rates will make very little difference to final costs.

The argument here is around the share of shipping freight rates in total costs, which is crucial to the size of the elasticity of demand. If, for example, the share of freight rate costs is only 10% then a 10% increase in freight costs, other things being equal would raise total costs by only 1%. In contrast if the initial share were 80% a 10% increase in freight rates would increase total costs by 8%. This may result in the producer increasing his prices to the final consumer, output and hence demand for shipping would fall. Thus the greater or smaller the share of shipping freight rates of total costs the higher, or lower, the freight rate elasticity of demand for shipping will tend to be. There has been some questioning of this condition since Marshall first postulated it. As long as demand for the product is fairly elastic while substitution is difficult the criteria for the third condition is fulfilled. It only holds if the elasticity of demand for the final product is greater than the elasticity of substitution between factors of production. It follows that it is 'important to be unimportant' only when the consumer can substitute more easily that the producer. [5]

According to this condition demand for shipping will be:

a)   more elastic, the greater the share of freights of total cost.
b)   less elastic, the lower the percentage, the less important freight rates are to total cost.

4.   Elasticity of Supply of Co-Operating Factors

The demand for anything is likely to be more elastic the more elastic is the supply of its co-operating agents of production.

The elasticity of derived demand for shipping will be dependent on the elasticity of other resources necessary in the production of the final consumer product. The greater the producer's ability to obtain resources for the production of the final consumer product from other sources the greater will be the elasticity. The means that should shipping freights increase substantially firms would change their production process in such a way as to avoid the use of the now expensive shipping, and the necessity to increase the final consumer product price. The presence of these substitute factors of production makes the derived demand for shipping highly elastic.

The elasticity of derived demand for shipping rests on the presumption that there are no alternative sources of any input that does not require shipping services. The presumption here is that there is no cost comparable, economically feasible, alternative sources of supply available to replace the cargo transported by sea.   There is a general reluctance, or unwillingness of domestic or other producers who do not require sea-borne transport to replace the cargo inputs in response to some increase in freight rates. There is a lack of substitutes for the inputs. To restate the condition in another form. The lower the producer firm's ability to attract supplies of other factors of production, to substitute the sea-borne cargo, when freight rates increase, the lower will be the elasticity of demand for shipping.

According to condition 4 demand for shipping will be:

a)   *more elastic, the greater the elasticity of supply of other resources used in production,*
b)   *less elastic, the lower the elasticity of supply of other resources used in production.*

5. Time or Run

A further condition is often added to those enumerated by Marshall. This fifth condition is concerned with the change that occurs in derived demand in the long-run, the other four conditions were postulated assuming the short-run. The demand elasticity for any factor of production, including shipping, just as the elasticity of demand for any final product will be greater, more elastic, the longer the period of time allowed for adjustment. The long-run is defined as a time period during which enterprises can adjust to all changes in the economic environment. The longer the time allowed for adjustment to take place the more responsive will firms be to any change in price or freight rates of factors of production. Producers can reorganise totally the productive process to minimise any factor of production which has became more expensive relative to other factors. Hence if the shipping freight rate were to increase substantially in the long-run, substitutes would be found on two levels upon the method of transporting a cargo and on the cargoes themselves. It follows that elasticity of derived demand for shipping will become increasingly elastic.

Summary

In conclusion the central point of the above discussion is that demand for shipping is a derived one. It originates in the demand for the products being conveyed. No cargo moves merely for the joy of movement. The individual shipowner will be aware of the effects of the elasticity of demand on decrease in freight rates on the companies total revenue. The aggregate demand for shipping grows out of the aggregate demand for raw materials and manufactured products requiring transportation. It is hence closely related to the general level of global economic activity. This activity constitutes the underlying determinant, the question was asked as to what determines the impact the factor price changes; freight rate elasticity of demand for shipping. This was brought down to five conditions which can be summarised thus:

1. The more difficult it is for shipping to be substituted by other factors of production the more inelastic will be the demand for shipping.
2. The lower the price elasticity of demand for the final consumer product the lower the freight elasticity demand for shipping.
3. The smaller the percentage of total cost accounted for by freight rate the lower the elasticity of demand for shipping.
4. The smaller the price elasticity of supply of substitute factors the smaller the freight elasticity of demand for shipping.
5. The longer the time run allowed for adjustment the higher freight elasticity of demand for shipping.

The general assumption presented earlier in this chapter claimed the elasticity of aggregate demand in the shipping industry over the short-run is inelastic has been confirmed. Any aggregate demand analysis based on the conditions laid out above will conclude that shipping has a low elasticity, it is inelastic. That is to say in a competitive market demand is freight rate insensitive.

117

Further Reading

K. E. Boulding *'Economic Analysis'* Vol. 1 Microeconomics First Edition, New York, Harper and Rowe, 1966 Chapter 13 page 252 - 261.

Metaxas B. N. *'Economics of Tramp Shipping'* London The Athlone Press, 1971.

Jansson J. O. and Shneerson D. *'Liner Shipping Economics'* London Chapman and Hall, 1987.

Evans J. J. *'The Elasticity of Sea Transport'*, Maritime Policy and Management, Vol. 15, (4), 1988.

---

[1] For Simple Summary of Demand Elasticity see Appendix 6.1
[2] Devanny, J. W. A Model of the Tanker Charter Market and a Related Dynamic Program. in Lorange P. et al. Shipping Management p100 - 117
[3] ibid. p105
[4] in order suggested by A C Pigou
[5] For a further explanation of this see M. Bronfenbrenner. Notes of the Elasticity of Derived Demand. Oxford Economic papers Volume 13 1961

Chapter Seven

COSTS

Introduction

Having discussed the concepts of aggregate supply and demand of the services of maritime transport at some length in the previous chapters, further explanation is required to improve understanding of factors behind these two concepts in terms of the firm operating in the industry. Supply are dealing with decisions that are dependent on productive techniques and the cost of production. Costs at their simplest are another way of saying supply. Costs are therefore central to the discussion about freight rates and the output and the relationship between them. This brings the discussion to an important stage, and the central object here is to understand how the above factors determine freight rates and the quantity of tonnage supplied.

A firm's costs will be dependent on the factors of production it uses and the price paid for their use. These determine the costs incurred in order to produce and thus, it is important for the firm to be able to identify and control them as far as possible. The primary objective being to minimise costs.

The costs of producing shipping services includes the market value of all the resources used in its production. Costs are therefore fundamental to supply decisions in terms of tonnage and cargo, ton miles produced by the vessel. They are the expenditure of the producer to generate goods or services. Costs borne by the ship operators are crucial in the determination of freight rates and tariffs. It is therefore useful to be able to express costs in cost per unit of time which are directly comparable with freight rates in the determination of profits.

Cost Characteristics

The discussion will begin by analysing the cost structure of the vessel concentrating on the short-run, and by considering the four basic aspects as follows:

1) The dimension of the vessel
2) The speed of the vessel
3) The voyage distance
4) Duration of time in port.

Dimensions of the Vessel

The possibility of improving the efficiency by increasing the size of the vessel has been acknowledged by mathematicians and economists for some considerable time. The limitations being those of naval architectures, shipbuilding technology and the port facilities. In the classic text book by Alfred Marshall published in 1890, the following points were made; "a ship's carrying power varies as the cube of her dimensions, while the resistance offered by the water increases only a little faster than the square of her dimensions, so that a large ship requires less coal in proportion to its tonnage than a small one. It also requires less labour, especially that of navigation; while to passengers is offered greater safety and comfort, more choice of company and better professional attendance. In short, a small ship has no chance of competing with a large ship between ports, where large ships can easily enter, and between which the traffic is sufficient to enable them to fill up quickly".[1] The final comment of 'fill up quickly' should not be overlooked, as port time is of critical importance in any consideration of vessel size. The largest vessels in the 19th and early 20th century were ocean going passenger liners. One of the reasons for this was the capability of loading and unloading passengers and their baggage quickly. The port time was short in comparison with vessels operating in other trades, a point returned to later in this chapter. Through much of the first half of the 20th century, vessel size increased only slowly. This is attributable to the inherent conservatism of shipowners in the traditional fleets. But it could be due to the lack of competition and market structure. In the second half of the 20th century, the depth of the radical change occurring in all trades during the late 1950s and 1960s. Since it has slowed considerably in most sectors as is shown in the following table.

Table 7.1   Vessel Average Ship Size
of Different Trades 1976-1990
(DWT 1000 +)

Existing Fleet as at 1st January	Tankers Over 10,000 d.w.t.	Combination Carriers	Bulk Carriers	Other cargo carrying ships	All Cargo Ships
1976	84.6	111.1	33.1	7.4	26.0
1977	94.7	113.0	33.7	7.6	27.6
1978	99.7	115.3	33.8	7.9	28.3
1979	105.0	116.5	34.1	8.1	28.2
1980	106.4	117.6	34.9	8.1	27.8
1981	105. 2	118.4	34.3	8.3	27.5
1982	104.5	117.9	35.6	8.3	27.6
1983	101.8	119.2	37.1	8.3	27.4
1984	100.7	118.9	37.8	8.4	26.9
1985	100.0	116.2	38.5	8.5	26.5
1986	95.5	120.4	39.6	8.5	25.8
1987	92.9	117.2	40.9	8.5	25.6
1988	92.0	117.8	41.5	8.4	25.4
1989	91.8	117.3	42.0	8.4	25.5
1990	92.8	116.2	42.8	8.4	25.8
% change 1980 = 100	110	106	129	11.3	99

The 'all cargo' ships column illustrates the general stagnation in vessel size following the intensive activity of the earlier decades. Average size of tankers reached its peak in the early 1980s   and since has experienced a gradual decline, being only slightly larger in 1990 than in 1976. Combination carriers have continued to grow in average size but at an extremely slow rate. Bulk carriers are the exception in the cargo carrying group, the average size has grown consistently, with some 30% increase in the period under consideration.

'Other cargo' carrying ships have also increased in percentage terms, though the change has been minimal. The reason for this is there has been no rapid technological change particularly in regards to loading or unloading gear, so that time spent in port has been stable and the increase in size has been relatively modest.

As pointed out in the earlier quote, increasing the cubic dimensions of a vessel leads to a lower proportional increase in cost. Such things as labour, capital and maintenance costs increase at a lower rate. Propulsion costs are approximately the same, or at a lower rate in relation to ship size. Under such conditions, the cost per registered ton will fall continuously as the vessel size increases. In other words, as the size and possible productive output of a vessel expands, unit costs will steadily contract. This is known as the advantage of returns to large scale production (economies of scale) as shown in the Figure 7.1.

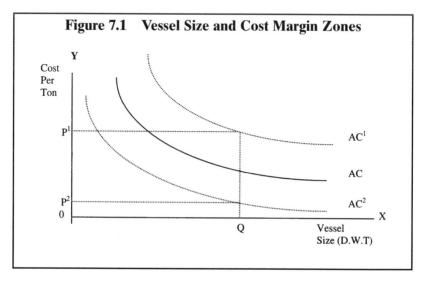

Figure 7.1   Vessel Size and Cost Margin Zones

The vertical axis (y) indicates costs per registered ton, the horizontal axis (x) dimensions of vessels in dwt tons. As can be seen the cost curve is declining as the vessel increases in size. The curve AC shows the general trend. The curve above indicates a higher cost sum; this is related to the registry or flag the company operates the vessel under. Higher costs AC^1 in general comes from the more traditional registers; Sweden or the United States for example. The high costs of the registers are often related in part to labour and insurance costs. The lower curve AC^2 marks the bottom limit of the cost zone and is similarly related to the choice of register. In this case low cost examples are Malta or Cyprus. A vessel of size Q, would if operating under a high cost register, have a cost per ton of P^1. If on a low cost register the cost would stand at P^2. What the figure highlights is a whole range of costs but of more importance here that they move in the same direction with regard to the size of the vessel.

Rather than considering cost under different registers, Edmond and Maggs[2] examine voyage cost per container on the North Atlantic trade for different companies. They also add the further criteria of the number of ports of call, as illustrated in the figure below:

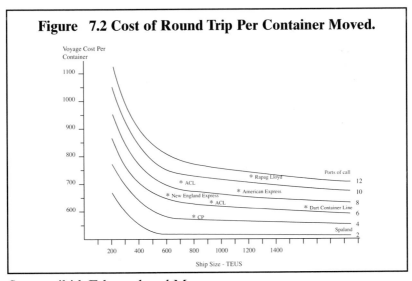

Figure   7.2 Cost of Round Trip Per Container Moved.

Source: ibid. Edmond and Maggs.

This shows a typical curve, being experienced by a number of companies, and the general effect of increasing the number of ports of call is to raise the voyage cost per container. The authors point out "The only company with significantly low costs (in this figure) Sealand, are well known for their use of feeder services to transport containers to their main ports of call".[3]

Kendall[4] constructs a similar model showing the cost of transport in tons of bulk commodity in different size vessels. A further criteria is added, that of round voyage distance. The model is built on a number of assumptions, the most important being that the curve relates to a particular time period and with a full cargo in outward direction and a ballast return voyage.

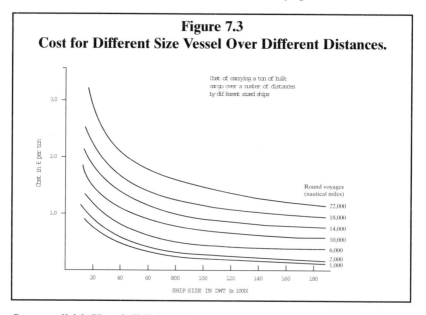

Figure 7.3
Cost for Different Size Vessel Over Different Distances.

Source: ibid. Kendall P. M. K.

This illustrates that the economies of large scale production are obviously present in the bulk cargo sector of the maritime industry. The longer the voyage in terms of nautical miles, the more economically efficient will the larger size vessel be.

The larger the vessel the greater the economies of scale gained at

124

sea. But the increased size presents a problem, that of the storage of the cargo (product) in port. The higher the value of the cargo, the greater the financial penalties for holding large stocks, consequently the economic size of the vessel will be smaller. It follows the lower the value of the cargo the larger the optimum vessel. A good example of this being crude oil tankers, where the cargo is a low value product in weight terms.

Storage and handling cost are considered by a number of authorities[5], which see the importance of the trade off between economics of large cargo at sea against the storage, handling and port costs. Ports are looked at in detail later in this chapter.[6]

Concentrating on the relationship per ton between the vessel size and the storage and handling costs. The latter costs in terms of tons increase linearly with the growth in the size of the vessel, and inversely with increasing total annual tonnage. Kendall illustrated both but here handling cost per ton of bulk cargo will be considered, with these costs for a number of different annual volume of trade, as illustrated below.

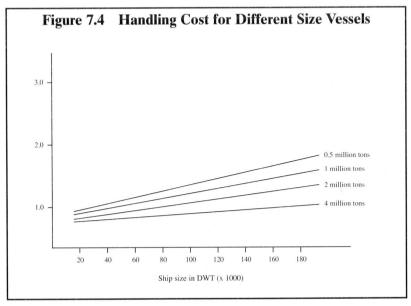

Figure 7.4   Handling Cost for Different Size Vessels

Source: Op. Cit. Kendall P. M. H.

125

This emphasises the considerable difference in the handling costs achieved by different size vessels. The ship costs curve is based on the assumption of a given distance. As the size of vessels increases, so of course, does the tonnage of cargo handled. To stabilise the time spent in port loading and unloading, the cargo handling speed must be increased. Kendall points out that there are four principal ways of achieving this:

1. "Increasing the speed of existing equipment. Since most handling equipment has a fairly fixed rated speed, this solution is unlikely to be acceptable except over a limited range of ship sizes.

2. Using more equipment of the same rated speed. Even if this were practicable, it is likely to be only a short-term measure.

3. Increasing the number of working shifts - also likely to be a short-term expedient.

4. Having new equipment installed, the rated speed of which has been designed to accommodate ships of expected size. Although it is possible for the capital cost of this equipment to rise faster or slower than the size of the ship it is required to handle in a given time, it has been assumed in this analysis that there will be a direct linear relationship between handling cost and ship size."

These handling and storage costs are combined with ships' costs so as to determine the theoretical cost optimum is illustrated in the Figure 7.5.

Here the ship's costs curve is based on the assumption of a given distance. Kendall further comments:

"The optimum size of ship under these conditions will be shown where the curve for total storage, handling and ship cost is at its minimum value. Of course, the storage and handling costs concerned are those that arise at both ends of the voyage. Thus, for a given volume of trade and length of voyage, the ships are economically discouraged from being above a certain size by the cost/ton of handling and storage rising faster than the ship costs/ton are falling."[7]

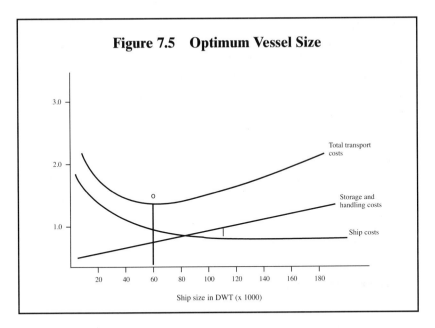

Figure 7.5   Optimum Vessel Size

Total transport costs

Storage and handling costs

Ship costs

Ship size in DWT (x 1000)

Source: Op. Cit. Kendall P. M. H.

Changes in Vessel Speed

The design of the vessel also determines its speed, but there is some room for manoeuvre. Increasing speed means higher fuel consumption; it is estimated that a 1% increase in speed will increase fuel consumption by 3%. Speed therefore is a variable in relation to bunker prices; an increase in fuel prices will provide an incentive to reduce speed in order to keep costs down. During the 1973 oil crisis, there was evidence to suggest that vessel speeds were reduced due to the 400% increase in bunker prices. Speed, however, affects journey time which has a cost impact. A reduced journey time will invariably reduce some of the variable overheads and partially offset an increase in fuel costs. A notable exception is the liner trade which has to meet its schedules and cannot thereafter alter its speeds significantly, and therefore tends to pass on unforeseen increases in fuel cost to the consumer.

Changes in speed will increase or decrease time spent on the voyage, bunker consumption costs will be increased or decreased accordingly. There is a clear relationship between these factors. Empirical data and academic theory indicates this relationship as shown by the following equation:

Equation 7.1

$$B(S) = B_d \left(\frac{S}{S_d} \right)^{\kappa}$$

where:

(B)S = fuel oil consumption per day at a given speed.
B_d = fuel oil consumption per day at vessel design speed.
S = given speed.
S_d = vessel design speed.

The 'k' factor may or will be dependent on vessel type, an example of a typical vessel is with a speed of eighteen to twenty knots, factor 'k' will be approximately at point 3.0.[8]

Changes of Voyage Distance

Assuming a given size of vessel and speed, an increased voyage distance will inevitably mean higher costs for bunker fuel and direct operating costs. This implies that the costs per ton of cargo carried by the vessel are a function of voyage length as can be seen from Figure 7.6 below:

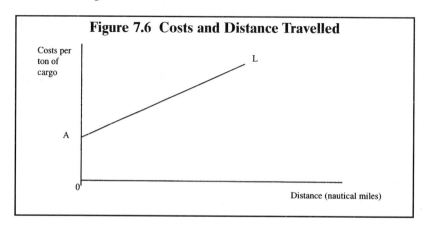

Figure 7.6 Costs and Distance Travelled

The linear relationship between cost and the number of nautical miles travelled is clear. The vessel with dimensions 'L' before the beginning of the voyage has a number of fixed or overhead costs, which are usually related to the vessel size. The vertical distance 0A represents these costs. Once the voyage has began, the vessel's costs increase in proportion to the distance travelled. This model can be modified to show the effect of different vessel sizes as in Figure 7.7. Here the cost per ton as a function of distance for these vessels of different sizes is shown, the flatter the curve the larger the vessel.

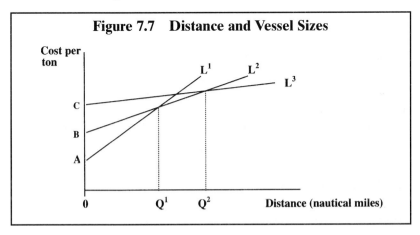

Figure 7.7 Distance and Vessel Sizes

The cost of per ton is less steep as the vessel size increases, this is because costs tend to be higher for larger vessels, and the cost per nautical mile are smaller due to more efficient fuel consumption. From the figure it is possible to see which size of vessel is most effective over what distance. Over distance $0Q^1$, L^1, the small vessel (A), has the lowest cost. Between Q^1 and Q^2, L^2, a larger vessel (B) is most efficient; beyond Q^2 a much larger vessel is preferable as the distance lengthens. A further point to note around distance 0Q1 and vessel L^1, L^2 there will be competition for cargo, similarly at distance Q^2; L^2, L^3 will be in competition.

Thorburn discussed the idea of vessel size, freight rate and distance travelled in his seminal work[9], arguing that larger vessels operate more efficiently over longer distances, and freight rates taper off with the length of the voyage.

129

To the above single vessel cost curve, 'L', he adds a freight rate curve 'f'. This shows that the freight rate per ton level rises continuously with distance, as illustrated in Figure 7.8.

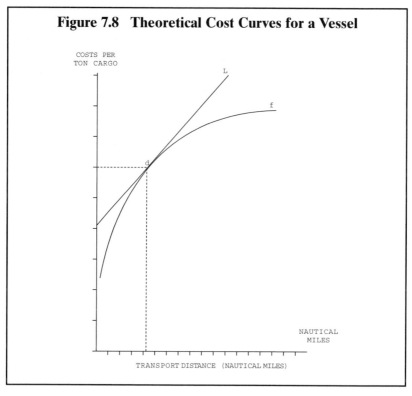

Figure 7.8   Theoretical Cost Curves for a Vessel

f   =   freight curve
L   =   costs curve
d   =   tangent point

The freight rate increases but by far less, in proportion to the distance. Thorburn points out :

"The number of offers seems in practice, however, to be as a rule so great that the conception of the offers as points on such a curve cannot be regarded as unrealistic, nor can it be regarded as unrealistic that the curve rises continuously".

The analysis is taken further in the following comment:

"When the cost curve of a vessel per cargo ton for trips of different length, L, is combined with the curve formed by the freight rates offered for transport over varying distances, f, the cost curve forms a tangent to the freight curve. [s]. The point at which the curves meet gives the transport distance at which the vessel makes maximum profit, and shows, therefore, the distance the shipowner is assumed to choose for his vessel. At a greater or shorter distance, the profit will be less, as shown by the fact that the curve c is above the freight rates offered."[10]

He then combines the previous different vessel size and cost curve with the freight rate curve, producing Figure 7.9.

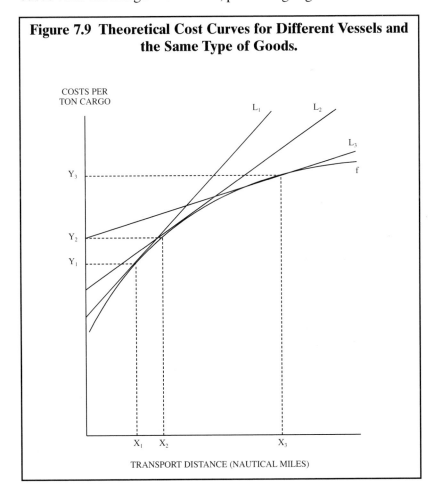

Figure 7.9 Theoretical Cost Curves for Different Vessels and the Same Type of Goods.

f	=	freight curve
$L_{1,2,3}$	=	cost curves for three different vessels
$x_{1,2,3}$	=	optimum transport distances for the three different vessels
$y_{1,2,3}$	=	freight rates at optimum transport distances

The dimensions and cost of the vessel are dictated by L^1 to L^3. These flatten out as the size increases. The freight rate curve f slowly tapers downwards with increasing distance. The tangential points between the size cost lines L, and the freight rate curve f serve to indicate the distance for which certain vessels will be the optimum size. The longer the distance, the flatter both the vessel cost line and the freight rate curve will be, which serves to show that the longer the voyage distances, the larger this will be the optimum vessel size. From this limited base can be seen the reason for small vessels being engaged in the coastal or short sea trades, and larger ones in the ocean going deep sea trades.

"It is now easy to see that if the number of vessels with different cost curves is very large, the tangent points will be close together, and may be approximated as a continuous curve. This must be rising with the increased transport distance, since every additional kilometre means greater costs. The derivative of the curve must also decline with increasing transport distance."[11]

Port Time

The primary objective of a port is to transfer cargo and passengers between land and sea transport as efficiently as possible. The time this operation takes, is of course the time that the vessel is required to be in port. This is a particularly important factor in the size of the vessel, for port time has a direct impact on this and their overall operational costs. The period in port relates closely to the type of cargo the vessel carries. The speed of loading and discharging which is directly dependent on the port organisation and the type of machinery used, and prevention of any delays to the vessel. Port costs are those levied on the ship operator for using the port and the relevant facilities. These charges are normally based on ships dimensions e.g. to both length and draft. The larger the vessel the greater the cost will be for the time spent in port. The level of these charges will have a significant effect on vessel size. The other element are the capital and depreciation costs, both of these are the more expensive being in port both in terms of working cargo or laying idle. Both costs can be considered as time cost. The opportunity costs of ships' time spent in port is what freight could have been earned in that time had the turnaround been more rapid or no call occurred, minus any extra cost involved.

If a vessel can load and discharge cargo rapidly it is not required to spend extended lengths of time in port. As a vessel size increases, port time decreases, and its costs will decline as illustrated in figure 7.10.

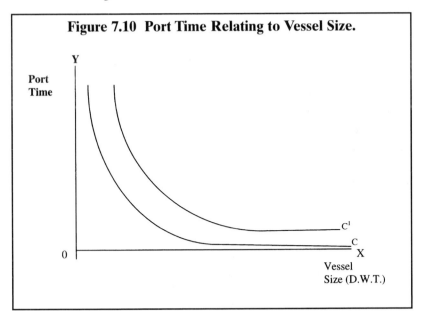

Figure 7.10 Port Time Relating to Vessel Size.

The three factors under consideration here are port time, size of vessel and cost (*Ceteris Paribus*), as can be seen port time has a direct relationship to costs. Port time is on the vertical axis, the y axis decreases rapidly as tonnage size increases along the x axis. As port time decreases, so do cost per ton (C), while the size of the vessel increases.

The reduction in port time is due largely to the massive capital investment and improvement in bulk cargo handling techniques in port. It was this investment which was a major contributory factor to the unprecedented growth in the size of the initial crude oil tankers and later dry bulk carriers over the last few decades. This increase in productivity was brought about directly by improved cargo handling techniques and was not shared by the traditional break bulk cargo liners. This is reflected in the modest increase in size discussed earlier. In the development of containerisation and other cargo unitisation systems, the increase in vessel size and capacity, and the rise in port productivity has been a major factor. It has caused the liner trade time in port loading and discharging to decline from weeks to a matter of hours. Such enormous movements of cargo both bulk and containerise require not only highly productive loading and discharging machinery but considerable land storage capacity. Hence both these elements reduce port time and have required massive capital infrastructure investments. These developments have been combined with a similar if relatively small investment in new building of larger vessels.

Such an analysis also makes the reverse point clearly. That the longer a vessel is required to spend in port the smaller the optimum size will be, short sea and coastal cargo vessels tend to confirm this assertion.

Cost Accounting Items

To approach ships costs in relation to basic accounting. Costs can be classified in broad operational terms under five different categories;

1. Capital costs

These cover the costs of financing new ships, including payments

134

of interests and loan principal, and the return on equity invested in the vessel. This return may not actually be a cash payment, but there is an opportunity cost in terms of interest lost, in having capital tied up in ownership of the vessel. These costs are fixed in the short-run but can be varied in the long-run.

2. General overhead

These include marketing, advertising, agency fees, accounting, management, and banking costs and are fixed in the short-run.

3. Operational costs

The costs of enabling the ship to sail, such as crews, maintenance, repairs, insurance, stores, victualling. These costs are fixed and thus independent of the level of output.

4. Voyage costs

These are costs connected with the running of the ship and can be avoided if the voyage is not made. The major voyage cost is that of fuel. Its consumption varies with distance and speed of journey. The amount spent on port and canal dues is a function of the journey distance. A short trip will not necessarily mean a greater amount of time spent in port and thus higher port dues.

5. Cargo handling costs

The direct cost connected with loading and discharging of cargo, stevedores, and, in the case of passenger ships, the passenger expenses, stewards wages, passenger information. These costs do vary with the quantity of cargo handling or number of passengers travelling.

Economic Analysis of Cost

Costs are classified in economics in terms of **Total, Fixed, and Variable.** Total Costs (TC) are all costs of a firm at any base level of production, total fixed costs are those costs which do not vary with output. These costs are borne even if there is no output. Consequently they are often referred to as overhead or unavoidable costs. The cost of any fixed factor is a fixed cost.

Total Variable Costs (TVC) are all costs that vary directly with the rate of output, that is costs whose magnitude varies with rates of production both in terms of increases and decreases. They are at times referred to as direct or operational costs, it follows that the total costs to the firm of producing at any level of service in ton miles can be seen simply as Total Fixed Costs (TFC) plus Total Variable Costs (TVC). The formula reads :

$$TC = TFC + TVC$$

Before considering what fixed and variable costs are applied to shipping, what must be considered is what is meant by output. This was discussed in the supply chapter as being ton miles. In other words the number of tons shipped multiplied by the number of nautical miles travelled. The short-run is important in the following discussions because certain costs vary with tonnage, others vary with distance travelled, and others with a number of voyages. In any discussion of costs it is important to distinguish between the short and long-run. In the short-run the business is committed by past decisions, and therefore certain factors of production are committed to obtaining some levels of output. In the long-run investment decisions will change and this will alter the fixed costs. All costs become variable in the long-run. In general the most significant fixed cost is the ship itself. Thus the time taken to obtain another ship will be defined as the short-run in this part of the discussion.

To combine these very general short-run economic criteria the cost classifications for a hypothetical ship are as follows:

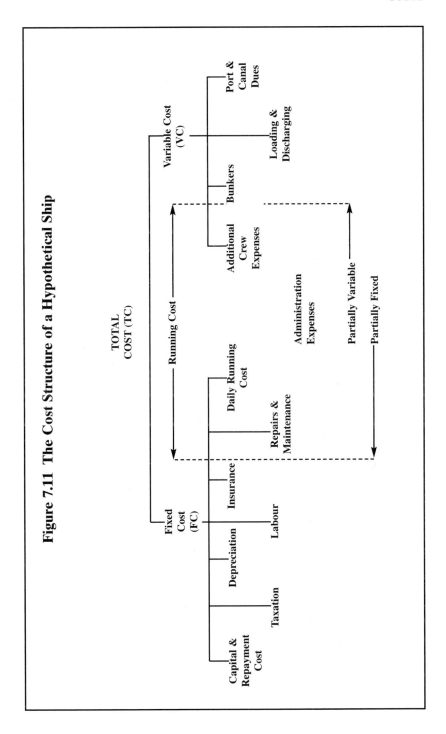

The figure indicates economic costs of the vessel. Vessel costs can be classified clearly, relating to those of economic theory at the extremities of the figure. Capital and repayment costs are obviously fixed in the immediate and short-run. At the other extreme port and canal dues and loading and discharging of cargo costs are clearly variable, relating directly to the levels of production. It is in the area of running costs that the classification by definition becomes difficult, for example; administrative expenses will have a certain element of fixed and variable costs. This should not however be allowed to undermine the value of economic classification in any analysis of the industry.

The concept of fixed and variable costs can perhaps be better illustrated by a simple example. Table 7.2 shows fixed variable and total costs of different levels of output in terms of ton miles.

Table 7.2 Total Costs

Output ton miles	Total Cost		
	Fixed (TFC)	Variable (TVC)	Total (TC)
'000s	£m	£m	£m
0	20	0	20
43	20	10	30
160	20	20	40
351	20	30	50
600	20	40	60
875	20	50	70
1152	20	60	80
1372	20	70	90
1536	20	80	100
1656	20	90	110
1750	20	100	120
1815	20	110	130
1860	20	130	150

What the above table illustrates is that fixed costs (TFC) remain at £ 20 million at all levels of output. Variable costs (TVC) increase as output per ton mile increases. Total costs are the sum of the fixed and variable costs. The information in the above table can be shown as a figure or graph in Figure 7.12.

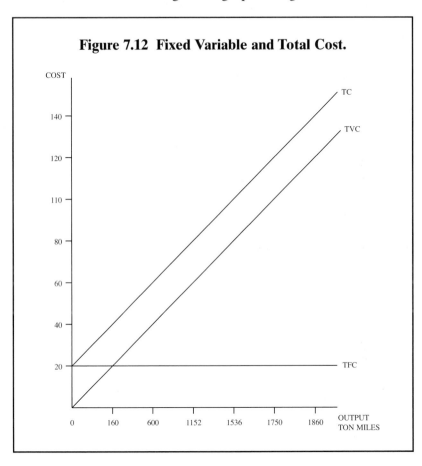

Figure 7.12 Fixed Variable and Total Cost.

In the above figure total costs are a summation of total variable cost and total fixed cost. It should be noted that total variable cost lies below the total cost curve throughout by the vertical distance of £20 million. This vertical distance is another way of representing total fixed costs, which remain constant at all levels of output.

To complete the analysis of costs of production in respect of ton miles of service there is another cost concept to consider that is **Average cost**, occasionally referred to as per unit costs. The **average total cost** curve (ATC) is the total cost of producing the given number of units of output divided by the number of those units. In this case, it is the total cost of producing a given quantity of ton miles divided by the number of ton miles produced. Average total costs are made up of average fixed costs and average variable costs. These are calculated on a similar basis; average variable costs divides the total variable cost at each level of production by the rate production, i.e. total variable cost divided by ton miles. Average fixed costs (AFC) are obtained by dividing total fixed costs at any level of output by the number of units produced. Marginal costs show the change in the total cost required to increase (decrease) production by one unit. The calculation of average and marginal costs are shown below:

Equation 7.2

(a) Average Total Cost (ATC) $= \dfrac{\text{Total Cost}}{\text{Number of units of Output}}$

(b) Average Variable Cost (AVC) $= \dfrac{\text{Total Variable Cost}}{\text{Number of units of Output}}$

(c) Average Total Cost (AFC) $= \dfrac{\text{Total Fixed Cost}}{\text{Number of units of Output}}$

(d) Marginal Costs (MC) $= \dfrac{\text{Change in Total Cost}}{\text{Change in Output}}$

Table 7.3 calculates average cost from data in the previous total cost example. The average costs, this table may be graphically represented as in Figure 7.13.

Table 7.3   Average and Marginal Cost

Output ton miles	Average Cost			Marginal Cost
	Fixed (AFC)	Variable (AVC)	Total (AC)	(MC)
'000s	£m	£m	£m	£m
43	0.465	0.233	0.698	0.233
160	0.125	0.125	0.250	0.085
351	0.057	0.085	0.142	0.052
600	0.033	0.067	0.100	0.040
875	0.023	0.057	0.080	0.036
1152	0.017	0.052	0.069	0.036
1372	0.015	0.051	0.066	0.045
1536	0.013	0.052	0.065	0.061
1656	0.012	0.054	0.066	0.083
1750	0.011	0.057	0.069	0.106
1815	0.011	0.061	0.072	0.154
1860	0.011	0.065	0.075	0.222

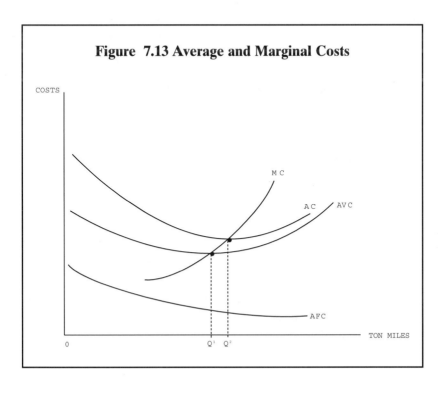

Figure 7.13 Average and Marginal Costs

In the above figure Average Fixed Costs (AFC) continue to fall throughout the curve, it is always a downward slope getting nearer and nearer to the horizontal axis. It will continue to do so throughout the range of output, because total fixed costs are a constant fixed quantity, £20 million which is being divided by a larger and larger number of units of output ton mile. Average Variable Cost (AVC) show a initial decline, then a steady increase begins at certain levels of ton miles output. It often takes the form of a 'U' shaped curve. The Average Total Cost curve (ATC) is simply AFC+AVC. This Average Total Cost curve (ATC) falls in the beginning and then rises steadily. The AFC is derived from a constant divided by an increasing level of output, ton miles, and hence declines systematically with output. AVC and ATC therefore move closer together as output increases. The short-run marginal cost curve cuts both these curves from below at the minimum points Q^1 and Q^2.

The 'U' shaped cost curve relates closely to what is known as the **law of diminishing returns** at times referred to as **the law of varying proportions, or the law of diminishing marginal returns.** It states that as the quantity of a one variable factor used in the production process is increased with the quantities of other inputs held constant a point will eventually be reached where the resulting increase in output becomes smaller and smaller. A number of points emerged from this; a 'law' is simply an assertion made by examination about some general tendencies in the technology of the real world. The law has been generally applied to most production processes and it appears quite plausible.

Marginal Costs

For the decision making process, the key consideration is marginal or incremental cost. **Marginal cost** may be defined as change in total cost generated by the production of an extra unit of output, or the avoidable cost production of not producing an additional unit. Marginal cost is calculated as the change in total costs per unit as shown in Table 7.3. Up to the optimum point the marginal cost is below the average cost. If the marginal cost is lower than average cost the average will fall. If it is higher, then the average will rise; it follows from the law of diminishing returns that the optimum point of production is where minimum costs are achieved, that is where the most efficient economic use is made of the plant in technological terms. The **optimum** point being where marginal cost equals average cost (MC=ATC) in the above figure where they intersect. To use a maritime example, the marginal cost is the cost of an extra passenger, ton of cargo or a container. If the ship is not fully laden the marginal cost will be quite small. At full capacity, however, an additional passenger, or an additional ton of cargo or container will require an additional ship, and therefore the marginal cost will be extremely high. The relationship between marginal and average cost is illustrated in Figure 7.13.

Break Even Analysis

To relate this simple form of cost analysis of the firm to the freight rate. A method of doing this is to find the level of capacity above which profits are earned. This is known as the break even point. It is a position where total revenue equals total cost and if the actual output exceeds this level, profits are made. It is a method which is based on empirical evidence from the industry. Before constructing a break even model it is necessary to make a number of assumptions.

I.   The freight rate market is perfectly competitive, that is to say there are many relatively small shipowners (sellers) and many relatively small shippers (buyers). A market structure making both shipowners and shippers 'freight takers', has no influence over the freight rate.

II. The shipowning firm consists of a single vessel, and therefore can only produce a single service, for example, a handy size dry bulk carrier.

III. Costs are stable in this short-run analysis.

IV. For clarity, cost and revenue curves are linear, i.e. a straight line.

V.   Ceteris Paribus applies.

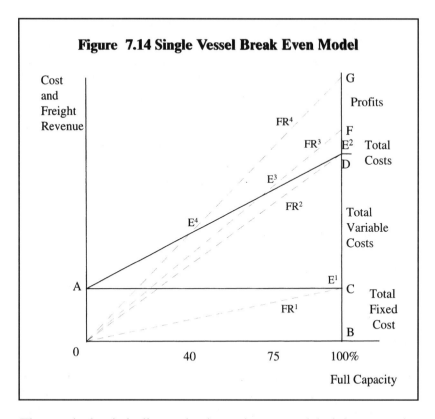

Figure 7.14 Single Vessel Break Even Model

The vertical axis indicates both total costs and freight rates; the horizontal axis, the tonnage capacity of the vessel to a 100% full capacity. The level of total fixed cost (FC) are indicated by the vertical distance of the line, AC. Variable costs (VC) are represented by the line AD; total costs are total fixed costs (TFC) plus total variable costs (TVC). This is also indicated by the line AD.

The freight rate curve is denoted by FR. Here there are four examples of different freight rates, so let us examine these individually. The lower freight rate FR^1 only just covers total fixed costs (0C) at full capacity (0B). It is an offer which shipowners will reject. The higher freight rate ($0FR^2$) just covers total costs (OD). These costs include normal profits and shipowners will accept this freight on a full cargo basis, E^2 at point AD. It is only at full capacity that such normal profit can

144

be secured. It should be added here that shipowners may accept any rate between FR^1 and FR^2 because it will cover fixed costs and some percentage of variable cost and maybe accepted in the short or medium run. The higher freight rate $FR^3(0F)$ will yield higher profits, the break even point E^3 is 75% of capacity utilisation. Any point below this 75%, losses will be made any point above it E^3 increase profits will be secured. The even higher freight rate F4(0G) indicates that profits will be made beyond the break even point E^4 at 40% capacity utilisation. The model illustrates the situation where short-run costs are stable, market freight rates are the dynamic element to which the shipowner reacts, the actual level of profits or losses will be related largely to a level of capacity utilisation which the break even point indicates. Break even analysis is a simple technique for determining the utilisation level here it was assumed to be a dry cargo vessel, but any single vessel can make use of such a simple method.

Summary

To progress the analysis further this chapter examined the costs of the firm, these costs are a critical determinant in the supply of tonnage offered. This supply being strongly influenced by the cost of the resources necessary for such activity. The basic outcome is that there is an economic advantage for large vessels, as against certain diseconomies suffered in port. Hence the decision to invest in an optimal vessel involves a balance being achieved between the cost per ton at sea, against the same cost in ports. It was argued that a vessel's cost function is calculated on a number of factors; size, speed and time spent in port and these will have an impact on the type of trade in which the vessel operates. Economic advantage is to be gained by achieving an optimum match of all these factors. This serves to explain the economic specialisation of different vessels in different freight markets.

Costs are divided between fixed and variable costs as output increases total costs increase, because variable costs will increase. In the short-run vessel size or active supply is fixed. As a consequence of the law of diminishing returns, beyond some level of output both average variable and total costs will rise. This is illustrated by the 'U' shaped cost curve.

Freight rate was introduced to the discussion of the 'Thorburn' model, and particularly when looking at Break Even model. This formulates a simple method of operating the single vessel. It relates total cost structures to different cargoes within a series of competitive freight rates, which provides a simple basis for operational efficiency.

Further Reading

Atmay R. *The Economics of Soviet Merchant Shipping,* North Carolina University Press, 1971.

Thorburn T. *Supply & Demand Of Water Transport,* Stockholm E.F. 1 Report ,1960.

United Nations *Freight Markets and the Level and Structure of Freight Rates* New York UNCTAD 1969.

United Nations *Coastal Shipping, Feeder & Ferry Services* New York UNCTAD 1970.

Buxton I.L. *'Engineering Economics and Ship Design'* Wallsend The British Shipping Research Association 1971

Edmond E. D. and Maggs R. P. *'Container Ship Turnaround Time at UK Ports, Maritime Policy and Management'.* Vol. 4 (1) 1976.

Kendall P. M. K. *'A Theory of Optimum Ship Size Journal of Transport Economics and Policy'.* May 1972.

Jansson J. O. and Shneerson D, *'Liner Shipping Economics'* London, Chapman and Hall 1987.

— —

[1] Marshall. A. Principles of Economics, London Macmillan & Co. Ltd. 1890, p290.n
[2] Edmond E. D. and Maggs R. P. Container Ship Turnaround Time at UK Ports, Maritime Policy and Management. Vol. 4 (1) 1976 p3-19
[3] ibid. p14
[4] Kendall P. M. K. A Theory of Optimum Ship Size Journal of Transport Economics and Policy. May 1972 p 128 -148.
[5] Op. Cit. Kendall P.M.K Also see Thorburn T. Supply and Demand of Water Transport. Stockholm FFI Report 1960 Chapter 7.
[6] Also see Chapter 13
[7] Op. Cit. Kendall P. M. H. pp131-134.
[8] Speed is also included in the Supply chapter 4
[9] Thorburn T. Supply and Demand of Water Transport Stockholm. FF1 Report 1960
The following figures are based on this study.
[10] Op. Cit. Thorburn T. p22.
[11] Op. Cit. Thorburn p.35

Chapter Eight

MARKET STRUCTURES

Introduction

The objective of this chapter is to examine the process of allocating scarce resources within the industry through different market structures. This contains only a brief survey of the theory of the firm. The firm being any entity which produces economic goods and services. The theory's purpose is to analyse the way in which decisions are made by firms in different markets. This chapter will explain how groups of firms behave rather than individual firms.

The shipping industry comprises a number of different markets, each with their own distinct market structure. This structure is determined by the market characteristics; the supply of service being offered, the type of the product, the number of operators, the barriers to entry or exit, the number of consumers demanding the service. Microeconomic theory describes these market forms using various models, ranging from perfect competition to monopoly. Between these two extremes, there are a number of intermediate market forms which will assist in analysing the basic structure of the shipping industry. Figure 8.1 suggests a basic market structure in the industry.

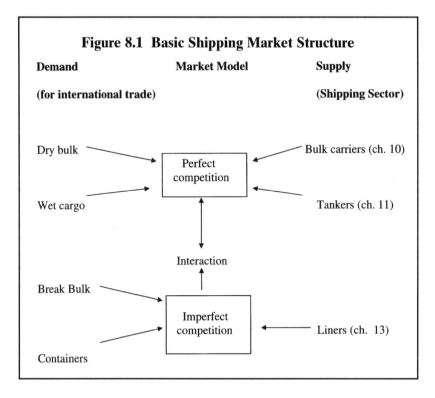

Figure 8.1 Basic Shipping Market Structure

The international demand for dry cargo is met using bulk carriers, and for wet cargo by tankers. Both the dry bulk and tankers markets are characterised by a large number of firms with free entry and exit, the shipping service being a homogeneous product. It could therefore be argued that they conform to a model of perfect competition. The market for liners, used to ship break bulk and containers, is however more complex, and can only be described as one of imperfect competition.

Imperfect competition exists on various levels. The most extreme is a monopoly situation where one firm dominates the sector. Although no such extreme exists in the liner sector or indeed the rest of the shipping industry, operators do exhibit some monopolistic behaviour, in the use of price discrimination. They also behave in consort, setting up conferences or alliances which may be considered to be part of an oligopoly structure. All are constructed on the presumption of profit maximisation.

The chapter will first briefly examine the economic models of perfect competition and monopoly, before considering the intermediate forms of imperfect competition, and oligopoly. This provides the theoretical underpinning for the industry specific chapters in the final section of this book.

Perfect Competition

The central characteristic here is that no individual firm, shipper or shipowner can influence the freight rate.

Perfect competition occurs when a large number of individual sellers, that is shipowners on the supply side, are confronted by a similarly large number of individual buyers, that is shippers or charterers on the demand side. All participants in the market are price takers in that they accept the ruling freight rate as axiomatic. This is the case in the dry bulk freight market where an open market comprising numerous individual firms of shippers and similarly large numbers of shipowners offering common carrier bulk transport services. In addition, they participate in an atomised market and have no inhibitions about entering or leaving the market. This is an integral criterion for the creation of a highly competitive market.

Microeconomics perceives perfect competition as an elaboration of Marshall's demand and supply analysis, which has been discussed previously, and provides insights into the way in which the equilibrium market price, that is the freight rate, is established. These insights transcend the narrow borders of the strictly defined model which are about to be constructed.

In a similar way to all economic models, perfect competition is underpinned by a set of assumptions which are detailed below.

Assumptions

1.   The industry includes a large number of relatively small firms of both shipowners and shippers.

The consequence of this is that each firm produces or consumes at a level of output which is extremely small in relation to the total quantity of the industry's production. The important implication of this assumption is that firms are so numerous as to be incapable of possessing any market power with which to influence the level of freight rates. Firms do not collaborate in groups to affect or influence the market. It follows that individual firms are incapable of affecting the freight rate by varying their own output levels or their demand for tonnage, since what the individual supplies or demands is insignificant in terms of the industry as a whole. All firms are, therefore, price takers as they accept as given the freight rate offered in the market. The rate is determined by the general market conditions of demand and supply.

2.   The Service Provided by the Various Producers is Homogeneous

In perfect competition the industry or industrial sectors can be defined as a group of firms producing a homogeneous (uniform) product or service. This assumption is essential to ensure that the first assumption operates. The product cannot be differentiated by advertising, trademarks or branding to influence the shipper. The standard nature of the product means that any attempt to increase the freight rate will be futile because the individual shippers can easily take their business to other competing ship-owners asking the lower market freight rate. Shipowners will not offer tonnage at a rate lower than that pertaining in the freight market. This would not be rational in that it will reduce profits. What is important in making the assumption about homogeneity is not only that the service offered is identical in physical terms but that it is perceived by shippers to be so.

3. Freedom of Entry and Exit of Firms, (Sometimes Referred to as Resource Mobility).

There are no features of an artificial or natural kind interfering with the free movement of firms in and out of the industry. Capital and other costs are such that they do not deter entry to the industry or sector. Exit is also open to firms, by selling their tonnage, sending it for scrap and or temporary withdrawal by laying up. The presumption here is that laying up is to exit from the industry, that is removing the tonnage from active supply. Once again this third assumption supplements the first one of a large number of firms, for if any barriers exist the numbers of firms on either shipowners or shippers side of the industry is reduced. Individual firms may grow in size or collaborate and hence acquire power to influence the freight rate, the market. The underlying implication here is twofold, first that the market mechanism, unimpeded, establishes the freight rate. Secondly, that at times when freight rates and presumably profits are high, firms will freely enter the industry. It follows that at low levels of freight rates firms will exit. Such freedom of movement in and out of the sector ensures that the profit maximisation function can be maintained.

4. Perfect Information or Knowledge.

This infers that the buyers and sellers are in close communication. It is here assumed that all shipowners and shippers, that is charterers, have full knowledge of the conditions and influences operating within the freight market. The number and details of vessels available for employment will be published in the market by the shipowner's broker. While on the other hand the charterer's broker will attempt to find a vessel in the market that suits the particular cargo needs. In the system will be published various cargoes, in the market, seeking transportation. In a similar way owners using this freely available information will attempt to find an advantageous cargo. There are no secrets within the market, every shipper and shipowner is aware of the past and current freight rates. On the basis of this and other information they assess trends themselves.

153

5. No Government Interference

The government or governments do not interfere in the market in any way. They refrain from subsidising vessels, flag protection and the like. The rates of government charters are not kept secret. There is no state interference in the interaction of the market and it responds freely to the forces of supply and demand.

Given all the above assumptions there can only be a single market freight rate. A ruling freight rate determined by the equilibrium point of the market demand and supply curves. The market demand curve is the aggregate of all the individual shippers' demands. The market supply curve is the aggregate supply of all the individual shipping firms supply curves above their variable cost curve[1]. Neither shippers nor shipowning firms in such a market can affect the freight rate. To take an example, the market freight rate stands at $10 a ton. Should an individual shipowner require, say, $12 a ton that firm would ship nothing because shippers would charter at lower market rates. Should some individual shipowners decide to be generous to shippers and charge less than $10 per ton, say, $8, this would lead to a loss of revenue for the shipowner and a lowering of the firm's profits with only a marginal increase in sales or tonnage chartered. In addition it would be considered irrational as it constitutes a movement in contradiction to the profit maximisation objective.

What has been constructed is a freight market applying to each individual shipowning firm and determined by the market supply and demand curve for the whole industrial sector. The industry or market demand curve is the sum of all individual demand curves or the aggregate demand. The industry or market supply curve is broadly the sum of all the supply curves of all ship owning firms in the industry, or aggregate supply. The industry's demand curve slopes downwards to the right because if the industry as a whole were to lower its freight rate, there would be an increase in quantity of tonnage demanded. This process follows logically from the basic law of demand. The construction of the firm's short-run supply curve is made comparatively simple by the structure of the competitive freight market. The firm's supply curve shows how much a shipowner is willing or intends to supply at different freight rates. As such, the supply curve reflects output plans based on information concerning expected freight rates. The supply curve moves upwards to the right from the base of each individual shipowning firm's lay-up point, that is the section of the marginal cost curve above the average variable cost, since firms will not produce unless variable costs are being covered. This is illustrated in Figure 8.2.

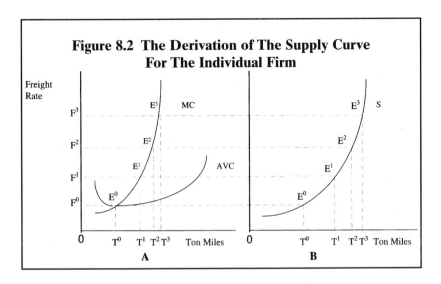

Figure 8.2 The Derivation of The Supply Curve For The Individual Firm

The competitive firm's supply function comprises two segments: the portion above freight rate where average variable costs are covered, and that lying below this minimum freight rate where nothing will be supplied because average variable costs cannot be covered. Section A in the above figure illustrates the firm's cost structure, and section B, the firm's supply curve. The supply curve begins at freight rate F^0 with the production of $0T^0$ ton miles. As the rate rises to F^1, F^2 etc., the equilibrium quantities move to T^1, T^2 etc. The marginal cost curve above F^0 therefore gives the supply curve for the firm. Any change in the freight rate will either increase or decrease the amount of active supply within the sector per unit of time. Hence the firms rather than being freight rate makers are freight rate takers.

The individual shipper, that is the charterer will face a demand

155

curve sloping downwards to the right, and any increase in demand a movement down the curve will cause a fall in price. In contrast the demand curve faced by the individual shipowner is perfectly horizontal in this competitive market. The structure of the market with a large number of relatively small buyers and sellers, homogeneous product, freedom of entry and exit etc. obliges the individual firm to accept the freight rate as given. The shipowner's demand curve is infinitely elastic, indicating that the firm can sell any amount of output, tonnage, at the prevailing market freight rate. This is illustrated in fFigure 8.3.

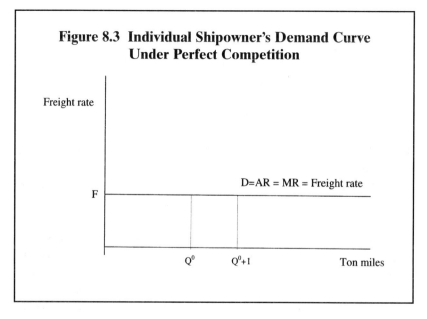

Figure 8.3 Individual Shipowner's Demand Curve Under Perfect Competition

The figure considers demand from the shipowner's (seller's or producer's) perspective. Where perfect competition exists, the shipowner has no influence on the market freight rate. Demand is perfectly elastic, and is therefore a horizontal straight line. Average revenue is found by dividing total revenue at each level of output by the number of units produced. In a perfectly competitive market, average revenue is simply another way of defining the freight rate (price), as it is consistent throughout for all of the individual firms. Therefore:

$$AR \quad = \quad \frac{TR}{Q}$$

Marginal revenue can be defined as the increase in total revenue resulting from a unit increase in output. Since total revenue increases by the same amount, marginal revenue is constant and may be expressed as:

$$MR \quad = \quad \frac{\Delta TR}{\Delta Q}$$

This is an important concept for the individual shipowning firms because it indicates what happens to total revenue when output expands. For the competitive firm in Figure 8.3, the marginal revenue received by the shipowner for selling the extra unit equals the freight rate and the average revenue.

A horizontal demand curve means that the range of output that shipping firms are capable of producing can be supplied at the same freight rate. Hence, from the demand curve facing individual shipowning firms can be drawn a set of important relationships with freight rate, average revenue and marginal revenue being constant, and not varying with output.

The shipowning firm in a competitive market can place any amount of tonnage on the market at the current market freight rate. A short-run analysis of freight rates and output serves to show the situation in which shipowning firms are impelled to vary the level of participation in the market. In the short-run they do not have the time necessary to change their scale of plant. The number of shipping firms will be fixed because new firms will not have the required time to enter nor will existing firms have time to exit. Therefore cargo movement must come from the tonnage capacity of the existing shipowning firms. This can be achieved in a number of ways: increasing vessel speed; reactivating laid up tonnage; postponing surveys or repair work or increasing utilisation. These are examples of increasing supply. It has to be made clear in this discussion that the firm is too small relative to the charter market in which it operates to effect the above freight rate. The problem confronting the shipowner is that of determining the theory of the firm.

Profit Maximisation

The central goal of the shipping firm is to maximise profit or minimise loss. The extent to which the objectives of shipowners or indeed the considerably broader group of all entrepreneurs may be explained by this goal of profit maximisation is a famous debate among not only maritime economists but the whole fraternity of economists. These arguments need not be rehearsed here, but a great deal of empirical evidence supports the goal of profit maximisation, and as yet there has not been developed other well defined objectives with any serious empirical support.

How then does a shipowner achieve profit maximisation or loss minimisation? There are certain conditions which dictate profit maximisation behaviour regardless of market structure. Firstly, the firm should produce output if total receipts are greater than total variable costs. In other words, the firm should produce only if the freight rate (average revenue) is greater than average variable cost. This is because it pays a firm to continue in the short-run even if it cannot cover its fixed costs, since these will be incurred regardless of any output. Secondly, the firm is maximising profits if marginal revenue is equated with marginal cost. This is because profits will rise whenever the extra unit of production adds more to revenue than it adds to cost. That is to say profit increases when marginal revenue is greater than marginal costs. Conversely profit contracts when additional units of output increase costs more than revenue, a situation where marginal cost is greater than marginal revenue. It follows from this that profit will be maximised where and only where, marginal cost is equal to marginal revenue. Shipowners should continue to supply tonnage for charter until the point is reached where the marginal cost of supplying the extra unit of tonnage is equal to the marginal revenue received for its use. Thirdly, the logic is that the marginal curve should intersect the marginal revenue curve from below. Figure 8.4 illustrates why this must be so. The diagram shows a situation where the marginal cost curve

158

cuts the marginal revenue curve in two places, suggesting output of T^1 and T^2 respectively. Clearly, T^2 is the output that maximises profits, where MC cuts MR from below.

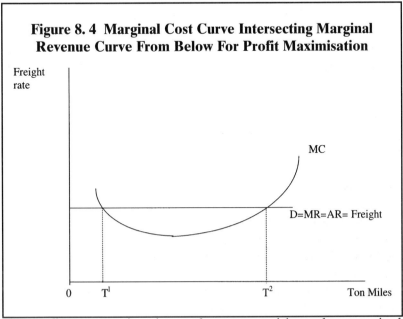

Figure 8. 4 Marginal Cost Curve Intersecting Marginal Revenue Curve From Below For Profit Maximisation

For a firm operating in perfect competition, the marginal revenue is equal to the average revenue and the freight rate. Therefore, as long as freight rates exceed average variable costs, marginal revenue and marginal costs will give the profit maximising quantity. (see Figure 8.5)

The firm chooses the output T^2 in equilibrium for which the freight rate (MR) equals marginal cost (MC) above the level of average total cost (ATC). At any point left of this equilibrium such as T^1, the freight rate is greater than marginal cost and it would therefore pay to increase output. At any point to the right of the equilibrium such as T^3, the freight rate is lower than marginal cost and it would lower profits by producing at this level.

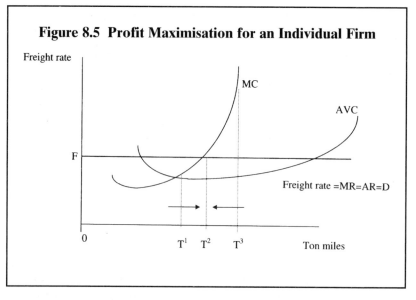

Figure 8.5 Profit Maximisation for an Individual Firm

Short-run Profitability

Although maximising profits in the short-run, given the freight rate and short-run costs, the firm may be in a profit making, loss making or break even position in the short-run.

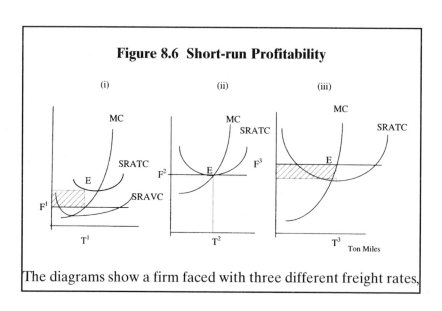

Figure 8.6 Short-run Profitability

The diagrams show a firm faced with three different freight rates,

F^1, F^2 and F^3. E is the point at which MR = MC = freight rate. In all cases this is above AVC, therefore each represents a short-run equilibrium position. At freight rate F^1 the firm is facing short-run losses indicated by the shaded area because the freight rate is less than the short-run average total costs (SRATC). At freight rate F^2, the firm is covering its average total costs and is therefore breaking even. At freight rate F3, the firm is making profits indicated by the shaded area, since the freight rate is above average total costs.

Long-run Equilibrium

The long-run is characterised by entry and exit of firms in response to short-run profits and losses. If all firms are in a profit making situation as in figure 8.6 (iii), new firms will enter the industry, increasing the active supply of tonnage. The shift in the industry supply curve given the same level of market demand will cause the freight rate to fall.

This in turn will reduce the profits available for the individual firms. Firms will continue to enter up to the point where profits fall to zero.

If the freight rate is equal to the lowest average cost of tonnage offered as in Figure 8.6 (ii), the firm will be earning normal profits, no excess or supernormal profits. Should the freight rate decline to below the firm's average cost, losses will be incurred. These losses can be minimised by continuing to trade where marginal costs are equal to marginal revenue. Eventually, the losses cause some firms to exit from the industry. Thus the supply of active tonnage is reduced, creating an excess demand at the prevailing freight rate. Upward pressure on the freight rate will increase profits and will eventually halt the reduction of supply at the point at which normal profits are restored.

Monopoly

The perfect competition model is typical of the tramp and tanker as discussed in Chapters 10 and 11, but for other types of shipping the market is less perfect. Monopoly is a market structure which is the direct opposite of perfect competition. As such, it exists when the industry or sector is completely controlled by a single provider of the product or service. From the supplier's perspective, monopoly is thus preferred to all other structures, but it requires the exclusion of all potential competitors.

A monopoly is a price setter rather than a price taker. Since it is the only firm in the industry, the industry demand curve is the individual demand curve. The curve is downward sloping, as freight rates increase, so the quantity demanded will decrease. The freight rate is equal to the average freight receipts or average revenue. In the case of a monopoly, the marginal revenue will be less than the freight rate for increasing output because the freight rate must be reduced in order to sell additional units of output. This is illustrated in Table 8.1

Table 8.1 Total, Average And Marginal Revenue for a Monopoly

Freight rate = average revenue $	output ton miles (Q)	total freight revenue (TR)	marginal revenue $\Delta TR / \Delta Q$ $
50	1000	50,000	
45	1500	67,500	35
40	2000	80,000	25
35	2500	87,500	15
30	3000	90,000	5
25	3500	87,500	-5
20	4000	80,000	-15
15	4500	67,500	-25
10	5000	50,000	-35

These curves are illustrated in Figure 8.7. The maximum point on the total revenue curve is the point at which marginal revenue is zero.

Figure 8.7 Revenue Curves for a Monopoly

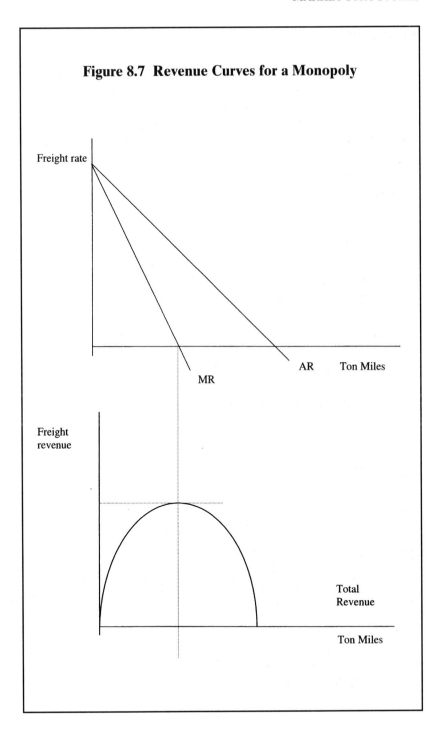

Equilibrium of Monopoly

The same three profit maximisation conditions apply as before, in that the freight rate (F) will be greater than the average variable cost (A) and average total cost (C), and marginal revenue (B) will equal marginal cost with the marginal cost curve intersecting the marginal revenue curve from below as illustrated in figure 8.8.

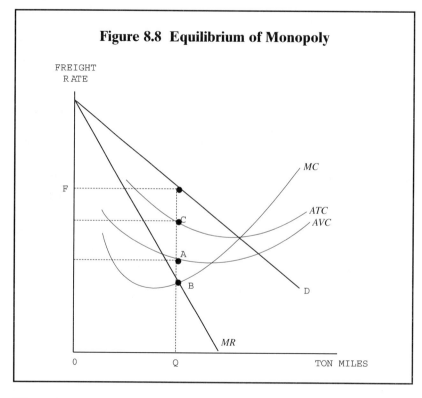

Figure 8.8 Equilibrium of Monopoly

Note that a monopoly does not equate marginal cost with freight rate as with perfect competition. The output at a particular price is determined by the demand curve, which is falling.

The diagram shows short-term profits being made, since at the point of equilibrium, the freight rate is greater than average total costs. Because there are barriers to entry, this situation can continue in the long-run. There is no tendency to zero profit as with perfect competition. Clearly, if short-run losses are being made, the firm would have to make some adjustments in order to maintain operations in the long-run.

Price Discrimination

So far, the assumption has been that the monopolist applies the same rate for all output. This need not be the case where the various markets or customers can be separated. On passenger ferries, for example, different rates will be charged to passengers according to the season or time of travel. This is possible because the markets are discrete. It is not possible for a customer to buy a cheap fare and then sell it on at a higher price because the lower fare only applies to a particular voyage. This type of price discrimination allows the companies to increase their revenues. Returning to the information in Table 8.1, it can be seen that a rate of $30 will lead to a demand for 3,000 tons of freight, and total revenue of $90,000. It is clear from the table that 1,000 tons may be sold at a rate of $50 dollars. If it is possible to separate the markets, them the 1,000 tons would produce $50,000 of revenue and the remaining 2,000 tons could be sold for $30 per ton giving a further $60,000. Hence the total revenue will be $110,000. This is illustrated in Figure 8.9.

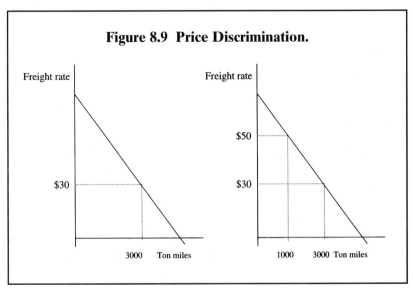

Figure 8.9 Price Discrimination.

Imperfect Competition

There is little evidence of pure monopoly power in the shipping industry. Market structures which do not conform to the perfectly competitive model, lie somewhere between this and the monopoly model. These intermediate structures are known as imperfect markets and fall into two broad categories:

- imperfect competition among many companies-monopolistic competition
- imperfect competition among a few companies-oligopoly

Monopolistic competition, first theorised by Edward Chamberlin, incorporates the characteristics of perfect competition (a large number of firms and free entry and exit), and monopoly with each firm offering a product which is differentiated from the others.

The demand curve for the individual firm is negatively sloped due to the monopoly power over its own product. However, because of the existence of close substitutes for this product, the demand curve will be relatively elastic. As before, profit maximisation will occur where marginal cost is equal to marginal revenue, and the price is dictated by the demand curve. Since firms have free entry and exit to the industry, more firms will enter the market in response to short-run profits. This will cause the individual demand curve to shift to the left, since the same demand will now be shared amongst a greater number of suppliers. This process will continue until zero profits or long-run profits are made. Short-run losses will lead to an exit of firms, shifting individual demand to the right until losses are no longer made.

Figure 8.10(a) shows firms making short-run profits, given by the shaded area. Firms enter the sector in response to the profits, and the demand curve shifts to the left. Eventually, the equilibrium is restored at zero profits, as shown in Figure 8.10(b).

166

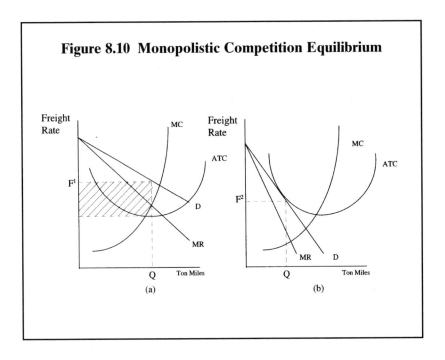

Figure 8.10 Monopolistic Competition Equilibrium

Oligopoly

Oligopoly is characterised by a few firms sharing a large proportion of the industry. Heavy industry which requires high capital investment tends to create a market structure in which there are a few major companies. Oligopoly exists in a number of forms, but in all cases two key features are present, namely barriers to entry and interdependence of the firms within the structure. Barriers are formed because smaller firms cannot readily compete with larger companies which enjoy benefits such as economies of scale, brand loyalty, control over factors of production and distribution. The extent of these barriers will of course vary from industry to industry. Interdependence of the firms within the industry arises because they are relatively few in number. In this situation, no firm can afford to ignore the actions of another. For example, a price reduction by one firm could seriously affect the sales of the other unless they react to this change.

167

This rivalry may lead firms in to adopt one of two opposing strategies, either they can elect to co-operate with one another or compete for the larger market share. The dilemma is that they will make more profits as a group through co-operation, but any one firm can increase its profits by competing. If co-operation takes place, the collective group can act as a monopoly enjoying monopoly profits. At the co-operative equilibrium, it will pay a firm to cut its price and therefore increase its market share if others do not follow. If others do follow, then the group as a whole will be worse off and may be worse off individually.

In the shipping industry, oligopoly could be said to exist in the liner trade where companies have formed cartels and more recently, alliances in order to collude. The concentration here will therefore be on collusive oligopoly.

A collusive oligopoly is one in which the firms agree prices (freight rates) or market share. An example of such an agreement is the cartel, which acts as a single monopoly firm in order to maximise profits as already shown in Figure 8.8. In this case, however, the cartel will set the freight rate which then determines the total industry output. Given this output, the individual firms can either compete for the largest share or agree quotas..

Where such an agreement is prohibited by law as for example in the UK, collusion is still possible but it is tacit. In other words, there may be a set of unwritten rules governing the collusive behaviour of the firms. One of the most common forms of tacit collusion is price leadership, where firms follow the price set by the dominant or leading firm in the industry. The 'followers' in this situation are price takers, acting as if they were in a perfectly competitive market. Figure 8.11 shows how the freight rate and ton miles will be determined under price leadership.

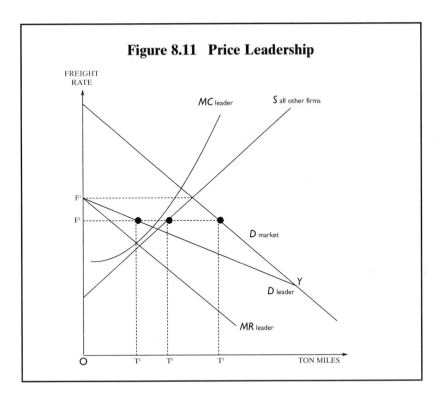

Figure 8.11 Price Leadership

The figure shows the demand curve for the market (D market) and the supply curve for all the followers (S followers). This is simply the sum of their marginal cost curves. The demand curve of the leader (D leader) consists of the demand not met by the other firms. At F¹, the whole of the market demand is satisfied by the followers, and therefore the leader is facing demand of zero (point x). At F², the followers supply nothing and so the leader faces the total market demand (point y). Thus the demand curve for the leader is the line which links points x and y. The leader then sets the freight rate at the point where MC equals MR for profit maximisation, giving a rate of F² and ton mile of TL. The followers will then supply Tᶠ making the total output TT (Tᴸ+ Tᶠ). The reality is more difficult since the leader has no knowledge of the followers' supply curves and cannot therefore derive its own demand and marginal revenue curves. The leader would therefore have to estimate the profit maximising freight rate and output.

169

An alternative is for the leader to maximise profits for a given market share of say, 50%, and to construct its demand curve and marginal revenue curve on this basis . The assumption would be that the other firms would follow the prices set by the leader in order to maintain their constant market shares. Figure 8.12 illustrates this situation where the leader aims for a 50% market share T^L which means a freight rate of F^L. Other firms will make up the remaining 50% share of the market.

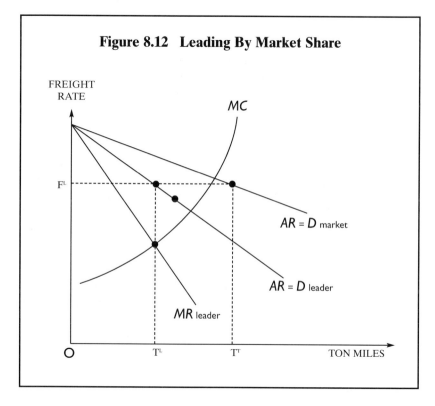

Figure 8.12   Leading By Market Share

Collusion in the liner shipping industry is possible because of the characteristics of the market. These may be described as follows:

(a)   there are only a few firms and they are all well known by one another.

(b)   the cost structures of the individual firms are similar so that there is a tendency to want to change prices by a similar amount and at similar times.

(c) the service provided is similar so that agreement on prices may be more easily reached.

In the liner trade, collusion among the operators takes place in order to restrict output and increase profits. These agreements are discussed more fully in Chapter 13.

Summary

The chapter endeavoured to identify the different types of markets or industry organisations, ranging from perfect competition at one extreme to monopoly at the other. These market structures will affect the way in which the firm within the industry behaves.

The underlying assumption of these theories of the firm, is the aim of maximising profits or minimising losses. For this condition to be satisfied, margin revenue equals marginal cost. With this concentration around this basic criteria of profit maximisation, there is an assumption about the behaviour of the shipowning entrepreneurs, in determining their level of output and freight rate expectations. Freight rates will have a strong influence on the activities of the shipping firm.

Most markets do not follow exactly the above models and would not be expected to. To create an exact model of some element of shipping market activity would require a far more complex and precise analysis. Nevertheless the insights into output decisions and freight rates are invaluable in understanding the way in which the industry works.

Further Reading

Sloman J. *Economics*, 3rd Edition Prentice Hall, 1997.

Parkin M. *et al, Economics*, London Addison-Wesley, Longman, 1994.

Begg D *et al, Economics,* 5th edition, London McGraw Hill, 1997.

---

[1] For the sake of clarity, 'lay-up' points will not be included here.

Chapter Nine

INTERNATIONAL TRADE AND TRANSPORT COSTS

The derived demand for sea transport is, as has been argued, dependent on the level of international seaborne trade. Gains from international seaborne trade arise because the cost of producing commodities are often different in different countries. These differences are further affected by the level of transport costs. This chapter will examine the basic theory underlying international trade before assessing the impact of transport costs. The analysis is based on transport costs rather than 'freight rates'. Transport cost is a broader definition of the divergence between domestic and foreign prices caused by conveying the commodities.

Transport as Cost of Production

Transport overcomes the obstacle of distance. The effectiveness of this process can broadly be assessed by examining the costs incurred. Low transport costs are indicative of an effective system. High costs are indicative of an ineffective one. It follows that transport costs are an element in the costs of production and, in a similar way to other costs of production, are substitutable. Superficially, if transport costs are low, it makes it possible for domestic commodities to be substituted for the less

173

expensive goods supplied over greater distances. Conversely, increased transport costs implies the lowering of the quantity of a commodity from distance supplied for those near at hand. In either case, transport costs are similar to any other cost of production and will ultimately be borne by the final consumer. The important underlying implication here is that a commodity will be traded internationally only if the pre-trade price differs; that is, it is less than the price of the domestic product. The difference is largely made up of the cost of transporting the commodity to the final consumer's market. In this way, transport costs are a consequence of the separation of the source of supply and the market. They cause the division between price in exporting countries and that in the importing countries. Thus they provide some protection for the producer in the importing country and the consumer in the exporting country. In other words, producers in exporting countries and consumers in importing countries will be adversely affected by transport costs.

The presence of transport costs in international trade have a number of implications and functions. Obviously it will permit trade to take place where the price of any commodity is higher in the importing country than in the country of origin, the exporting country. It will impede trade in commodities where the price gap between the domestic producer price and the supply price of a potential trading country is equal to or less than the transport cost needed to convey the commodities between the two countries. Hence these costs will have a combined effect, not only on the value of the commodity in international trade, but also on the mix of these commodities and their movement into and out of the trading arena.

Willingness to cover transport costs or charges is the test of the level of utility created by the movement of the commodity. Transport costs, like all costs of production, are paid by the final consumer, but act as a revenue compensating the provider of the transport service.

In the above discussion 'transport cost' has assumed two meanings. From the transport supplier's point of view, it is the cost of the factors of production required to produce the transport service. From the consumers of transport's perspective, it is the cost of utilising the service. It is also useful to examine who is the hirer of transport services, and, at which point during the transit process certain decisions are made about who bears the costs.

There are two general cases in point. First, **free on board** (F.O.B.) terms. In this situation the terms of the sale of a commodity leaves all the costs of loading, conveying and discharging to the shipper or charterer. Consequently the choice of vessel is left to the buyer, generally the importer. The other general method is known as the **costs insurance freight** (C.I.F.). Here all forms of insurance and other costs of delivering goods to the destination are paid by the seller of the goods, hence the seller has the responsibility for the total organisation of the cargo movement. The seller therefore normally nominates the vessel to be used. The difference between F.O.B. and C.I.F. constitutes the total transport costs and usually implies, a considerable influence on the choice of vessel to be nominated and other services to be used. The use of these general methods or derivations of them have been an important influence on the development of international seaborne trade, as is argued below.

The level of sea transport costs have been measured in terms of freight rates, the relation or proportion of liner freight rates to export price. In a large number of developing countries, a large part of the non-bulk exports and imports are moved by liner services. The long-term trends in these freight ratios are determined on the one hand by the development of liner freight rates, and the other by the unit value of the commodity traded. In such an analysis a number of categories of commodity have been established. The movement in the freight ratio has been related to a number of interrelated factor movements as follows:

1. Where the freight ratio for a commodity has shown a major increase. This can be divided into two elements: (a) where the commodity price has declined and freight rate increased, (b) where both commodity and freight rate have increased, but freight rate at a greater rate.

2. Where freight rates exhibit a relatively slow but constant upward trend, but where commodity prices have been characterised by fluctuations in price.

3. Where freight rates have been related consistently to commodity prices.

4. Freight rates have declined where increases in commodity prices have been greater or more rapid than increases in freight rates.

Table 9.1 illustrates the general trend for the past quarter of a century of commodity exports from developing countries to Europe.

Table 9.1   Ratio of Liner Freight Rates to Prices of Selected Commodities 1964 -1994

Commodity	Route	Freight rate as percentage of price							
		1964	1970	1975	1980	1985	1990	1993	1994
Rubber	Singapore/Malaysia-Europe	8.0	10.5	18.5	8.9	n.a	15.5	14.5	11.4
Tin	Singapore/Malaysia-Europe	1.2	1.2	1.6	1.0	n.a	1.7	1.4	1.3
Jute	Bangladesh-Europe	8.7	12.1	19.5	19.8	6.4	21.2	24.3	21.8
Cocoa beans	Ghana-Europe	3.1	2.4	3.4	2.7	1.9	6.7	7.5	6.2
Coconut oil	Sri Lanka-Europe	8.8	8.9.	9.1	12.6	12.6	n.a.	11.2	7.3
Tea	Sri Lanka-Europe	6.5	9.5	10.4	9.9	6.9	10.0	5.3	5.5
Coffee	Brazil-Europe	4.9	5.2	9.7	6.0	5.0	10.0	4.3	2.7
Coffee	Columbia (Atlantic)-Europe	4.2	4.2	5.7	3.3	6.7	6.8	7.1	3.6
Cocoa beans	Brazil-Europe	8.6	7.4	8.2	8.6	6.9	11.0	10.6	8.6
Coffee	Columbia (Pacific)-Europe	4.5	4.5	6.3	4.4	6.1	74	7.6	3.8

Source UNCTAD Review of Maritime Transport (Annual)

Taking the period as a whole, what is most noticeable is that freight rates have increased in all commodities over all the routes covered in the above table. Examine the first eleven years of the table, 1964 - 1975. It can be seen that with the single exception of cocoa beans, that the freight rates increased substantially in the majority of cases. The general analysis suggests that increases were due primarily to the contraction in commodity prices. The post - 1975 period illustrated far less stability. This is particularly noticeable for the mid - 1980s, and by the 1990s some substantial contraction in commodity prices are the major influence with some moderate increases in freight rates. Broadly, the evidence appears to be that primary commodities which constitute a substantial part of the export of developing countries, despite fluctuations, is in a long-run downward trend. Hence, for developing countries, liner freight rates can have a significance for national income and the balance of payments. For a large proportion of the key non-bulk export, cargoes are conveyed by liner services.

The UNCTAD Annual Review of Maritime Transport put forward another method of considering global freight rates. This is to estimate the world average freight costs in relation to total C.I.F. values of exports. A broad assessment of this trend is related to countries grouped in Table 9.2.

Table 9.2 Estimates of Freight Cost as a Percentage of Import Value by Groups 1970, 1980, 1982-1994

YEAR	World Total	Developed Market Economy Countries	Countries Developing	Africa	Oceana
1970	7.75	7.26	10.04	10.88	10.21
1980	6.64	5.49	10.44	13.42	12.84
1982	6.65	5.32	10.69	10.82	12.85
1983	6.67	5.37	10.77	10.65	12.84
1984	6.15	5.10	9.79	10.82	12.76
1985	5.72	4.81	9.17	11.03	12.30
1986	5.33	4.33	9.22	11.09	12.26
1987	5.33	4.39	8.90	11.30	12.30
1988	5.27	4.40	8.85	11.30	12.29
1989	5.27	4.42	8.87	11.29	12.30
1990	5.22	4.40	8.60	11.00	12.26
1991	5.24	4.35	8.48	11.10	12.26
1992	5.33	4.35	8.52	11.15	12.13
1993	5.44	4.33	8.33	11.06	12.23
1994	5.40	4.29	8.25	11.05	12.24

Source: UNCTAD Review of Maritime Transport Annual

The typical development during the last two decades has been a general contraction in the ratio of freight rates to import prices, although the annual picture is less consistent, especially during the late-1980s. To generalise, as the value of international trade has increased, there has been a consequent contraction in the proportion of freight rates to import values. The contraction in world freight costs and those of developing market economies has been substantial. In the developing countries on the other hand, contraction has been much slower, and during the decade of 1970 experienced some increase. The developing countries costs were consistently and substantially higher. The percentage of import values of the developing economies approximately doubled throughout the period. There is also some consideration in the table of two sub-groups in the developing countries category. These are Africa and Oceana because they are often quoted and, of more importance, have the highest percentage freight costs to import value. These sub-groups have been stable during the last decade and significantly higher than both the developed and world market economy by two or three times in percentage terms.

The substantial differences in transport costs by different groups of countries can be partly explained by the following factors. From the developed market economies point of view, their imports consist of a large proportion of bulk cargo commodities whose freight rates are relatively low. They can exercise control over or influence over the level of conference or other liner rates presumably more than developing countries. Developing countries lack influence and have a number of other factors which work against them. The generally higher rates are attributed to the greater distances which commodities are transported. The cost also increases as the per unit value of the good increases. These increases occur at different stages of the production process, because of increased care needed in handling high value goods. Much of the developing countries imports are in the category of high-value manufactures. The escalating structure of freight rates because of "what the traffic will bear" in liners[1] also works against developing economies exporting manufacturing products rather than basic raw material. This is because the higher level of the productive process commands a higher value of freight rate. There is also the tendency for trade

178

routes to be traditional ones, geared to a previous imperial system, which makes it cheaper to trade in transport terms with developed countries than with developing countries in the same region. A problem heightened by the neglect or lack of transport infrastructures within developing economies and regions. All factors relate to the utilisation by developing countries of liner services which are relatively more expensive.

International Trade Theory - Absolute Advantage

Before venturing into any discussion of the impact of transport costs on the maritime industry, there must be a clear understanding of the economic factors operating in international trade. The central tenet of the classical economies of international trade was that of free trade. Free trade, it was claimed, created a situation in which each nation would naturally specialise in a certain commodity production and in that way increase world production. Adam Smith in the 18th century, perceived unfettered competition, the development of national specialisation as a method by which countries would produce the commodities in which they possessed "absolute advantage" over other countries. This is the essence of the free trade argument. The problem with the simple free trade argument based on the theory of absolute advantage, however, is that it cannot explain the existence of trade in the case where one nation is better suited to the production of all commodities. This situation was recognised and a better theory was constructed by Richard Torren, and then by the more influential David Ricardo in the early nineteenth century. Their work focused attention not on absolute advantage but on comparative advantage, or relative advantage as the deciding factor in determining the terms of trade. Briefly the argument is that even if a situation is possible where a country is capable of producing everything more cheaply than any other country, it would be in its best interest to concentrate upon the output of commodities in which it has the greatest comparative advantage; that it produces the commodity most favourable to its conditions leaving other countries to

179

produce commodities in which they have a comparative advantage.

Comparative Advantage

The theory can be explained by constructing a model. Assume, as Ricardo did, two countries, England and Portugal, and two commodities, cloth and wine. For simplicity, the following assumptions can be added.

1. Complete factor mobility within national boundaries, but immobility internationally.
2. Unchanged technology.
3. Full-employment.
4. No protection.
5. Similar wants in the two countries.
6. Labour being the only asset
7. Technology being the major element in cost differences.

The choice of England and Portugal is the method of illustrating an industrial and agricultural economy, or rich and poor countries. Generally Ricardo gave Portugal, the poorer country, producing the agricultural commodity - wine, absolute cost advantages in both commodities. As argued, labour is the only variable input. Portugal can produce a unit of wine with 80 labour hours and a unit of cloth in 90 labour hours. In England, a 100 labour hours are needed to produce 1 unit of cloth and 120 labour hours are needed to produce 1 unit of wine. Hence, before any specialisation, the following cost comparisons can be made.

Table 9.3a Before Specialisation
(Labour cost of production in hours per unit of output)

	Wine	Cloth	Total
Portugal	80	90	170
England	120	100	<u>220</u>
			390

Portugal, in the above table has an absolute advantage in both commodities over England, but England will be incapable of importing these commodities on a long- term basis because she has nothing with which to exchange. Trade is only taking place on the basis of a different comparative (relative) cost. A closer examination of the above table reveals that Portugal has a comparative cost advantage in wine, that is to say relative to cloth. England is said to have a comparative advantage in cloth. This is due to the wine to cloth ratio: 6/5 in England and 8/9 in Portugal. It follows that England specialises in the production of cloth whilst Portugal specialises in the production of wine. To develop this a little further, Portugal has a comparative advantage in wine production because it can produce one unit of wine in only 80 hours, that is 80/120*100 = 66% - that is 66% of labour hours needed in England to produce the same unit. Conversely, Portugal would take 90 hours to produce a unit of cloth, e.g. 90/100*100 = 90% of English effort to produce one unit of cloth. Portugal has comparative advantage in that it is more efficient than England in wine production than in cloth manufacture. If exchange is possible, the obvious course of action for specialisation is for Portugal to produce two units of wine and England to produce two units of cloth with a combination of 360 labour hours.

Table 9.3b With Specialisation of Trade
(Labour Cost of Production in Hours)

	Wine	Cloth	Total
Portugal	160	-	160
England	-	200	<u>200</u>
			360

So long as a mutually acceptable basis of exchange can be agreed, both countries will benefit from a specialisation of trade for, with specialisation, England can obtain increased amounts of wine per labour hour indirectly by exchange. Portugal, similarly with cloth indirectly by exchange. This will hold true so long as the exchange ratio between England and Portugal prior to specialisation remains. In England the ratio 5/6 units of cloth to

181

1 unit of wine. In Portugal, the ratio is 9/8 of cloth for 1 unit of wine. Hence the exchange ratio lies between these two countries as far as the Ricardian theory of comparative advantage is concerned. Apart from indicating the high and low units between which the terms of trade are operating. By terms of trade is meant that comparisons of a countries imports and exports in terms of price.

Factor Endowments: The Hecksher Ohlin Model

Hecksher and Ohlin, two Swedish neo-classical economists extended the model to include more than one factor of production. These factor endowments were land, labour, capital and enterprise. The central focus of the Hecksher Ohlin theory was therefore the difference in the relative factor endowments between countries. The concept is that a country will export a commodity which during its production uses the country's relatively abundant and hence cheapest factor while importing the commodities whose production uses up its relatively scarce and hence expensive factor. If countries were assumed to possess exactly equal access to technology, then countries well endowed with capital would specialise in capital intensive commodities. On the other hand, if a country is endowed with a relative abundance of labour, which is therefore cheap, it would be encouraged by free trade specialisation to produce labour intensive commodities.

The theory can be illustrated using a simple two factor model, which makes the following assumptions:

1. Two factors of production (labour and capital), two countries, two goods.
2. For any given good, the amount of capital and labour used in its production is the same in every country.
3. Each good has or needs either more labour or more capital in its production.
4. Each country differs in its full employed factor endowments, which are fixed in quantity.
5. Factor endowments are fully mobile within a country but immobile between countries.
6. Similar tastes in both countries

Diagrammatically this can be represented using production possibility curves, sometimes referred to as transformation curves[2] (Figure 9.1a). These describe the limited amount of goods and services which an economy can produce during a given time period. Resources are scarce and so therefore the decision to produce certain goods or services involves opportunity costs; that is forgoing of alternative goods and services. The opportunity cost of production can be expressed as a trade-off to gain a certain quantity of another good or service. The curve shows how one good, say y (wine) can be transferred along the production possibility border or frontier into the other good, x (cloth). The curve will be concave reflecting the increased marginal rate of transformation. This is because for some factors of production, a percentage of say labour, will be more effective in the production of y (wine), but the other remaining labour will be more effective in production x (cloth). The extra amount of x that can be produced by decreasing the amounts of y will steadily decrease as less efficient factors are drawn into production. This is because the opportunity cost or marginal rate of transfer of x (cloth) in line with y (wine) steadily increases as production increases. It increases the production of x and decreases the production of y. Suppose that country 1 is rich in capital, and country 2 is rich in labour, good y (wine is the capital intensive commodity and x (cloth) is the labour intensive good. In the absence of trade, the internal equilibrium for each country is determined by the interaction of supply (as represented by the production possibility frontier) and the demand (as represented by the country's indifference curves). These equilibria are established by the points of tangency between the indifference curve and the production possibility curve, i.e. where the marginal rate of substitution is equal to the marginal rate of transformation, and are shown at A for country 1 and A' for country 2. The slope of the lines at these points P^1 (for country 1) and P^2 (for country 2) show the relative prices of the commodities, i.e. the price of wine relative to the price of cloth. The fact that P^1 is steeper than P^2 indicates that good y is cheaper in country 1 than in country 2; giving up production of some of x produces proportionately more of y. In other words the opportunity cost of y is lower in country 1 than in country 2. The reverse is true for country 2 where the opportunity cost of x is lower. Thus capital intensive country 1 prefers to produce capital intensive good y, and labour intensive country 2 will have a preference for labour intensive good x.

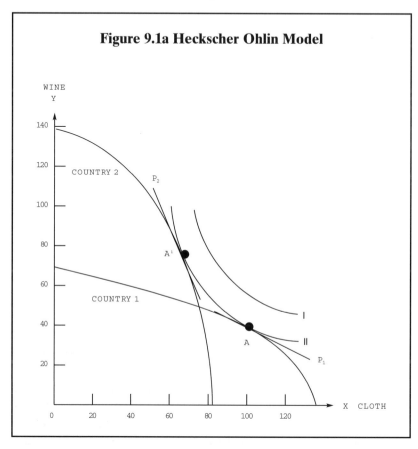

Figure 9.1a Heckscher Ohlin Model

With the introduction of trade, specialisation increases in line with factor endowments, such that country 1 produces more cloth relative to wine and country 2 produces more wine relative to cloth. This allows the consumers in both countries to reach the higher indifference curve II, and so the production equilibrium is established at B for country 1 and B' for country 2, and they will now exchange commodities at point E. In this way, both countries gain from international trade. This is illustrated in figure 9.1b.

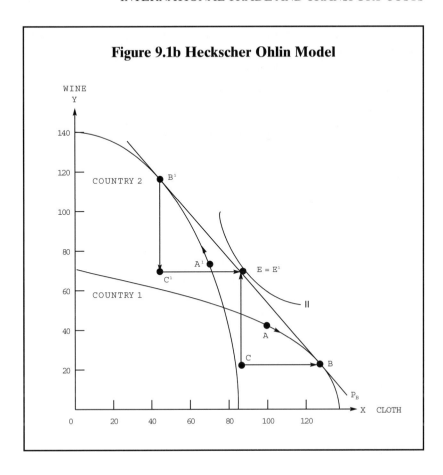

Figure 9.1b Heckscher Ohlin Model

This is a theoretical discussion of free trade, but the reality is that free trade is prevented by many factors, for example, the use of tariffs as a method of bargaining with other countries to remove theirs, and the more pertinent (in the present context) advocation of subsidies for merchant shipping on the grounds of defence. Transportation costs also create some distortion of the international price of trade goods. This is investigated in the following section.

Transport Cost Theory

The aim here is to relate the broad international trade analysis to one of transport costs. The main point about transport costs as argued, is that they serve to protect domestic producers from foreign competition. The costs can be perceived as the difference in the value of the product at its place of origin and the value as it arrives at its final utilisation destination. Hence it has been referred to as a trade-resistant factor. Whilst in the present context the main interest is an element of shipping freight, transport costs are much wider including not only freight but such items as port handling costs, insurance premiums and interest charges of goods in transit. In the present discussion, to avoid any needless complexity, the concept of transport costs will be used and will define broadly international trade as the cost divergence between domestic and foreign prices caused by conveying the commodity. Such a cost diversion explains why many goods and services are not traded internationally; they are referred to as non-traded goods and services. Changes in transport costs imply that previously non-traded goods and services become internationally traded or traded goods. At its simplest, transport costs can be assessed in Equation 9.1

Equation 9.1

$P_i - P_e = F$
Where P_i is the equilibrium price in the importing country
P_e is the equilibrium price in the exporting country
F is transport costs per unit

Hence the equilibrium price in the importing country, P_i must exceed the exporting price, P_e by the amount of transport costs, F. Developing the formula further, repeating the earlier assumption of the competitive cost model; there are two countries, 1 and 2, producing two commodities y (wine) and x (cloth). Both countries have a common currency and there is free trade. In addition the domestic producer exports a commodity and receives a price for their product as it leaves the country. This will be free on board (F.O.B), whilst the importing country will include transport costs to be costs insurance freight (CIF) in their price. Under the circumstances, the price ratio of a product for the consumer will be :

$$\frac{PY(F.O.B)}{PX\ (C.I.F.)} \quad \text{in country 1}$$

and

$$\frac{PY\ (C.I.F.)}{PX\ (F.O.B)} \quad \text{in country 2}$$

What the formula highlights is how, in certain sectors the transport costs can play a vital role in international trade. If the commodity price plus transport costs is lower than domestically produced commodities, then trade will take place. Any modification in commodity price or transport price could radically change this situation.

The relationship between transport costs and other factors may be summarised as follows:

Cost of Production	–	F.O.B	+	Transport Costs	=	Delivery Price of export C.I.F	<	Foreign Domestic Product Price

Domestic production of any commodity for export	Imports into foreign country

The central point here being that the delivery price (C.I.F) is less than the foreign domestic price of the commodity. Any changes in transport cost having some impact on the level of trade.

The inclusion of transport cost into the analysis is straight forward and obvious. The existence of these costs cause discrepancies between domestic and foreign prices. The effects are very similar to these of tariffs or other impediments. To develop this theme, a model will be constructed for a single country initially in a free trade situation with no transport costs. Transport costs will then be introduced and their impact examined.

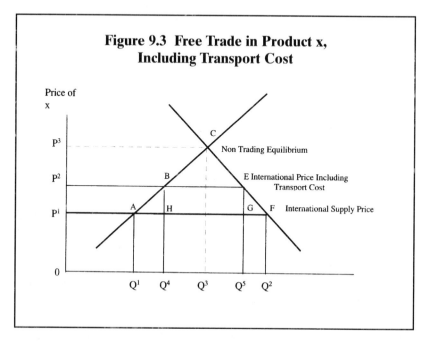

Figure 9.3 Free Trade in Product x, Including Transport Cost

Figure 9.3 shows the partial equilibrium model of demand and supply in a single country. The non-trading equilibrium is that associated with a closed economy. Domestic equilibrium is at point C with price P^3 and quantity Q^3. The international supply price is P^1. This is the price at which the foreign producer of x sells it in the domestic market without transport costs. The equilibrium free trade price will thus be P^1 as this is the indicative price at which foreign produced x will be sold and domestic produce will be unable to charge a higher price. The domestic and international price under free trade being identical. The domestic producer will supply up to the point at which the costs are equal to those of the international market. The domestic purchaser will be able to offer $0Q^1$ at Price P^1 or area $0\ P^1A\ Q^1$. Foreign producers will supply the remaining Q^1 to Q^2 at Price P^1 or area $Q^1AF\ Q^2$.

Now to drop the assumption of no transport costs. The costs are the vertical distance of P^1 to P^2. The new international and domestic price including transport costs will be P^2. International suppliers now require P^2 to compensate for the transport costs. With this upward shift in price, the total quantity in the market contracts from $0Q^2$ to $0Q^5$. Domestic producers who do not pay transport costs, to increase production from $0Q^1$ to $0Q^4$. There is also a decline in the international product consumption due to the increased price.

Thus, the impact of transport costs in a free trade area is threefold.

1. Transport costs add to the domestic price of imported commodities.
2. Transport costs reduce the level of imports by encouraging increased domestic production. (The analysis generally asserts that domestic producers will be less efficient because of the higher costs)
3. Transport costs will cause consumers to reduce their consumption of a product because of the increase in its price.

There is an additional point worth making that should transport costs happen to be so high as to eliminate trade altogether, that is equal to or in excess of the vertical distance P^1 to P^3, all production will be supplied by domestic producers, the original domestic equilibrium C.

Transport Costs: The Supplier Perspective - One Country Model

The impact of transport costs will now be examined from the supplier's perspective. The analysis assumes constant demand elasticity and the presence of free trade. The model looks initially at the position without transport costs. When these costs are then included the impact is simply on the supply curve, increasing costs and moving it to the left as illustrated by the following Figure 9.4a.

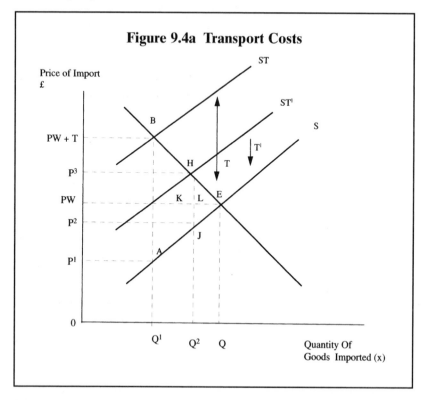

Figure 9.4a Transport Costs

The supply curve S is the import supply not including transport costs. The original trade equilibrium is at the point E with quantity Q and price PW, the international or world price for the commodity x. On the higher supply curve ST', the additional costs due to transport are shown by the vertical distance T and T'. The addition of transport costs changes the equilibrium point to B, with quantity reduced to Q¹ and the price increased to PW+T. The quantity supplied has contracted and the price increased.

What is of interest is that the transport cost has been shared between the consumer and the importer; the consumer pays the additional cost of PW,PW+T, B,K and the producer the cost of P¹, PW+T, K,A.

If some technological or organisational change reduces transport costs to T¹, so that the relevant curve is ST¹, then the final price will be lowered to P³ and the quantity increased to Q². Here again both consumers and importers share increased costs. Consumers from PW, P³,H,L and importers from PW, P²,J,L.

The above analysis can now be related to the price as shown in Figure 9.4b. In this example, PW is £10 per unit which creates a demand for 200 units. The initial transport costs are £5 per unit and this means a reduction in quantity demanded to 150 units. The imported commodity now costs £7.50. Total transport costs will be (£12.50 - £7.50) x 150 units, of which half (£2.50 per unit) will be paid by the consumer, and the remainder by the importer. The second stage is where the transport situation improves and the costs are lowered to £2.50. The quantity imported increases to 175 units and the final consumer price falls to £11.25, the import price increasing to £8.75. Total transport costs are (£11.25-£8.25) x 175 units. Once again the consumer and importer contribute half the cost, i.e. £1.25 per unit each.

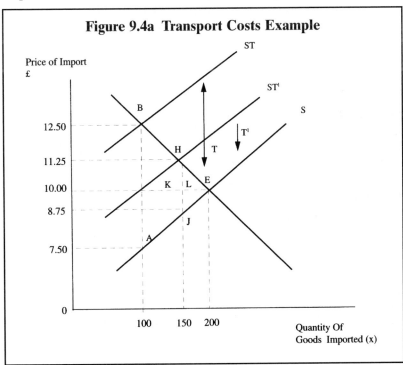

Figure 9.4a Transport Costs Example

Here the assumption has been made that the larger the elasticity of demand, the greater the proportion of transport costs which will be borne by the importer; the more inelastic (that is steeper) the supply curve, and the more elastic (that is flatter) the demand curve. The reverse process will mean a larger proportion will be paid by the consumer. There will be further discussion of this later.

Two Country Model

The discussion thus far has considered the impact of transport costs using a partial equilibrium analysis with regard to a single country. The analysis is now extended to allow us to examine two countries. What is clear is that the commodity has to be cheaper before it can be exported from a country and that transport costs have an important influence on the final import cost.

Here two countries are combined in the same figure with four curves in relation to the same common vertical axis of price, that is price expressed in common currency with the horizontal axis of quantity. This axis runs in two directions from the origin zero. country B is structured in the usual fashion from left to right, but for country A the process is reversed; the curve runs from right to left. That is to say that the demand curve and the supply curve for B are as usual, but for the co-purpose of analysis the quantity axis for country A has been reversed with the curves for demand and supply being inverted. The demand curve slopes negatively from right to left and the positive movement is along the quantity axis to the left of the common origin; that is to say from right to left. To begin with the observation in the absence of any international trade between the two countries A and B. It is possible to formulate this model with a single country and the rest of the world formed as a single entry. Without international trade each country operates on its own individual equilibrium; country A at EA, consuming 50 units of x at £5 per unit and country B operating at equilibrium EB consuming 50 units of x at £11 per unit. To move now to a situation where there is trade, but not yet including transport costs. This is the longitudinal line at the price of £8 at point G, the price line a-d. At this level a-b

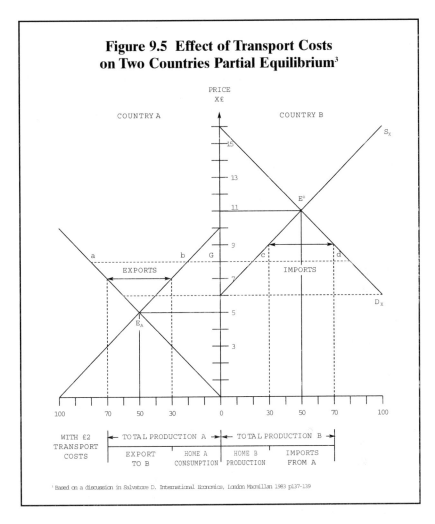

Figure 9.5 Effect of Transport Costs on Two Countries Partial Equilibrium[3]

' Based on a discussion in Salvatore D. International Economics, London Macmillan 1983 p137-139

is the excess supply of country A and is equal to c-d, the excess demand in country B, that is to say that a-b represent exports and c-d imports. In country A, a-G will be produced with b-G being for domestic production. In country B, total home production will be c-G and this will be consumed domestically.

Bringing transport costs into the model, first it is assumed that transport costs are £2 per unit. This means that the price of unit x in country B will exceed that of country A by £2. In this particular model the costs are shared equally between the two countries meaning that country A accepts a price fall to £7 and country B's export price will be increased to £9. This will cause a reorganisation of production and consumption. In country A the lower level of production will be 70 units of x. Similarly, consumption will increase to 30 x, and will therefore export 40x. Country B increases its production to 30x lowering its imports to 40x. In this way the total consumption contracts by 10x to 70x.

In the above, if the level of transport costs reach or exceed £6, trade would cease because for the price difference between country A's internal equilibrium price of £5 and country B's internal equilibrium price of £11 would be taken up by transport costs. Hence £6 or more converts commodity x from a trading to a non-trading good or service. Whether trade will take place at all is dependent on the relative magnitude of the distance between the relative equilibrium prices EA and EB, and the cost of transporting commodity x from the domestic economy or exporting economy A to the importing economy B. If transport costs under free trade conditions are less than the vertical distance between each, then international trade will take place. At or greater than this distance, each country will remain self-sufficient in commodity x. The assumption in the above discussion is that the importing country A and the exporting country B shared an equal proportion of the total costs of transport. This raises the question as to who bears the transport costs; the sellers, that is shippers or suppliers; or the buyers or purchasers. This will be dependent upon the elasticities of supply and demand. In short, the elasticities of supply and demand are the ratio of changes in the quantities supplied or demanded in relation to a small change in price. A shipper exporting goods will pay the transport cost insurance freight C.I.F. Should the shipper be in the importing country, then the ship pays freight on board F.O.B. Therefore the importer bears the transport costs.

The Effect of Elasticity

The effects of the elasticities of supply and demand on the bearer of transport costs in particular countries market are illustrated below, where elasticity is indicated by the demand or supply

194

curve. This analysis, like the above, begins with the ruling market price in the absence of transport costs. First, an examination of the situation where the supply curve is perfectly inelastic as shown in Figure 9.6.

The central point here is that quantity supplied at any price range, at least in the short-run, is fixed at OQ. Thus the introduction of transport costs (T) will have no effect on price. Two courses of action are open. First, to include the transport costs in the price, P+T. This causes the quantity demanded to contract, Q^1. But since supplies do not respond to changes in price, there is a lack of any equilibrium because of an excess of supply a-b does not force prices to fall back to the equilibrium price P. In this way the attempt to push the price and force the purchaser to pay fails. The second situation is economically acceptable. Here price P can be seen as the C.I.F. price, with the F.O.B. price being P+T. The distance between P+T and P is equal to the transport costs. As can be seen the shipper or the supplier will bear all the transport costs. It follows that in the extreme case where supply is perfectly inelastic, the conditions of demand, be they elastic or relatively inelastic, have little or no effect as the shipper or supplier bears the incidence of transport costs.

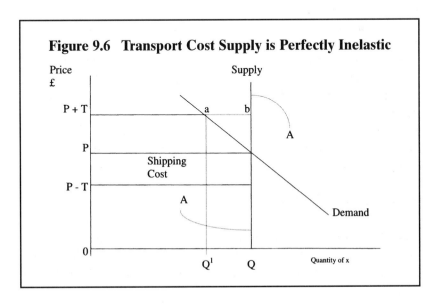

Figure 9.6   Transport Cost Supply is Perfectly Inelastic

The situation where the demand curve is perfectly inelastic, is shown in Figure 9.7.

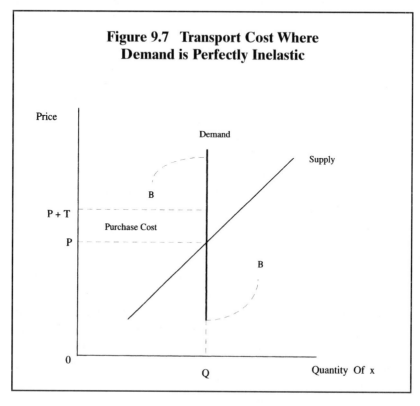

Figure 9.7   Transport Cost Where Demand is Perfectly Inelastic

In the above model the quantity demanded, regardless of short-run price will be before transport costs are introduced. The price at which OQ will be supplied will be P; this is the equilibrium market price. The introduction of transport costs (T) into the model causes the market price to increase from P to P+T. Because demand is perfectly inelastic, the increase in price will have no effect on the quantity demanded. The transport costs will be included in the purchasing price. In this case, because of F.O.B. pricing (P+T being the C.I.F. price). The central point here being that the whole of the transport costs are borne by the purchaser of the commodity when demand is perfectly inelastic and supply is elastic or relatively inelastic. The purchaser will pay the whole of the transport cost. The figures used are extreme examples where either the supplier or the purchaser bears the whole of the transport cost. Generally this will not be the case. The amount of the transport costs borne by the supplier or the shipper and the purchaser will be dependent upon the elasticity of demand and supply. At its simplest, the more inelastic the supply, the more likely it is that the supplier will bear the majority of the importing transport costs. Here the curves are assumed to indicate the elasticity as in the curves of the previous figures, move to the right following the arrow A in Figure 9.6. Moving to the right following the arrow, then the less the transport costs will be borne by the suppliers; that is the more elastic the supplier, then the greater the share of the transport costs borne by the purchaser. Where the demand is inelastic, the share of the transport costs is borne by the purchaser, as in Figure 9.7. If the arrow B is followed, then the curve will become increasingly elastic and the amount of transport costs paid by the supplier will increase.

It is clear from the above discussion that the elasticity is centrally important to who bears the costs of transport. The lower the elasticity of demand then the more the transport costs will be borne by the purchaser. The higher the elasticity of demand, then the greater the share will be borne by the supplier. The higher the elasticity of supply, the more the transport costs are borne by the purchaser. The lower the elasticity of supply, the more will be borne by the supplier.

What arises from the discussion is the importance of the degree of flexibility possessed by the participants. Those who can rapidly adjust their behaviour to deal with transport costs are likely to be capable of avoiding them, those who cannot, contribute substantially to them.

The analysis has been related by UNCTAD to the trading position of developing countries, the discussion is based on the presumption that the main stay of developing countries exports are agricultural products whose elasticity of supply is very low, i.e. inelastic. A situation where the supplier will usually bear the bulk of transport costs, whereas their imports in the form of manufacturing processes are relatively elastic and as such most of the transport cost will be borne by the importer. Similarly, when considering developing countries exports, the higher the elasticity of demand, the lower the elasticity of supply, the greater the amount of transport they will use. Converting the case to imports, the higher the elasticity of supply, the lower the elasticity of demand, there will be greater contribution to transport costs as discussed earlier in this chapter.

Exchange Rates

International trade can only occur if it is possible to exchange the currency of one country for that of another. The exchange rate between two currencies is the amount of one currency that must be paid to obtain one unit of another, i.e. the price of one currency in terms of another. A dollar/sterling exchange rate of $1.60/£1 means that £1 buys $1.60. This price or exchange rate is determined by a number of factors, which makes exchange rate determination very complex, but at the simplest level, it is, as with any other market price, the interaction of supply and demand.

International transactions fall into two categories: the purchase and sale of internationally traded goods and capital investment overseas. The demand for foreign currency is dependent on the demand for imported goods and services and investment overseas. For example, the demand for sterling will increase if the UK is exporting more goods and services or foreign residents are investing in the UK, both of which must be paid for in sterling. The supply of foreign currency is dependent on the demand for imported goods and services and the extent of capital outflows. As far as sterling is concerned, the supply will increase with a growth in UK imports, or by an increase in UK investment overseas. Since one currency is traded for another, the demand for foreign currency implies an eagerness to supply sterling, while the supply of foreign currency implies a demand for sterling.

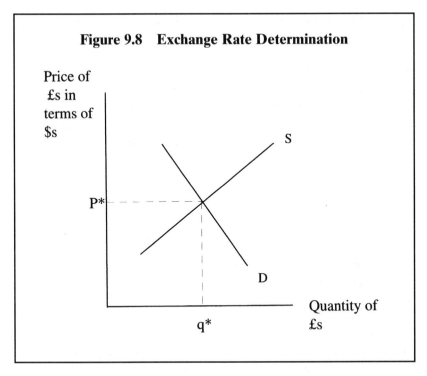

Figure 9.8 Exchange Rate Determination

Figure 9.8 shows the exchange rate between sterling and the dollar. The vertical axis gives the price of sterling in terms of dollars and the horizontal axis shows the quantity of sterling.

The exchange rate P* is at the point where the quantity demanded is equal to the quantity supplied. As illustrated in Chapter 5, shifts in the demand or supply will cause the equilibrium exchange rate to change. This is further complicated by government policy, in particular, whether or not the exchange rate is allowed to 'float' or to be 'fixed' at a certain level against other currencies. In reality, the regimes are not so clear cut and contain elements of both. The following analysis, however, will examine the two extremes of floating and fixed rate systems.

Floating Exchange Rates

Under a floating exchange rate regime, the currency is allowed to **appreciate** or **depreciate** according to demand and supply conditions. An appreciation raises the value of a currency in terms of another. A depreciation lowers the value of a currency in terms of another. If sterling appreciates against the dollar, less sterling is required to buy a dollar. Suppose the dollar/sterling exchange rate is $1.60=£1, a movement to $1.50=£1 constitutes a depreciation of sterling against the dollar. £1 now buys fewer dollars than before. Conversely, a movement in the exchange rate to $1.70=£1 represents an appreciation in the value of sterling.

Such movements in the exchange rate are caused by shifts in the demand, supply, or both. In Figure 9.9 changing tastes in the US mean a greater preference for UK goods which must be paid for in sterling. The increased demand for sterling creates an upward shift in the demand curve. At the existing exchange rate of P^1 there is now an excess demand of Q^3-Q^1. The excess demand for the currency will create upward pressure on the currency and its price will therefore rise. The price of pounds in terms of dollars increases, making UK exports less attractive, and the new equilibrium is established at an exchange rate of P^2 where the quantity demanded equals the quantity supplied of Q^2. Sterling has appreciated against the dollar.

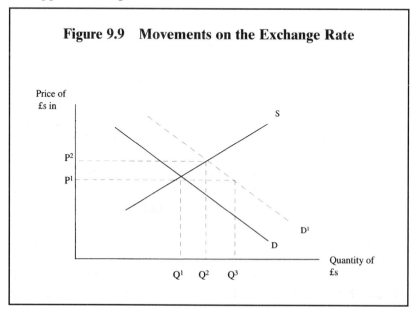

Figure 9.9   Movements on the Exchange Rate

Excess supply, on the other hand requires a depreciation in the price of a currency in order to restore the equilibrium.

The advantage of a floating rate system is that a currency should not be over or undervalued for very long. Such 'mispricings' can lead to distortion of a country's competitiveness and comparative advantage. For example, if a country is experiencing high inflation relative to other countries, its goods will be relatively more expensive, reducing the quantity of exports. However, in this situation the price of sterling will fall in terms of dollars. The exchange rate will depreciate to maintain the international competitiveness of the UK. In a floating system, the exchange rates adjust to maintain competitiveness and ensure that demand equals supply, leaving governments free to concentrate on the pursuit of domestic objectives .

The disadvantage of such a regime is the tremendous uncertainty surrounding the exchange rate. This is a particular problem in the business environment, where cash flows can be seriously affected by adverse currency movements. It can also be argued that floating rates also promote speculative trading in a currency which can have a destabilising effect on the economy.

Fixed Exchange Rates - Background

The damaging nature of exchange rate volatility has been such that the governments have looked to fixing the exchange rate. Indeed, for much of the 19th century, currencies of the most important trading nations were fixed in terms of gold. The system relied on the physical transfer of gold between countries to maintain the equilibrium rates of exchange, a process which was slow, and which, combined with the shortages of gold, lead to its eventual breakdown. The next attempt to fix exchange rates came after World War II with the Bretton Woods system, named after the New Hampshire resort where the agreement was signed in 1944. Under the agreement, the countries were committed to preserving a fixed rate until there was evidence of 'fundamental disequilibrium'. In this eventuality, the countries were expected to **devalue** or **revalue** their currencies, in order to establish new parity relationships.

The system worked on the principle of the Gold Exchange Standard, in which the US pledged to keep the dollar price of gold fixed, by agreeing to exchange US currency on demand at a rate of \$35 per ounce. Other countries then fixed their currencies in terms of dollars.

The Bretton Woods system operated with reasonable success until the late 1960s, when it came under pressure due to falling demand for dollars. This was attributable to a number of factors, notably worldwide inflation in the 1960s, which meant a rise in the prices of commodities other than gold, leaving gold undervalued in terms of all the major currencies. This situation was further exacerbated by the printing of money in the US to finance war in Vietnam. The resulting expansion in the money supply pushed up the dollar price of goods and made gold seem extremely cheap. Countries jumped onto the bandwagon of buying gold, preferably with borrowed dollars, with the prospect of being able to sell the gold at a profit and repay the dollar loans which were eroded by inflation. This increased pressure on the dollar lead to an attempt to increase the dollar price of gold, but even that was unsustainable. The system finally broke down in the early 1970s and currencies allowed to float.

More recent attempts to fix exchange rates have come in Europe as part of the European Monetary System. The Exchange Rate Mechanism pegged currencies of the member countries to the Deutsche Mark (DM), as a step to European Monetary Union and a single currency in Europe. The system came under pressure in the early 1990s with the withdrawal of UK and Italy whose currencies were unsustainable within their parity limits. Despite these problems a single currency, the Euro, is still proposed for 1999.

Operation

Under a fixed rate system, movements in the exchange rates in order to maintain equilibrium are not possible. Other mechanisms are therefore required to restore imbalances within the system. Two such possibilities can be identified: movements in reserves of foreign currency held by the central bank, and adjustments in interest rates.

Central banks can use their currency reserves to artificially create demand for or supply of the currency. In Figure 9.10, the excess demand for sterling created by the outward shift in the demand curve creates pressure for the exchange rate to move to P^2. This pressure is removed by the central bank's purchase of foreign currency using its sterling reserves. This increases the supply of sterling to meet the increased demand, and the supply curve shifts out to S^1, leaving the exchange rate unchanged at P^1, but accommodating the increased demand of Q^3. In the same way, pressure on sterling through an excess supply is removed by the sale of sterling by the central bank.

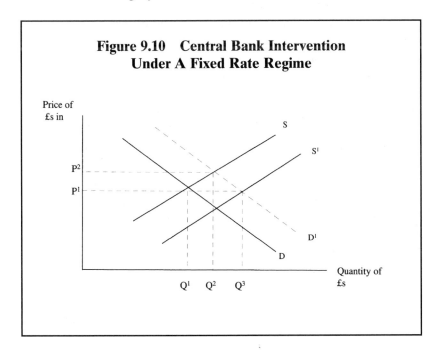

Figure 9.10   Central Bank Intervention Under A Fixed Rate Regime

Interest rates are another tool used for the manipulation of exchange rates. International traders hold transactions balances which they will often lend out in the short-term. The destination of these funds depends on the return on the investment. Clearly they will invest where interest rates are highest. An increase in the UK rates of interest relative to other countries would create an inflow of capital into the UK, stimulating the demand for sterling. Conversely, a decrease in UK interest rates relative to other countries would cause an outflow, and reduce the demand for sterling.

If pressure on a currency becomes too great, neither movements in reserves nor interest rate manipulation will sustain the level of the exchange rate . Under a fixed rate regime, the only option is to devalue or revalue. This involves the setting of new parity relationships in terms of other currencies. A devaluation is the result of a falling exchange rate, and a revaluation is the consequence of a rising exchange rate. Such changes, if they are too regular or too large, can cause the breakdown of a fixed rate system. This was a problem with the Exchange Rate Mechanism, which came under speculative pressure when it was believed that the devaluations and revaluations could be forced.

Exchange Rates and Shipping

In assessing the impact of exchange rates on shipping, a direct and an indirect affect must be identified. The cost of shipping is directly affected by the movement in an exchange rate. Since freight rates are quoted in dollars, the cost of shipping relies on the movement in the dollar. An appreciation relative to other currencies will increase freight rates, making shipping more expensive; a depreciation, on the other hand, will reduce the freight rate. Clearly, the size of the effect depends on the volatility of a particular currency in terms of dollars.

The indirect affect is more complex, but can be explained simply in terms of the derived nature of the demand for shipping.

Exchange rate movements may cause an increase in the level of international trade, if they move in such a way as to make the exports of the major trading nations more attractive. Since demand for shipping depends on the level of international trade, the demand for shipping will increase as an indirect affect of the movements in the exchange rate. For example, a depreciation of sterling will make UK exports cheaper. These exports will need to be shipped to the customer, thus increasing the demand for shipping.

Balance of Payments

International transactions are recorded by governments in a balance of payments account. Actual payments among countries must necessarily balance, since it is not possible to buy more pounds than are available to sell. However, the types of purchase and sale may not be the same.

For example, exports of UK cars may exceed imports of foreign cars. In this case more pounds will be bought for exported cars than are sold for the car imports. This creates a surplus on the car account. International trade consists of many different items. This makes the accounting complex, but broadly they can be categorised as debits and credits. Debit items create a supply of a country's currency from requirements to fund imports and foreign investment, whilst credit items create a demand for a country's currency from exports and investment from overseas. A deficit in the balance of payments means that the supply of home currency exceeds the demand, a surplus means that demand exceeds supply. The structure of the balance of payments is discussed below:

1. **Current account transactions**

    These comprise exports and imports of goods known as visibles, and exports and imports of services known as invisibles.

2. Transactions in UK assets and liabilities

These are a record of direct investment by, changes in government reserves of foreign currencies, and repayment of loans from the International Monetary Fund (IMF)

3. Balancing item

This is the amount needed to exactly balance the receipts and payments, and arises due to errors and omissions in the accounts mainly through timing.

These three main categories are incorporated into an outline structure of the balance of payments as shown in Table 9.4

Table 9.4 The Structure of the Balance of Payments

CURRENT ACCOUNT		
Trade in goods	+	exports - imports
	=	**Visible Balance**
Trade in services	+	exports - imports
	=	**Service Trade Balance**
Investment income	(+/-)	interest payments, profits, dividends
	=	**Investment Income Balance**
Transfers		Government receipts and payments
		Private receipts and payments
	=	**Transfers Balance**
TRANSACTIONS IN ASSETS AND		
LIABILITIES		
Direct investment	+	Foreign companies investing in UK
	-	UK companies investing abroad
Portfolio investment	+	Foreign residents purchase of UK shares
	-	UK residents purchase of overseas shares
UK banks and non banks lending and		
borrowing		
General government account		
BALANCING ITEM		

206

Shipping and the Balance of Payments

The contribution of sea transport to the balance of payments is contained in the invisibles section of the account. The figures are subdivided into dry cargo and wet cargo. On the credit side, the receipts include earnings from the country's merchant fleet, either owned or chartered to country's residents, freight on exports, freight from cross trades, revenue from passengers collected abroad, time charter hire and payments made by foreign ships for port services.

Payments or debits comprise home operators' payments abroad, chartering of foreign vessels, freights and passenger payments to foreign operators, and port charges .

Examination of the sea transport account shows that the industry contributed a net £1.31 billion to the balance of payments in 1995, whilst the net payment to foreign shipowners to carry goods and passengers into the UK was £1.5 billion, leaving an overall balance of £0.2 billion. In terms of direct contribution to balance of payments, there has been an increase of 389% over the last twelve years, from £267 million in 1983 to £1305 million in 1995. At 1990 prices this is still an increase of 185%, and is attributable to improved efficiency and productivity in the industry. Shipping is clearly an important element of the balance of payments .

Summary

The demand for shipping is dependent on the level of international trade. The basis of such trade is the existence of different commodities or resources, or differing costs of production in different countries. The comparative advantage that results is further affected by the costs of transportation which must be added to the product prices. In so doing, the comparative advantage may change. Transport is therefore an important part of the analysis.

Payment for international goods requires the exchange of currencies between the different countries. These rates are determined by the forces of supply and demand. Their impact on shipping can be seen as both direct and indirect. The direct affect stems from the fact that freight rates are largely denominated in dollars, and costs may be in a variety of different currencies. Clearly, the conversion can result in exchange profits or losses. The indirect effect is due to the derived nature of demand for shipping. Movements in the exchange rates may create a comparative advantage, leading to increase trade.

The trade to and from a country is shown by the balance of payments. Analysis of the account for the UK reveals the high contribution and thus importance of the shipping industry.

Further Reading

Hawkings, J. E. *Shipping Subsidies and the Balance of Payments.* London: Lloyd's of London Press, 1989.

Rogers, P., Strange J and Studd, B. *Coal: Carriage by Sea.* London: Lloyd's of London Press, 1997. 286 pp.

Salvatore, *D. International Economics* London Macmillan 1983

Viner J. Studies *The Theory of International Trade.* London Allan Unwin

Bulking of cargoes. New York: United Nations, 1975.

Articles

Goss, R.O. *Economics and the international regime for shipping.* Maritime Policy and Management 11 (2), 1984.

Laing, E.T. *Shipping freight rates for developing countries: Who ultimately pays?* Journal of Transport Economics and Policy Xl (3), 1977.

---

[1] see Chapter 12
[2] See for details Chapter 2
[3] Based on a discussion in Salvatore D. International Economics, London Macmillan 1983 p137-139

Part III
INDUSTRY SECTORS

Chapter Ten

THE DRY BULK MARKET

Introduction

The analysis so far has been based on a study of the many variables determining demand and supply in relation to the maritime industry. This chapter will discuss how both demand and supply respond to freight rates but do not individually determine them, it is their behaviour within a market phenomenon. Thus there is a corresponding shift of emphasis to the technique determining equilibria. An examination will be made of the behaviour of the single dry bulk cargo shipowning firm as a decision making, optimising or profit maximising agent, on the supply side of the market. Competitive freight rate taking behaviour on the part of the individual shipowning firms leads to a supply function in which the output of the firm, and hence aggregate output in this sector of the industry responds to changes in the market freight rate for the services offered. Combining the supply function together with the shippers' demand function examines the elements needed to solve the basic problem of equilibrium in the freight rate markets. This must be set against a background of dynamic economic conditions engendering the consolidation of the bulk cargo trades with technological change bringing about increased specialisation of vessels and cargo handling methods. This process is sometimes referred to as "bulkerisation" of the trade. These same economic factors prompt increasing "sectionalisation" of the freight market.

The dry bulk carrier section of the maritime industry and in particular that section known as 'tramps' can be defined or characterised in various ways. There are two such definitions. The first is what can be termed the traditional type of technological definition. This concentrates on the type of vessel operating in the sector and the legal boundaries of those operations. It is purely descriptive and based on an elaboration of the criteria of typical tramp tonnage. The classic example of this traditional form of definition is postulated by H. Gripaious. "A deep sea tramp ship is prepared to carry any cargo between any port at any time, always providing the venture is both legal and safe".[1] These vessels trade from most deep sea ports in all the major bulk dry cargoes. They are of medium size lacking any specialised equipment and are not engaged in a regular trade. Thus terms like 'free trader', 'freelance shipping', 'general trader' and 'irregular trader' have been coined. All these definitions are market driven and often related closely to vessel size, terms like 'average tonnage', or 'handy-size'. With the passage of time, these tonnages have steadily increased. A further element is the possession of cargo handling equipment, as conventional tramps are geared, that is, capable of loading or unloading virtually anywhere. These vessels are common carriers, meaning that they undertake to carry anybody's cargoes providing there is space available. Usually cargoes are transported by the shipload. Such a definition would cover what was fondly known as the traditional tweendecked 'workhorse', the basic medium size, irregular or general trader. This type of definition is called into question by the growth in the volume of bulk trade and by the industry's response with a substantial increase in the size of vessels engaged in such trades.

The second definition is constructed around the charter or freight market in which the tonnage participates. This broader definition may be coined in addition to the conventional tramp ship, as it may also be defined as bulk carriers, combination carriers, and at times tankers operating in the grain market. Simply on the grounds that they are engaged in irregular or general trading and comply with Gripaious' earlier definition.

The Dry Bulk Carrier came into operation in the 1960s. They are single decked dry cargo vessels, originally categorised as 10,000 dwt or more, but this base line has been increased all the time. The development of this type of tonnage is shown in the following table:

Table 10.1   Developments of Dry Bulk Carriers 1976 to 1995 (dwt 10,000+)

Size 000 DWT	1976	1980	1985	1990	1995	1976 = (100)
10 - 60	794	99.2	117.0	113.3	116.5	+32
%	75	72	62	56	51	
60 - 100	14.3	21 2	37.9	41.4	49.6	+71
%	13	15	20	20	22	
100 +	11.9	17.2	32.8	48.0	62.5	+81
%	11	12	17	24	27	
Total (100)	105.749	137.7	187.8	202.7	228.7	+116
Average Size		34.0	38.9	43.1	44.7 (1993)	

Source: World Bulk Fleet, Fearnley, Oslo (various issues)
The table includes only vessels of 10,000 dwt and above.

The obvious point highlighted by the table is the massive growth of this section since the 1970s with total tonnage increasing by 116 %. The average size of vessels has also increased from 11,900 to 45,000 dwt. There has also been a considerable reorganisation on tonnage groupings during the period with increased concentration in the higher tonnage range. The handy size and panamax group broadly that of 10,000 to 60,000 dwt has

213

increased by 32% in tonnage terms but in terms of the level of participation it has declined from 70% to 51%. The larger groups 60,000+ increasing in bulk tonnage terms and participation in the sector. The largest a 100,000 ton+ making the greatest impact, by increasing by 81% and in terms of level of participation, from 11% to 27%.

These vessels obviously differ in size from the traditional tramp and a large proportion will not be geared, that is, do not have loading and unloading equipment. This will limit their flexibility in trading terms since, as the individual vessel increases in size, the number of ports and routes which it can possibly trade from will diminish. Underlying these increases in size and level of technological sophistication as has been argued, is the massive expansion in demand. A part of this has been the growth in the volume on particular trade routes which has encouraged long-term contracts of different types to develop, tying large dry cargo carriers to specific routes. Hence the classic economies of scale argument has caused substantial technological change and has been underpinned by powerful economic imperatives.

In attempting to find a definition within the terms of the technology used and to combine it with the earlier definition, account must be taken of the contemporary sectionalisation of the dry bulk shipping sector and the spectacular increase in vessel size this has entailed. A traditional deep-sea dry cargo tramp ship is an irregular trader, of medium size possessing its own cargo handling gear, and prepared to carry any cargo between any port at any time, operating in the open market. The second group are of tonnage of larger vessels who in general have no cargo handling equipment and are often inhibited in their area of commercial activity and trading. A large proportion of these vessels operate under different forms of long-term contracts. Contracts strongly influenced of course by the short-run spot market.

What emerges from this discussion is that the tramp trade and dry bulk trades are no longer synonymous. Over the last few decades a new structure has developed with separate, if overlapping sectors. This can be examined from the perspective of technological use, that is, the type of tonnage operating within each trade sector.

Their growth is the root cause of sectionalisation and specialisation in both cargoes and technological utilisation as well as the penetration of competitors from other sectors. The five major dry bulk commodities, iron ore, grain, coal, bauxite and aluminium and phosphate rocks constitute a substantial section of international seaborne trade. Over recent decades these commodities combined account for between 40% and 50% of the volume of seaborne trade movement and between 50% and 60% of the total demand for shipping space expressed in ton miles.

The above five cargoes constitute the major bulks. In United Nations statistics these cargoes are categorised under 40 headings. These are grouped under 4 main groupings: minerals, agricultural and forestry products, semi-manufactures and manufactures. In the case of some of the individual items under these broad headings the level of seaborne movement is closely related to the level of economic activity, for example scrap metal, non-ferrous ore and cement. Others are not totally immune from the general level of business activity, but also react to other stimuli, for example such cargoes as livestock feed and fertiliser. A point worthy of note is that wood in the form of logs, lumber and wood pulp is one of the primary sectors in these minor bulks and is a most important cargo as far as tramp tonnage is concerned.

In addition to the minor, sometimes referred to as 'Neo-bulks', there has developed in recent years other categories, some included in the above list, known as new-bulk cargoes or specialist bulk cargoes. These categories are related to two main factors. First is the tonnage of bulk cargoes for example, refrigerated cargoes, and the second is combined with the problem of stowage and handling which presents difficulties, for example, motor vehicles.

Development

The development of the last quarter of the century from both the point of view of the supplier tonnage and shippers demand illustrates in some detail in the following table:

**Table 10.2   Developments in the Dry Bulk Trades -
1970 to 1994**

	Supply Tonnage			Demand Transport Performance		
	Dry Bulk Cargoes 1	**2**	**3**	**Main Bulk Commodities**		
				4	**5**	**6**
Year	**Million/DWT**	**% Annual Charge**	**% of World Fleet**	**000 Million Ton Miles**	**Million Tons**	**% Annual Charge**
1970	76.3	-	-	2,264	448	16.0
1971	89..0	16.6	24	2,335	490	-
1972	106.9	20.2	26	2,400	505	3.0
1973	123.3	15.3	27	2,917	662	23.0
1974	135.6	10.0	27	3,150	668	7.0
1975	146.8	8.2	27	3,121	635	-5.0
1976	158.1	7.7	26	3,122	646	2.0
1977	174.4	10.3	24	3,157	645	-1.8
1978	184.5	5.8	28	3,263	667	3.4
1979	188.5	2.2	28	3,757	762	14.2
1980	191.0	1.3	28	4,011	796	4.5
1981	199.5	4.5	29	4,070	806	1.30
1982	211.2	5.9	30	3,952	759	-5.8
1983	220.6	4.5	32	3,816	732	-3.7
1984	228.4	3.5	33	4,392	833	13.8
1985	237.3	3.9	35	4,480	857	2.9
1986	235.2	-0.9	36	4,493	835	-2.7
1987	231.8	-1.4	36	4,787	875	4.9
1988	230.1	-0.7	36	5,120	940	7.4
1989	231.4	0.6	36	5,239	965	2.7
1990	238.9	3.2	36	5,259	968	0.3
1991	244.0	2.0	36	5,416	1,005	3.8
1992	245.7	0.7	35	5,299	990	-1.5
1993	251.3	3.1	35	5,296	993	0.3
1994	254.3	2.8	34	5,431	1,028	3.5

Source: Maritime Transport OECD Annual.

On all the criteria included in the table there has been substantial long-term growth of the supply side. Tonnage of all and bulk carriers has increased by in excess of three fold (Column 1). As for the percentage of the world fleet (Column 3) it has experienced a virtually uninterrupted rise from approximately 25% to over a 33%. This change does not only relate to the bulk carrier load but to the experiences of other sectors of the industry during the period. The percentage annual change (Column 2) mirrors what occurred in other sectors in a less dramatic fashion, particularly in terms of contraction. The levels of expansion in the early 1970s are a continuation of the substantial levels of the mid and late 1960s. The Maritime crisis of 1973 and 1974 bring rapid contraction but unlike other sectors, for example tanker tonnage, the figures remain positive.[2] During the late1970s the level of increases are low compared with earlier in the decade, a situation persisting into the 1990s. The late 1980s sees a significant contraction which persists for three years.

Demand here is indicated by the level of transport performance, the prime indicator ton miles, (column 4) shows a fairly steady long-run increase. Similarly million tons of cargo lifted (column 5) is one of long-term growth of substantial magnitude. Annual percentage changes in million tons lifted (column 6) shows evidence of the strong impact of the early 1970s crisis. After the long period of substantial and sustained growth there is rapid contraction in the mid 1970s. This occurs again in both criteria in the early and late 1980s and the early 1990s. The late 1980s is of interest as contraction is evident in both supply and demand at this time. But it is on the demand side that the more erratic changes in both directions are experienced, often of short duration. This major expansion and increased level of specialisation has engendered new areas of activity and levels of competition between operators in the dry bulk market. This is highlighted in a simplified form shown in the following table:

Table 10.3   Level of Activity in Different Trades by Vessel Type

	Demand [Shippers]			
Cargoes/ Trades / Vessel Types	Bulk	Minor Neo Bulk	Grain	Oil
Traditional Liners	V. Low	Low	Nil	Nil
Tramps	High	High	High	Nil
Bulk Carriers	High	High	High	Nil
Combination Carriers	High	High	High	High
Tankers	Nil	Nil	V. Low	High

1) Container tonnage often engages in Minor or Neo.
   Bulk movement, stowed in Containers.
2) This also includes specialised tonnage in particular trades.

The presence of traditional liners as competitors or interlopers within the above figure is related to what has been called the neo-bulk cargoes.   Such cargoes possess the physical characteristic of liner cargoes, but the volume has expanded to convert them to bulk quantities, hence the competition for their transportation by tramps and other bulk carriers. The reverse is also true and liners have always competed with tramps in that they have taken these minor bulks as supplementary to or, topping off, cargoes. These are referred to as optional cargoes, loaded in periods of low demand for other cargoes on particular services or legs of such services. The liner operators rather than sail partially loaded or even empty, have incentives to fill up with optional cargo. The reason is that they are running a service and any freight earnings above actual handling costs must add positively to revenue. Hence, dependent on the standpoint taken, it is possible to use the term interloper for those liners conveying cargoes broadly designated as mainly suitable for tramp tonnage. The reverse is also true where tramp tonnage interlopes in areas designated as mainly suitable for liners. A clear line of demarcation between these two sectors of dry cargo carrying being difficult to draw.

Table 10.3 shows a group known as combination carriers. These are results of attempts to secure the advantages of specialisation while avoiding some of the disadvantages. The owners of this tonnage aim to be versatile in their response to substantial modifications in the freight market. The 1960s brought more flexible vessels, bulk carriers combining the ability to transport dry and liquid cargoes. The type developed into either, dual purpose bulk and oil or triple purpose ore bulk and oil. The crude oil and ore carriers tended to be large vessels in excess of 120,000 dwt. Recently there has been a movement towards the building of smaller, product vessels. Generally, they have not been as universally successful as the simple operational principles on which they are built would suggest. First there are very few direct or triangular trade routes which would secure cargoes both outward and homeward. Secondly the additional investment costs in building such flexible vessels and the extra operational costs of the ability to load different cargoes are high. The conversion costs of moving from carrying one cargo to another are frequently high both in terms of a functional and a time sense. For example following a full cargo of oil there is the necessity of washing, gas freeing and other cleaning, particularly if the same tanks or holds are to be used for coal, ore or grain. Despite these cost disadvantages the flexibility of such vessels means they will take advantage of substantial changes perceived as being long lasting between freight markets. Empirical evidence indicates that once committed to a particular freight market this type of tonnage remains there for some considerable time. The competitive relationship between combination carriers and tankers is noted in the figure as is the tanker as an occasional competitor in the dry cargo bulk market. The competition is almost totally limited to the grain trade. Tanker activities in this trade were important in the mid 1960s when, in 1965, 14 million tons of grain were transported over 83 million ton miles in tankers. By the 1970s this form of activity was insignificant and remained so. Its significance still remains in its ever present ability to recognise its potential and join the active dry cargo supply should freight rate changes encourage such a movement.

What should be mentioned in the above context is the presence of industrial carriers, huge industrial companies basing their operations on vertical integration who often own their own tonnage to transport raw materials or the finished product. Usually the objective is to gain control over their transport needs and minimise their freight costs. Oil companies are the obvious example but in the dry cargo sector, pulp, steel products and sugar companies often own considerable amount of tonnage. The company either acts as operator or has its tonnage operated by ship management companies.

The figure highlights again the fact that the merchant shipping industry is not a single entity but a cluster of interacting industries differing in numerous ways. Each responds to different market demands and this is the cause of different services being provided as well as the differing levels and types of technology utilised. The technology has remained dynamic despite the long freight recession of recent times. Technological and organisational changes have been less specialised than those experienced prior to the mid 1970s. This and the series of oil shocks which followed had a considerable impact on bunker prices and hence shipbuilding. They increasingly concentrated on low fuel consumption and improved propellers and hull hydrodynamics. The wider economic forces of increased costs forced construction of commercially high performance vessels which could achieve profitability in times of depressed freight rate markets. These freight rate markets form another important demarcation level between different sectors of the industry.

Charters[3]

The definition constructed around the charter or freight markets in which the tonnage participates will now be examined. Shipowners and shippers use a wide variety of freight contracts, (charterparties) in their dealings with each other. These are complex legal documents with two elements which are of interest in the present context. The length of time the contract is operable from which follows the broad terms of the contract and secondly the method of establishing freight rates. In simple terms four types of charterparty can be classified as follows:

1) Single or consecutive voyage charters

Under these charters shipowners undertake to provide a vessel to carry specific cargoes as full loads for a single or consecutive voyages between a range of ports. The shipper pays freights per ton of cargo loaded and the shipowner or operator pays all costs, although there are some variations regarding who pays the expense of loading and discharging said cargo. This constitutes the dry cargo tramps area of activity for this is the short-term competitive spot market. It is thus possible to define dry cargo tramps using the second method suggested, namely the type of charterparty and freight market. That is not by the technical characteristics of the vessel and its acceptance of cargo, but by the market sector in which it operates. Arguably, a dry cargo tramp vessel could be defined as tonnage seeking its employment in the highly competitive spot freight market.

2) Time charter

Under this form of charter shipowners agree to provide a vessel for the exclusive use of the charterer on the charterer's business. Short charters run for two years and what is often called medium term charters from two to five years. The shipowner provides the vessel and crew as well as being responsible for capital charges, running costs and maintenance. The charterer (shipper), takes responsibility for all voyage expenses and port and cargo handling costs. To time charterers can be ascribed the element of a long-term bulk carrier market as distinct from the earlier spot market, although both these markets interact on each other.

3) Bareboat or demise charters

Here the shipowner provides the vessel for hire and takes no further active part in the proceedings. The charterer becomes the vessel manager and operator in every detail. This form of charter is not used as often as the two discussed previously. The criteria shows that it fits into the market for long-term charters.

4) Contracts of affreightment

This an undertaking by the shipowner to transport a quantity of cargo over a given time period on a particular route or routes. Usually no ship is named so it is possible to ship cargoes between different vessels. The limitations being the quantity of cargo available and any maximum or minimum restraints at loading or discharging ports. The shipowner agrees to transport the cargo at a specific freight rate per ton. Here again the trade is in bulk dry cargo, the contract being medium or long-term.

Under these different charterparties, the operating cost items for which either shipowners or charters are responsible, are shown in the following figure 10.1 designed by I. L. Buxton.

This gives a broad indication of the particular costs under different agreements, and how they are allocated between shipowners and charterers. The inclusion of a column on cargo handling expenses, is to allow for voyage charter, which can be designated either to shipowners or charterers.

The owner operated, for example, oil companies, sugar, and steel producers are sometimes referred to as industrial operators who see maritime operation as an element in their production process. This should not be seen as implying they have little interest in the level of freight rates, for generally shipping activities will be undertaken by a subsidiary section of the company. The return on investment by this sector will be of importance. If for example costs of moving cargo are persistently below that of market freight rates, further investment in tonnage could be undertaken, to remove any independent chartered vessel from the operations. On the other hand, if the freight rates are persistently below their costs, they could charter tonnage, while laying up, dispensing on the Sale and Purchase market, or scrapping their own vessels.

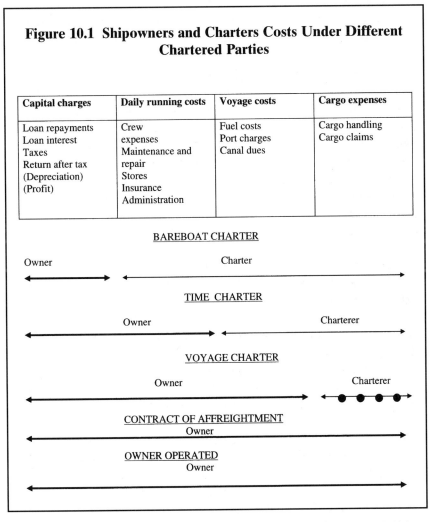

Figure 10.1 Shipowners and Charters Costs Under Different Chartered Parties

Capital charges	Daily running costs	Voyage costs	Cargo expenses
Loan repayments Loan interest Taxes Return after tax (Depreciation) (Profit)	Crew expenses Maintenance and repair Stores Insurance Administration	Fuel costs Port charges Canal dues	Cargo handling Cargo claims

BAREBOAT CHARTER

Owner   Charter

TIME CHARTER

Owner   Charterer

VOYAGE CHARTER

Owner   Charterer

CONTRACT OF AFFREIGHTMENT
Owner

OWNER OPERATED
Owner

Source: Based on Buxton I. L. Engineering Economics and Ship Design. British Ship Research Association. Wallsend June 1970

It could be suggested that in Figure 10.1, capital charges, and daily running cost are fixed costs (F.C.) and voyage cost and cargo expenses variable cost (V.C.) but this is an over simplification, as argued in Chapter 7.

The Spot Market

The technological concept of a tramp is now only relevant to a minority of tonnage operating in the dry bulk trades, but what can be usefully termed the 'Tramp Market' is still of importance that is on the trip or time charter basis. The term 'Tramp' will concentrate on the short-term spot market for tramps tonnage and its interaction with the longer term markets. A spot market will be defined here as one where vessels and cargo are available for immediate delivery as opposed to the long-term or forward market. Spot in this case meaning immediately effective. The spot market is where a large number of individual sellers, that is shipowners on the supply side, are confronted by a similarly large number of individual buyers, that is shippers or charterers on the demand side. This is a situation where all participants in the market are price takers. Such a large number of relatively small buyers and sellers within the dry bulk freight market means it functions at a highly competitive level. In other words an open market comprising numerous individual firms of shippers and similarly large numbers of shipowners offering common carrier bulk transport services. It is a competitive market where rapid movements in freight rates are seen as normal. Within such large markets there will be sub-markets, for example on the basis of the time criteria, but with a high degree of interdependence. Such highly competitive markets function in the Baltic Exchange in London, and there are also similar if smaller markets in Hong Kong, New York, Oslo, Piraeus and Tokyo.

The above preamble is of assistance in constructing a working description of the tramp sector of the industry. It has already been argued from an operational point of view that this sector comprises small or medium size non-specialist dry cargo tonnage. These general or irregular traders concentrate their operations almost wholly on the main bulk commodities conveyed by them as a single bulk cargo. Finally, and of prime importance, they participate in an atomised market and have no inhibitions about entering or leaving the market. These are an integral criteria for the creation of a highly competitive market.

Maritime economists have perceived in the functioning of this international bulk shipping spot market, elements akin to those of the theoretical model known as perfect competition.[4] The tramp market firm within perfect competition is the basis of much micro-economic analysis. It is an elaboration of Marshall's demand and supply analysis, which has been discussed previously, and provides insights into the way equilibrium market price, that is the freight rate, is established. These insights transcend the narrow borders of the strictly defined models which are about to be constructed.

Perfectly Competitive Market

In a similar way to all economic models perfect competition is underpinned by a set of assumptions; these appear to be present in the tramp market. A competitive market has some general principles or conditions which it must fulfil to achieve equilibrium. Every firm must operate at an output which is deemed appropriate to the conditions of cost and demand, the quantity all firms will sell at the market freight rate must equal the total quantity all buyers wish to purchase, and by the means of equilibrium price the market is cleared. Within the above is the important, and overriding assumption that all entrepreneurs, both shipowners and shippers, are rational or act rationally. That is to say their central goal is to maximise profits as with all micro economic decisions. What follows is the assumptions specific to perfect competition related to the dry bulk market.

1. Large number of relatively small firms both shipowners and shippers.

The consequence of this is that each firm produces or consumes a level of output which is small in relation to the total quantity of the industry's production. The important implication of this

225

assumption is that firms are so numerous as to be incapable of possessing any monopoly power with which to influence the level of freight rates. Firms do not collaborate, to affect or influence the market. It follows that individual firms are incapable of affecting the freight rate by varying their own output levels or their demand for tonnage: since what the individual supplies or demands is insignificant in terms of the industry as a whole. All firms are, therefore, 'price takers' as they accept the freight rate offered in the market as given. The rate is determined by the general market conditions of demand and supply. The individual firm is powerless, as changes to the industry's total output caused by the entry or exit of one additional firm is so insignificant as to have no perceivable effect on freight rates. If for example a tramp operating firm was to double the size of its fleet, the resulting increase in cargo capacity would have no discernible effect on the position of the supply curve and the effect on the freight rate would be negligible. This is often referred to as the small or smallness assumption because it means all firms, whether they are consumers or suppliers, lack the ability due to their size to influence the market freight rate.

2.   Identical service

The argument here is that the numerous firms among tramp tonnage are all producing services indistinguishable from one another. What is offered is a homogeneous product, a bulk transport service, a situation making it impractical for the small individual shipowner to attempt to increase the individual freight charge because the individual shippers can easily take their business to other competing shipowners asking the market freight rate.

3.   Freedom of entry and exit of firms

In the tramp sector investment requirements are low compared to many other industries particularly considering the financial and other support often readily available from governments and other sources. This means that it is relatively easy for firms to move into the industry.

Exit is also open to firms, by selling their tonnage, sending it for laying up or scrapping it. The presumption here is that laying up is to exit from the industry that is removing the tonnage from activity supply. Those who enter may be combination vessels who would move out of carrying oil cargoes in the tanker market into the dry cargo market or tanker tonnage into the grain trade. This occurs when dry cargo freight rates exceed tanker freight rates and expectations are of the situation remaining for some time. Once the freight rate situation is reversed, operators will exit to the oil sector.

4.   Perfect information or knowledge

In the dry bulk market, the Baltic Exchange is one of the major centres for market information. Brokers representing shipowners and shippers are in close contact with each other and thus information is freely communicated.

The Freight Market

Given the above assumptions there can only be a single market freight rate. A ruling freight rate determined by the equilibrium point of the market demand and supply curves. The market demand curve is the aggregate of all the individual shippers' demands. The market supply curve is the aggregate supply of all the individual shipping firms supply curves above their variable cost curve, i.e. marginal cost curves.   Neither shippers nor shipowning firms in such a market can affect the freight rate.

The industry's demand curve slopes downwards from left to right because if the industry as a whole were to lower its freight rate it would supply, or offer for charter, more tonnage. This process follows logically from the basic law of demand. The supply curve moves upwards from left to the right from the base of each individual shipowning firm's lay-up point, that is the section of the marginal cost curve above the average variable cost. Where the two curves intersect the freight rate is established for every shipowning firm in the industry. Any change in the freight rate will either increase or decrease the amount of active supply

227

within the tramp sector per unit of time. It follows in this sector of the industry, rather than being freight rate 'makers' they are freight rate 'takers'.

To take an example, the market freight rate stands at $10 a ton. Should an individual shipowner require, say, $12 a ton then that firm would ship nothing because shippers would charter at lower market rates. Should some shipowners decide to be generous to shippers and charge less than $10 per ton, say, $8, this would entail an obvious loss of revenue for the shipowner and a lowering of the firm's profits with little or no increase in sales, or tonnage chartered. In addition it would be considered irrational as it constitutes a movement in contradiction to the profit maximisation objective. The above discussion confirms that the individual shipper, that is the charterer will face a demand curve sloping downwards to the right, any fall in price will cause an increase in quantity demanded, a movement down the curve, in contrast the demand curve faced by the individual shipowner is perfectly horizontal in this competitive market: as argued, the individual shipowning firm cannot charge a higher freight rate and will not concede a lower. The structure of the market with a large number of relatively small buyers and sellers, homogeneous product, freedom of entry and exit etc. obliges the individual firm to accept the freight rate as given. The firm's demand curve is infinitely elastic, indicating that the firm can sell any amount of output, tonnage, at the prevailing market freight rate. This is illustrated in Figure 10.2

The market sector is indicated by section (b) of the above figure. The industry's demand curve and supply curve are each horizontal summations of the numerous components. Once the market has determined the freight rate each shipowning firm or shipper, sees freight as a fixed parameter in its decision making. They are impotent to determine or influence that freight rate. The market interacts as a whole, it is the sole determinant of the freight rate. The model is an illustration of a systematic picture of the short-run freight rate market equilibrium. The centre model (b) shows the interaction of demand and supply in the tramp sector. The demand curve D is inelastic, the supply curve

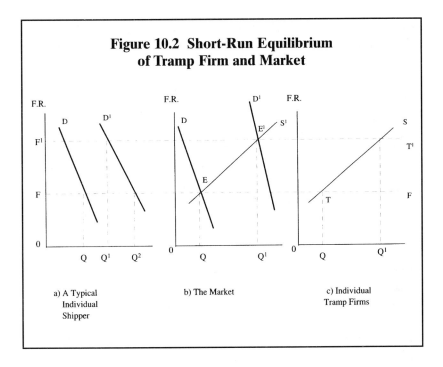

**Figure 10.2 Short-Run Equilibrium
of Tramp Firm and Market**

a) A Typical
Individual
Shipper

b) The Market

c) Individual
Tramp Firms

S^1 is elastic and they intersect at E, the stable market equilibrium. The freight rate is F and quantity of total tonnage Q. Section (a) of the model illustrates the shift in the individual shipper's demand curve from D to D^1. Such a movement will not effect the market freight rate if only one individual shipper increases his demand so shifting his total of chartered tonnage from Q^1 to Q^2. This is not possible due to the first assumption rather, all or a large majority of shipper's increase their demand, the markets aggregate demand would increase and the action would cause the market demand curve to shift from D to D^1 a new market equilibrium would be established at E1, freight rate F^1, quantity Q^1. Section (c) illustrates the position of a typical tramp owning firm with its elastic curve S. With the increase in freight rate to F1 tonnage is increased from Q to Q^1 and a new equilibrium for the firm will be established at T^1. A new output yielding at least in this time period a higher level of revenue and presumably profits. Under the present assumption the shipowner has no incentive to change the freight rate, for example an increase would reduce supplies taken up by charters from individual shipowners to zero. From the demand curve facing individual shipowning firms can be drawn a set of important relationships with freight rate, average revenue and marginal revenue being the same.

Marginal revenue as has already been pointed out is a central idea in micro economics. Its use does not, of necessity, imply a small item. Marginal revenue is a change in the total revenue per quantity of unit chartered. The change in total revenue is calculated as the change in the quantity of tonnage chartered. The following table illustrates this, and it is important to note that the market Freight Rate (FR) is assumed to be $40.

Table 10.4   Hypothetical Tramp Shipping Firms Cost and Revenue

1	2	3	4	5	6	7	8	9
Quantity per unit of time Q	Total Revenue T.R. (FR)	Total cost T.C (F.C.+ AVC)	Total Variable Costs T.V.C	Average Total Costs A.C. (AC=$\frac{TC}{Q}$)	Marginal Cost M.C. (MC=$\frac{\Delta TC}{Q}$)	Marginal Revenue M.R. (MR=$\frac{\Delta TR}{Q}$)	Profit and Loss T.P. (TP=TR-TC)	M.C. and M.R.
0	0	35	0	0	0	0	- 35	
1	40	59	24	59.0	24	40	- 19	MR < MC
2	80	75	40	37.5	16	40	5	" "
3	120	95	60	31.7	20	40	25	" "
4	160	120	85	30.0	25	40	40	" "
5	200	150	115	30.0	30	40	50	" "
6	240	190	155	31.7	40	40	50	MC = MR
7	280	245	210	35.0	55	40	35	MC < MR
8	320	330	295	41.3	85	40	-10	" "
9	360	430	395	47.7	100	40	- 70	" "

As can be seen from the hypothetical table a tramp shipowning firm in a competitive market can place any amount of tonnage on the market at the current market freight rate. The whole table is constructed on the basis of a horizontal demand curve. A number of things flow from this. The total revenue curve is linear from zero, secondly the demand curve, freight rate curve, average revenue and marginal revenue are all equal. Hence demand equals freight rate = average revenue = marginal revenue (D=FR=AR=MR). A short-run analysis of freight rates and output serves to show the situation in which shipowning firms are impelled to vary the level of participation in the market. In the short-run they do not have the time necessary to change their scale of plant. The number of shipping firms in the tramp sector will therefore be fixed because new firms will not have the required time to enter nor will existing firms have time to leave the industry. Changes in the level of industrial output, that is movement of cargo, must come from the tonnage capacity of the existing shipowning firms. This can be achieved in a number of ways: increasing vessel speed; reactivating laid up tonnage; postponing surveys or repair work or increasing utilisation. These are examples of increasing supply. It has to be made clear in this discussion that the firm, for example the firm operating a single vessel, is too small relative to the charter market in which it operates to affect the above freight rate. The problem confronting the shipowner is that of determining the tonnage to place on the market, that is how does a tramp owning firm decide how much to produce in a perfectly competitive market? The answer to this question is fundamental to the theory of the firm.

How then does a tramp owner achieve profit maximisation or loss minimisation? One method of finding the point of profit maximisation involves a comparison of total charter receipts, or total revenue, that is freight rate multiplied by the total tonnage chartered, with the total costs, that is cost per unit multiplied by total tonnage supplied. Since profit or loss is the difference between revenue and cost. The previous Table 10.4 combined with the following Figure 10.3 will be used to illustrate the total revenue, total cost approach.

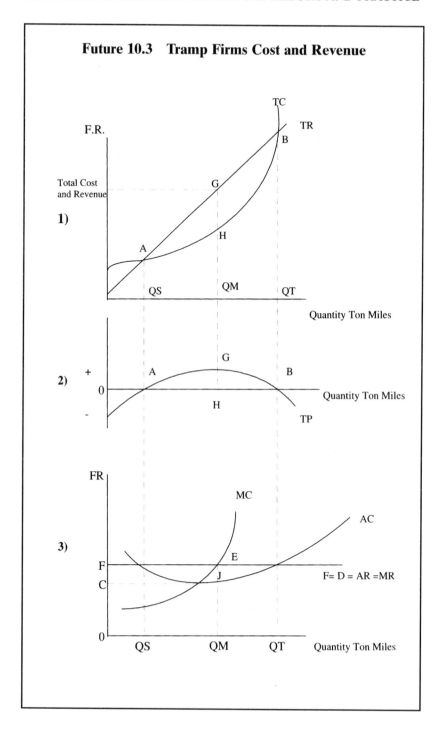

Future 10.3   Tramp Firms Cost and Revenue

Column 1 shows quantity of active tonnage in the market and is the horizontal axis in the figure. The freight rate is $40 a ton on the vertical axis. Column 2 shows the tramp shipowning firm's total revenue increasing by $40 at each level of tonnage. If one unit of tonnage per unit of time is chartered the shipping firm's total receipts will be equal to the freight rate. At two units of tonnage total revenue will be twice the price of the product. In this way each additional unit of tonnage chartered will increase total revenue by a constant amount. From this it can be seen in the figure that the total revenue curve is upwardly sloping and linear. In other words because the freight rate is fixed the total revenue function is a straight line from the point of origin, its slope is constant. A logical situation, as in a perfectly competitive tramp firm, freight rate revenue is the same at every level of output. Column 3 shows the shipowning firm's total cost of operation, it is also indicated by the curve of total cost in figure (i). Total costs are a summation of the firms fixed and total variable costs. The firm's total fixed costs are those costs which remain whether the firm is trading or not. This is indicated in the total cost column by $35 as these are the costs before any tonnage is chartered. Total fixed costs are $35 throughout all quantity levels. Within the limitations imposed by the amount of tonnage the shipowner can vary the amount on charter, that is operating in the market. This generates the total cost column in the table and the curve in the figure. The curve illustrates clearly the minimum total cost of producing the various levels of output in the short-run. The shape of the total cost curve is related to the law of diminishing returns. The law has a direct influence on the total variable cost (column 4), these are the cost of actual production over and above total fixed costs .

Similarly it can be seen in the associated average (total) cost column 5. Total profit is the difference between total revenue and total costs, the quantity produced between 2 and 7 in column 1 and QS and QT in Figure 10.3 . These serve as the boundaries of profitable operation. Below 2 units, or QS the firms makes a loss, total costs exceed total revenue. Beyond 7 units, that is QT the firm is again making a loss for the same reason. Given the range of profitable operations the firm will maximise total profit when the tonnage chartered is 6 units or QM. In the figure, QM is where the vertical distance between total revenue and total costs is greatest. The amount of profit is measured by the vertical distance GH. At output below QM and above QS the slope of total revenue exceeds that of total cost, hence the two curves become further and further apart as output increases. This continues until output is in excess of QM but below QT when the slope of the total cost curve exceeds that of total revenue and the curves are converging as output rises. The profit function is shown in Column 8, derived by taking total costs away from total revenue, and by figure (1) above the profit model figure (2) which subtracts cost from revenue at every quantity level. The presence of fixed costs means that shipowners incur a loss of equal to $35 when no tonnage is active, thus there is a negative commencement to the total profit curve. It rises to a positive at A (QS) and continues to rise until it reaches G (QM) then falls to B (QT) where it again becomes negative. This is of course in line with Column 8. It follows that the shipowning firm maximises its profits at the output QM, where the distance between total revenue and total cost are the greatest. This position is confirmed by the height of the profit curve which reaches its peak at G or GH. In both models GH is the same distance and indicates the point where profits are maximised. The total revenue total cost approach is one method of calculating the level of production at which a shipowning firm will maximise its profits, but it is an awkward method to use when firms are combined together in an industry or sector of an industry as in tramp shipping. The method generally preferred for calculating the point of profit maximisation is based on the use of marginal costs and marginal revenue. This uses freight rates as an explicit variable and indicates the skill of shipowners, that is entrepreneurial behaviour that leads to the profit maximisation objective.

Marginal revenue is the additional revenue obtained from the charter of additional units of tonnage. In the Table 10.4 and Figure 10.3 the same results are achieved as in the earlier discussion of columns 1,2,3 and model 1 but in this case they are explained in terms of average and marginal costs and marginal revenue. Basically the analysis is the same as that above but the diagram takes different forms. Profits are maximised or losses minimised at the level of production by the shipowning firm at which marginal cost is equal to marginal revenue.(MC=MR). The conditions for profit maximisation can be stated simply in terms of the marginal concept. Profits will rise whenever the extra unit of production adds more to revenue than it adds to cost, that is to say profit increases when marginal revenue is greater than marginal costs. Conversely profit contracts when additional units of output increase costs more than revenue, a situation where marginal cost is greater than marginal revenue. It follows from this that profit will be maximised where and only where, marginal cost is equal to marginal revenue. Shipowners should continue to supply tonnage for charter until the point is reached where the marginal cost of supplying the extra unit of tonnage is equal to the marginal revenue received for its use. In the Figure (3) marginal cost equals marginal revenue where quantity QM is produced, point E. In the table marginal cost and marginal revenue both equal $40 where quantity per unit time is 6 and profit stands at $50. If any level of production below 6 is considered an increase in production will increase total revenue by more than total cost and hence profits increase. Increasing production also increases marginal revenue. Production beyond 6, total costs are in excess of total revenue, similarly marginal cost is greater than marginal revenue and profits contract.

Figure 10.3 (3) looks at the situation from the point of view of costs. Here costs are indicated by the average cost curve (in full the average total cost curve) and the costs of production of QM are indicated by J. As normal profit is perceived as a cost it is included in the average total cost curve, the distance between J and E therefore represents supernormal profits. The presence of supernormal profits will encourage more tonnage to become part of the active supply and compete for this profit. All the industry will be aware of the excess profit because of the perfect knowledge assumption. The freedom of entry assumption allows tonnage to compete for this excess.

Now to examine how the individual shipowning firm responds to changes in the market level of freight rates. It has been emphasised that a profit maximising tramp shipowning firm will offer to supply the quantity of tonnage whose marginal cost equals its marginal revenue. For this firm in a perfectly competitive market, marginal revenue is simply the prevailing freight rate over which the firm has no influence. The firm can offer for charter extra amounts at this freight rate and since the firm is a small part of the total tramp tonnage the hiring of one more unit of tonnage will have no perceivable effect on the freight rate. The firm's profit maximising aim dictates that it should produce the quantity for which the marginal cost is equal to the freight rate. It therefore follows that in the short-run it is the marginal cost which is relevant to tonnage-offered decisions given the fixed cost of offering tonnage, whose total amount may not be changed in the short-run.

Table 10.5   Hypothetical Tramp Shipping Firm Profit or Loss at different Freight Rates

1	2	3	4	5	6	7	8	9	10	11
Quantity per Unit of Time	Total Cost	Average Total Cost	Average Variable Cost	Marginal Cost	Freight Rate $40 = M.R		Freight Rate $30 = M.R		Freight Rate $20 = M.R	
Q	T.C.	AC	A.V.C	M.C.	Total Revenue	Profit &Loss	Total Revenue	Profit & Loss	Total Revenue	Profit & Loss
1	59	59	24	24	40	-19	30	-29	20	-39
2	75	37.5	20	16	80	5	60	-15	40	-35
3	95	31.7	20	20	120	25	90	-5	60	35(C)
4	120	30	21	25	160	40	120	0	80	-40
5	150	30	28	30	200	50	150	0(B)	100	-50
6	190	31.7	26	40	240	50(A)	180	-10	120	-70
7	245	35	30	55	280	35	210	-35	140	-105
8	330	41.3	37	85	320	-10	240	-90	160	-170
9	430	47.7	43	100	360	-70	270	-160	180	-250

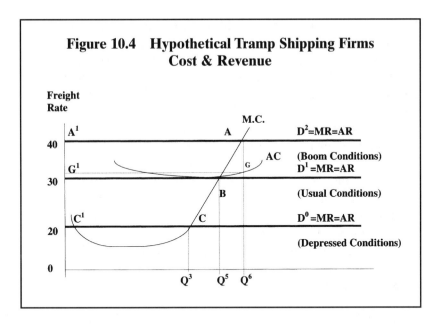

**Figure 10.4   Hypothetical Tramp Shipping Firms
Cost & Revenue**

Table 10.5   and Figure 10.4 illustrate the response of an individual tramp company to a movement in the level of market freight rates. First to examine the left hand side of the figure which shows how the freight rate of the tramp shipping's services is determined at the market level by the reactive tonnage ship supply and demand curves. It is assumed that a changing level of demand is matched with a constant supply curve. The initial position is at a market demand shown by D^0, and the market equilibrium point C with a freight rate of $20. An increase in demand to D^1 produces equilibrium B and the freight rate has strengthened to $30. Yet another shift in demand from D^1 to D^2 creates a freight rate of $40 at equilibrium point A.

The central element in this figure is the illustration of the change in the short-run equilibrium of the freight market.   If the individual freight taking firms begin with the high freight rate $40, supernormal profits will be made when the freight rate is in excess of the average cost curve (which includes normal profit) illustrated by point A^1 in the figure. If the freight rate is equal to the lowest average cost of tonnage offered the tramp firm will be earning normal profits, no excess or supernormal profits, point B.

237

This is the lowest point on the average cost curve where it is intersected by the marginal cost curve at Q^5 units of output in the table. Should the freight rate decline to below the firm's average, cost losses will be incurred. These losses can be minimised by continuing to trade where marginal costs are equal to marginal revenue. These losses can only be sustained to a freight rate equal to the average variable cost. Below that level point C^1 the firm must exit from the industry.

Market freights are in the range from $40 to $20 in the table, and in the figure between point A^1 and C^1. Taking as a starting point the freight rate $40, a boom rate the demand curve faced by the tramp shipowning firm is horizontal throughout its length at that freight. At quantity level Q^6 there is exactly the amount of tonnage to maximise profits since freight rates (marginal revenue) are equal to marginal cost. The type of profit earned by the tramp tonnage is supernormal indicated in the figure by the area A^1AGG^1. This arises simply because of the amount the freight rate exceeds costs GA times the total quantity of tonnage offered Q^6. The assumption of entry and exit is of importance here for in a period of supernormal profit those in the market will attempt to increase the quantities they offer. Of more importance, competitive firms outside the short-run market will enter in the next time period or the long-run eventually forcing down the level of super profits by the competitive process.

Should the market freight rate decline to $30, what can be termed a usual or normal freight market condition will prevail. The quantity offered will be Q^5 per unit of time and at this freight level the tramp firms would earn a return not only to maximise profit but to make optimum use of resources because marginal cost is equal to average cost and normal profits are being secured. At this level total revenue just covers total costs and profits are zero (see table). Here it is perhaps wise to repeat that normal profit is seen as a cost and will be included in the average cost curve. At this point no firm will be willing to exit from or enter into active supply. As stated previously, the short-run marginal cost curve is also the short-run supply curve for the tramp firm operating as it does in a perfectly competitive market.

The curve shows how much the firm will offer at every possible freight rate. There is one exception to this should the freight rate fall below the level of $20 in the table and the figure. At levels below this shipowners profit maximising (loss minimising) decisions will be to withdraw tonnage from active supply. This level of freight rate fails to cover variable costs. There would be a loss of all tonnage operating in additional to the loss of all fixed costs. The obvious response is the shutting down of production. Since it is assumed that in the short-term the shipowning firm cannot exit from the industry and cut or avoid all costs they will produce nothing, that they will lay-up or scrap tonnage. A freight rate only slightly above $20 will cause trading to continue even though the firm is suffering losses because the freight rate fails to cover average cost. So long as variable costs are covered the shipowner's profit maximising decision has to be to continue production. It is essential to cover fixed costs, to remain in active supply, hence point C is the freight rate cost level below which tonnage will not operate.

This point is indicated by the intersection of the marginal cost curve by a separate demand curve at different levels of freight rate. It is clear that the supply curve of the individual shipping firm is identical to the marginal cost curve and to the right of the withdrawal or lay-up point C. Below that point tonnage offered for trading will be zero at any freight rate above that of point C and particularly above point B will increase the amount of tonnage offered. It has been shown that a tramp firm's supply curve is that portion of the marginal cost curve above the minimum average variable cost curve. That is from point C to A and beyond. The individual shipowning firms which make up the supply side of the market will have to respond to changes in the market demand and freight market conditions.

In any discussion of the industry's supply curve, a summation of the individual firms' supply curves, time is of importance. In an earlier chapter time periods in economic theory were discussed in detail, they may be defined as instantaneous, short and long. The instantaneous run, sometimes referred to as the immediate or market period, it a very short time period when output remains constant and all factors are fixed. The supply curve is perfectly inelastic. The short-run is where no adjustments can be made to fixed factors. Here the supply curve becomes more elastic. The long-run is of sufficient length for all factor input to be varied. The supply curve becomes increasingly elastic. It is the area between the two extremes of time that is of interest here. This presents some difficulties as K.E. Boulding points out "between the instantaneous no adjustment and the long-run full adjustment there is an indefinite morass of short periods"[6]. It is on the short-run which the following discussion of tramp markets will concentrate. This period which can be defined as one not long enough to change the capacity of the industrial sector, that is no change in the quantity of plant or equipment e.g. tramp tonnage, but of sufficient length to change the degree of utilisation of tonnage capacity. In the tramp sector utilisation of tonnage capacity and the adjustment of total capacity will proceed simultaneously. Utilisation can be seen as for example tonnage being laid up and reactivated. Changes in capacity are related to levels of scrapping and new building. Both these types of adjustment will be related to changes in the level of demand and to the expectation of change being either permanent or short-run. With these reservations in mind the present discussion will concentrate largely on changes in the level of utilisation of tonnage within short-run industrial capacity.

To analyse the tramp market and freight rates and the length of time the supply curve utilisation takes to respond to changes in demand. In the instantaneous run there is by definition no immediate supply response as shown in Figure 10.6. The supply only reacts with time.

The industry's supply curve consists of a vertical perfectly inelastic curve S representing a fixed supply at quantity Q. The equilibrium E, at freight rate is the market rate F for the demand D. This is a level at which the marginal company will be at its lay-up point. With the increase in demand from D to D^1 creating a new intersection with supply yielding a higher freight rate F^1 and equilibrium E^1, freight acts as a device to ration increased demand. A number of questions arise from this market situation.

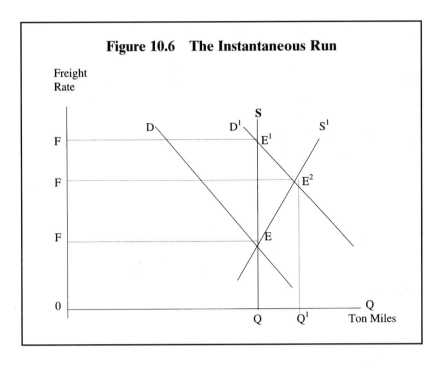

Figure 10.6   The Instantaneous Run

First what is the relationship to full capacity utilisation? If the inelastic supply curve is not only instantaneous but an indicator of full capacity utilisation some time will elapse before additional capacity can be introduced. But here it will be assumed that there is unemployed or under employed capacity still available. Secondly the level of response to the changes in demand will depend upon the future expectation of shipowning firms. It can be argued that the initial period is one of assessment of expectations as to the stability of the new demand. Shipowners will be hesitant to undertake the additional costs of a precipitous response. If the previous assumption is followed the supply situation is one where part of the active tonnage is under utilised by part loading or slow steaming. Other tonnage is in a repair yard for maintenance or surveying as well as a percentage laid up. There is a considerable amount of tonnage within the active supply as well as from surplus or inactive tonnage. Since different shipowners are likely to have differing lay-up points a large amount of tonnage will be offered S^1 at this new level of freight rate F^1. This will cause the supply curve in the very short-

241

run to have an increasingly positive slope. In this the size of the freight increase will be of major importance and the new supply curve S^1 will establish a new equilibrium at E^2. The freight rate stabilising at F^2 with an increase in the quantity of tonnage to Q^1. This is a significant increase combining the expectations of demand change persisting and illustrating the process of short-run adjustment to dynamic demand.

To analyse in more detail the positive movement of the supply curve once the instantaneous run is completed. Such an analysis assists in the understanding of the industry's supply curve and its interaction with increasing demand. The following figure clarifies the position.

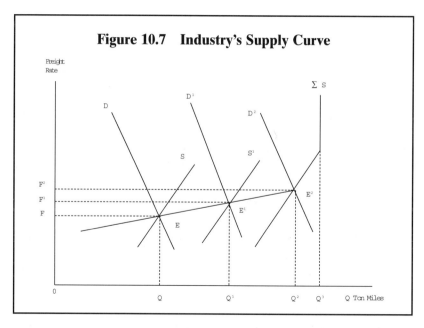

Figure 10.7   Industry's Supply Curve

Here the tramp sector of the dry bulk shipping industry has an increasing cost curve shown by the positive slope of the industry's supply curve S until it becomes vertical at full capacity utilisation Q^3. The process of adjustment of the supply curve in response to freight market demand can be seen. The demand shifts from its original position of D to D^1 increasing the quantity demanded from Q to Q^1 and causing a rise in the freight rate from F to F¹ through the process discussed earlier, drawing increasing supply into active tonnage S to S¹. The movement from D^1 to D^2 brings forth a similar movement in supply to (S) which means the full capacity of the industrial sector is Q^3. It (ΣS) should be noted that the supply curve has changed from relatively elastic to inelastic as full utilisation of total supply is completed. The series of equilibria E, E¹ and E² show the increased cost of supplying tonnage as more and more capacity is included in the active fleet. This increase is due to the factors listed above, in particular reactivation of laid up tonnage. It could also be added that the normal process of delivery of newly constructed tonnage would be a factor but this would be contrary to the way the short-run has been defined in the present discussion.

The interaction of demand and supply in the tramp market can be examined from a more generalised point of view. The demand for tonnage has already been discussed in some detail in the earlier chapter.[7] It is as stated a derived demand for the dry bulk commodities that are to be transported, and is thus subject to numerous exogenous pressures over which individual tramp owners have no influence. The elasticity of derived demand is defined on a number of generalised factors as follows:

1) Elasticity of Derived Demand

This is the elasticity of the consumer's demand for the final product. In those products in which the bulk commodity input is of importance, such consumer demand is generally considered to be inelastic.

2) Proportion of the Total Cost

The importance in percentage cost terms of the freight rate is the price of the final product. Freight rates are usually, but not always, a small percentage of the value of bulk cargoes. It would follow that a substantial increase in freight rate would have relatively little impact on the final price of the consumer product. These broad conclusions on the dry bulk freight rate have been criticised on a number of grounds. The major one being that as already suggested freights can constitute a substantial element in the final consumer price, coal being used as an example. When freights are particularly high charterers become transport cost conscious and one method used to minimise these costs is to change the source location of the cargo, that is to lower the voyage distance. This is done even if at times such a strategy entails accepting a commodity of inferior quality.

3) Substitution

This comes in two forms. Firstly, commodity substitution, the extent to which the imported bulk commodity can be replaced by a domestic product. For the majority of such bulk commodities, domestic supplies, that is supplies requiring no tramp or bulk carrier service are not readily available. Secondly, transport substitution, the availability of other means of transport for bulk commodities. There are generally no substitute for bulk shipping services at the level of freight rates that is cost or even time cost efficient, although certain regions and commodities can potentially challenge this position.

The above discussion supports the general assumption that demand for dry bulk tramp vessel services come from a group of the general bulk commodities whose elasticity is relatively low. Such an assessment of the tramp industry must be seen as a short-run generalisation tempered by earlier comments. To enlarge on these comments economic recession or cycles due to harvests can have an important impact on demand elasticities. In terms of influencing the freight rate the percentage of the final consumer price can, in certain low value bulk commodities, become an important element in the final price. Hence changes in freight rates have an important influence on elasticity. This is to argue that the total production cost of dry cargo bulk commodity per ton miles could have an influence on the source of such commodities. These important exceptions can only be considered where specific trade and trade routes are to be analysed. Here a generalised analysis is being undertaken and will concentrate on the general demand for bulk tramp cargoes, where demand elasticity is considered to be very low, that is to say demand is inelastic. The demand then for dry bulk cargo transportation is price insensitive. The Research Institute at Bergen made some estimates of these general elasticities. V.D. Norman commented that "the short-run price elasticity of transport demand in bulk shipping should be around 0.2 while the long-term elasticity should be close to 0.5".

That is to estimate in the short-run that a 1% increase in freight rates would mean an 0.2% decrease in tonnage demanded. The supply curve of tramp shipping is, what has been termed, J-shaped. The elasticity of supply is at base, a measure of the ease with which the tramp sector can expand or, for that matter, contract tonnage on offer and is dependent on the different lay-up rates for individual units of tonnage. As explained above, the individual transport firm's supply curve is that part of the marginal cost curve above the average variable cost. The steeper the marginal cost curve becomes the steeper the industry's supply curve. Such steeply rising marginal cost curves are a sign that that industry's supply curve is having increasing difficulty in expanding its active tonnage. Supply is becoming increasingly inelastic as the tramp sector of the industry nears full capacity. At times when the marginal cost curve is less steep and the average cost curve of the firm lies at relatively similar levels, a situation where active tonnage can comparatively easily be expanded, the supply curve will be elastic. Figure 10.8 illustrates this situation:

The supply curve in Figure 10.8 is initially extremely elastic. At or near short-run full capacity or full employment it becomes extremely inelastic. The important point about the curve is the rate at which it shifts from being nearly perfectly elastic to becoming extremely inelastic. This is a vital point, as can be seen if the dry cargo tramp is compared with that of the crude oil tanker. The supply curve of tramp tonnage in Figure 10.8 indicates a comparatively gradual shift between the elastic region and the inelastic region of the curve. The gradual slope of the curve results from the general presumption of substantial differences in lay-up rates, that is lay-up points between different

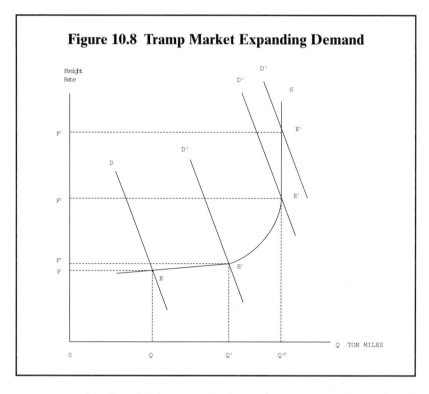

Figure 10.8 Tramp Market Expanding Demand

tonnage units. In addition, any bulk market, as argued, consist of a number of major and minor or neo bulk commodities, plus the occasional tramp movement in other commodities. This multiplicity of commodities creates a situation where the one or more commodity sectors could be booming with others in decline, a situation creating a more gradual change in the elasticity of the supply curve, when compared, with some of the single commodity markets of the tanker industry.

The level of freight rate is illustrated in the above figure by the intersection of the demand and supply curves within the expanding market. The initial demand D and freight rate F is very low with equilibrium at E. As the supply curve is extremely elastic there is a large amount of tonnage laid up for want of employment. This can be seen as a depressed market. It is not at or below the lowest freight rate for at this point, no tonnage would be trading, and in this position, Q is the amount of active

246

supply. From this initial low point demand increases to D^1 which has a substantial effect on quantity supplied which increases from Q to Q^1. Conversely it produces a minimal effect on freight rates which rise to F^1. It could be suggested that an increase in freight rate of say 5% has brought forth an increase in supply of say 50%. A further and similar increase in demand for tonnage moves the demand curve to the right from D^1 to D^2. Here again the amount of tonnage supplied increases substantially from Q^1 to Q^2. With a substantial effect on freight rates increasing from F^1 to F^2. To put approximate figures on this analysis, it could be suggested the quantity has increased by 30% and the freight rate doubled. A further increase in demand of less magnitude than the previous ones takes demand from D^2 to D^3. The industry is at full capacity; no further tonnage is available, the same supply is offered Q^2 but it provokes a substantial increase in the level of freight from F^2 to F^3. A small shift in demand when the tramp sector is at or near full capacity, that is when the supply curve is extremely inelastic, causes a massive rise in the freight rate level. Here it can be seen that demand within the tramp sector of the industry is the most dynamic factor in the market. But the impact of these changes on freight rate will differ enormously, for it is dependent on the condition of the supply curve where it is intersected by demand. The above discussion is of an expanding tramp freight market where the final equilibrium E^3 is on the perfectly inelastic full capacity section of the supply curve, a position where the spot freight rates becomes sensitive to any variations in tramp demand or supply. It has been suggested that here a 1% increase in demand could cause a 30% increase in the freight rate. The supply curve here was constructed on the definition of active supply bringing dry cargo tramps and associated vessels into active trading. The inelastic curve is where all the available supply equals active supply. This constitutes the total tonnage engaged in the dry cargo tramp sector.

Potential Supply

What is an ever present factor, as pointed out at the beginning of this chapter, is the additional tonnage which under certain circumstances, associated with unusually high levels of freight rate, will begin trading in the dry cargo tramp sector. This potential supply includes combination carriers of all types, large bulk carriers, cargo liners and tankers in addition to newly constructed tonnage. It is asserted that the supply of tramp tonnage is only perfectly elastic to some improving level of freight rate when the potential supply from outside the strict definition of tramps listed above becomes active supply. There is a one period time lag before such adjustments or additions to supply can occur. The point and extent to which this will occur is dependent on the relationship between dry cargo tramp freight rates and rates operating in other markets. The exact relationship between these criteria has not as yet been adequately researched. The basic relationship appears to be as discussed below. At some boom level of freight rate transfers from one area of activity to another begin. The transference of combination carriers to the dry tramp market is a comparatively simple operation. This movement of external potential supply into active supply in a one period time lag is illustrated in the Figure 10.9.

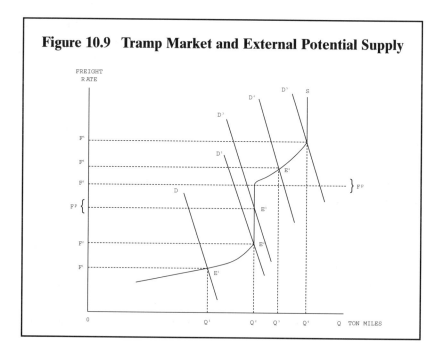

Figure 10.9   Tramp Market and External Potential Supply

The lower part of the above figure simply reiterates the previous one showing the rise in the freight rate as demand increases and the supply becomes increasingly inelastic. This is a position where the active supply becomes the total supply of tramp tonnage. There is an increase in demand from D^1 to D^3 bringing forth total tramp supply $Q^{2/3}$ and increasing the freight rate to F^3. The underlying trends and expectations are for demand to continue to rise moving further to the right, with the commensurate rise in freight rates. Thus the freight rate in the tramp markets are at a higher level than those experienced in other market sectors.

Combination carriers, tankers and vessels from other areas of activity move increasingly into the tramp market. This level or region of freight rates is denoted in the figure above as Fp . Here it can be seen that the potential supply moves strongly into the tramp sector. The change in the supply curve is illustrated by the rightward kink from P to E^5. The supply curve becomes more elastic between these points and the matching quantities are $Q^{2/3}$ and Q^5. The importance and extent of this potential supply is dependent on two factors; the inter-market freight rate relationships and the actual amount of tonnage constituting the potential supply. It should be noted that should demand continue to rise beyond D^5 equilibrium E^5 the supply is once again at full capacity Q^5 and there are no further opportunities for additions to tonnage.

The lack of further supply is indicated by the perfectly inelastic supply curve. It follows that such rises in demand would only create commensurate increases in freight rate and some rationing of tonnage in the short-run. That is, until some further increases in the level of tonnage supplied are possible.

The discussion of the dry cargo tramp market thus far has concentrated on boom conditions or movements towards such market conditions. That is increasing demand and followed by an expansion in the level of market activity. The mistake must not be made that a contraction in demand and a lowering in market activity is simply the process of putting the mechanism into

249

reverse. In an expanding freight market one of the main effects is that of achieving equilibrium freight rates and market clearance. This ensures that all tonnage offered at that freight rate will be chartered. This means once equilibrium rate is secured all tonnage offered will secure a charterer. It follows that on a rising or booming market, all things being equal, the market will be cleared. It can therefore be suggested that in a rising market, tramp shipping acts in a similar way to models used in primary economics where apples, oranges and eggs are used for the basic commodity. The problem is that the analogy with soft fruit or eggs is flawed as tramp tonnage is a long life asset which unlike apples cannot be simply consumed or allowed quickly to rot away. This has important implications since tramp tonnage is the industry's capital asset which despite radical changes in short-run freight rates remains part of total supply in one form or another, e.g. active or inactive. The specification of the process simulating the demand and supply model is that decisions have been made simultaneously. But it can be argued that tramp shipowning firms base current decisions on past expectations calculated on the basis of the freight rate operating in the previous period. Thus, as was discussed above in the current period, it can be regarded as fixed, that is to say, the quantity of tonnage supplied per unit of time is dependent on the freight rate in the previous period. Figure 10.10 examines the delay in the reaction of supply. Although this is an oversimplification it approximates how freight markets adjust to a contraction in demand causing the eventual establishment of a new equilibrium.

To consider a different market situation where the original equilibrium position is E with demand D at freight rate F and a quantity supplied by shipowners Q. There is a contraction in demand, causing the demand curve to shift to the left becoming D^1. If the market functioned as smoothly as the basic model suggests it would clear the excess supply and move rapidly to create a new equilibrium at E^2, the quantity supplied contracting from Q to Q^2 establishing a new freight rate at F^2. This does not occur when the sudden contraction on the much more volatile demand side of the model is not matched by a similar reactive

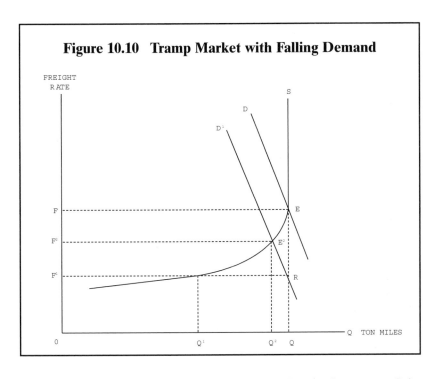

Figure 10.10   Tramp Market with Falling Demand

contraction on the part of supply. Rather the total tonnage Q in the immediate run remains active. Such an excess of supply Q to Q^2 can only obtain a freight rate of F^1 in response to point R on the demand curve. This general reluctance to remove tonnage from the market creates a period of low freight rates. There are obviously often considerable time lags between the fall in freight rates and an increase in the inactive fleet as they move to lay-up. This is because it takes some time for all spot charters which exist at a particular time to be concluded, while many ships remain without charters but are still in the active supply as they have not withdrawn from the market in response to falling freight rates. Tonnage idleness of this type is based on shipowners' expectations of an impending improvement in freight rates or a desire not to act precipitously in what may be a short lived situation.   However, the market mechanism will gradually remove surplus tonnage from the active supply by laying up and scrapping a movement encouraged by the persistent low freight rates. Eventually a new equilibrium E^2 will assert itself.[9]

New tonnage will enter the market continually even in periods of freight rate depression as for example it will be replacement tonnage or tonnage ordered around the previous boom period. Even in the unique position where the amount of tonnage scrapped equals exactly, in tonnage terms, new building, supply would increase because the new tonnage will be more transport efficient. Such an increase in supply is reflected in a shift of the whole supply curve to the right. A movement in the tramp sector supply curve can only be achieved by a movement into another short-run period, what can be termed a one period lag in the adjustment of the supply of tonnage. Figure 10.11 illustrates such an increase in supply.

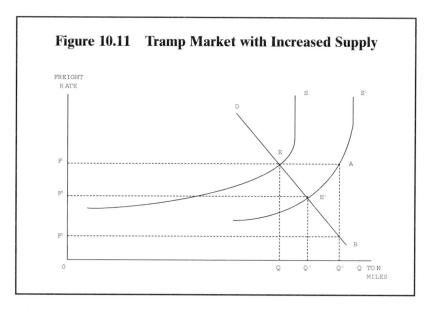

Figure 10.11   Tramp Market with Increased Supply

The figures of the tramp freight markets illustrate similar instabilities as the previous figure but from a different aspect, supply. Demand is assumed to remain constant during the period of adjustment. The demand curve indicated by D. The original market supply curve is S with the prevailing freight rate F^1 at equilibrium E and the quantity of tonnage supplied Q. The entry of new tonnage in the new short-run period moves the supply curve completely to the right S to S^1. There is a surplus of tonnage of Q to Q^2 or (E to A). This quantity is consistent with point B on the demand curve. At such a point, the appropriate freight rate would be F^2, and at such a low rate, shipowners would begin to remove tonnage from active supply. The process towards freight rate market stabilisation will continue until a new equilibrium E^1 is secured at freight rate F^3 at quantity Q^3.

The market interactions of supply and demand in the above model refer simply to per unit of time. The following Figure 10.12 is an attempt to highlight time and its influence on the market. The movement in the demand curves is similar to those illustrated in the expansion or movement towards boom in freight rate conditions in the figure below. The important difference here lies in the expansion in supply as a reaction to movements in demand and expectation. This can be seen from the inelastic full capacity section of the curve moving outwards from zero as potential supply increasingly becomes active supply.

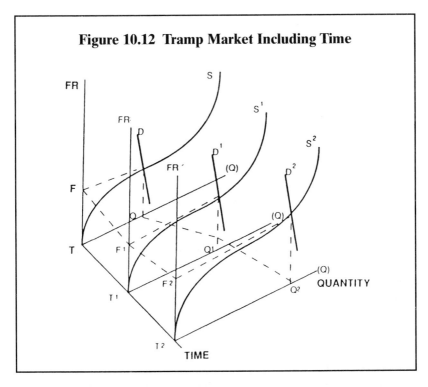

Figure 10.12 Tramp Market Including Time

(Based on Shimojo T 1979)

253

Figure 10.12 has three axes, the vertical one refers to the freight rate (FR), the central axis represents the quantity of tonnage (Q), and the third axes is time (T). S denotes the supply curve or tonnage capacity offered within the specific time period, D denotes demand curves. The freight rate is low at F. Demand D intersects the supply curve in its elastic region at Q. In the second time period, T^1, demand has moved to the right and is entering the increasingly inelastic region of the supply curve. The supply curve has moved marginally out, this is the 'wait and see' period when movement of available supply to active supply is minimal. At this time the freight rate rises to F^1 and quantity supplied to Q^1. The third period denoted by T^2 sees the beginning of the boom with shipowners' expectations rising. Demand has continued to increase and is now intersecting with an expanding supply. It is assumed that the available supply has in the time period T^2 become active supply. S^2 has moved outward as has Q^2 increasing to the limits of full capacity. Freight rates have been dampened by the increase in supply and has reached F^2 levels. The three demand models could be constructed to include the entrance of all potential supply to the market or a contraction in freight rates. What the figure attempts to do is to add a further dimension, time, to the previous discussion.

This discussion of the tramp sector of dry bulk cargo shipping shows that the element of the freight market in both the demand and supply sides creates forces inducing rapid fluctuations in freight rate. Often in practice these freight rate fluctuations are violent responses to marginal developments in demand and supply of tonnage. All the evidence of the freight rate movement over time serves to confirm that the market in this sector is highly competitive. In this unstable competitive tramp freight market the contraction of demand creates considerably more problems than an expansion in demand. The above discussion indicates that overcapacity is a far greater problem than under capacity in the freight rate cycle. This capacity being created to satisfy previous short-term freight booms. In a market suffering from overcapacity, a falling market, individual owners finding themselves in trading difficulties. That is the position where freight rates fall below their lay-up points, leaving owners with three options, either to lay-up, scrap, or sell their tonnage into the second-hand market. Such tonnage presumably remaining in the active supply. These responses to changing competitive market conditions rest on the individual shipowner as a freight or price taker who passively accepts current freight rate levels as given and over which the shipowner has no influence.

For much of the time overcapacity is endemic in this sector of the industry giving rise to another form of response, not individual but collective. Here shipowners organise themselves in some way to exercise a co-ordinated control over the amount of tonnage offered on the market. This represents a collective measure by individual owners co-operating as a more or less committed group who no longer perceive themselves as price or freight rate takers unquestioningly accepting current market rates but who attempt to organise an improvement in these rates. This is done by a systematic withdrawal of tonnage and the discouraging or inhibiting of new building. The institution of such systems means the shipowner's response moves from being passive to active.

In the course of the history of the dry cargo tramp sector and the tanker sector too, there have been numerous examples of the establishment of freight stabilisation associations in one form or another. For example it is claimed that one of the last gestures towards the economic survival of sailing ships was to organise a minimum freight rate agreement in 1905. This, like many later agreements, was an attempt to set the level of freight rates. It is a form of organisation usually referred to under the general heading of 'Tonnage Stabilisation Schemes'.

Such schemes come under three broad headings: minimum freight rate agreements, organised lay-up, and scrap and build. The intention of all these schemes has been to raise the level of freight rates and in doing so bring confidence and stability back to the tramp sector. These schemes were established in periods of prolonged depression in the freight rate market where demand has contracted and the industry is operating at a level below or substantially below full capacity.

A minimum freight rate agreement in the dry cargo trade is when all participants in the agreement undertake not to fix a cargo below the collectively agreed freight rate. In addition there is often combined in these agreements stipulations that no owners would despatch a vessel in ballast to any loading area unless there is a secure, that is, fixed charter for the return voyage. Such agreements stipulate the minimum freight rate members could accept and they have complete freedom to secure higher rates should a shipper make such an offer. There were a number of schemes attempted during the interwar years. The best known is the 'Tramp Shipping Administrative Committee'. It secured support from British and other governments and achieved some limited success. There are a number of reasons for this. Not least it began its operation as the cyclical trends in the freight market began to improve. Another reason is that minimum freights were fixed on a limited number of routes, for example the grain trade between Australia and Europe and the River Plate trade. Other routes of presumably lesser importance were allowed to fall unhindered and time charters were not included in the scheme. This will be examined using Figure 10.13.

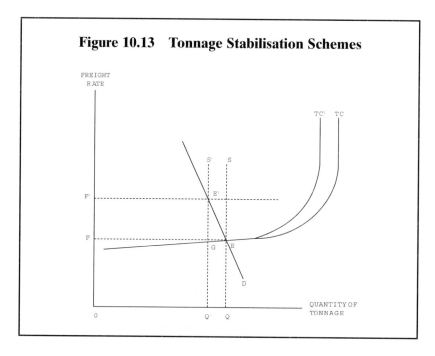

Figure 10.13   Tonnage Stabilisation Schemes

The underlying assumption here is that demand has contracted and the industry is in a period of prolonged depressed freight rates. Obviously a considerable amount of tonnage is laid up. The industry is operating well below full capacity. In the figure the active supply is OQ and the total revenue is OFEQ. The objective of the scheme is to raise freight rates to F^1, that is to fix the minimum freight rate at this level. The new minimum freight rate means some withdrawal along the demand curve from E to E^1 and a corresponding contraction of supply from Q to Q^1. This contraction in supply entails a loss of total revenue $Q.Q^1.G.E$. This is a loss more than compensated for by the increased revenue $F.F^1.E^1.G$. with a new equilibrium being created at E^1.

The organised lay-up scheme is where members agree to lay-up some of their more costly tonnage recouping compensation for this action from those owners whose vessels remain in operation. Typical of this form of scheme was one established by the International Shipowners Association in the late 1950s[10] under the control of the Tonnage Stabilisation Association Ltd. This became operational during the freight slump of the early 1960s. Initially the scheme was open to deep sea dry cargo tramps over 5000 dwt with the obligation that all tonnage active or laid up be offered for entry to the scheme. The scheme was not linked to any form of minimal freight rate or compulsory lay-up. There was a small entrance fee for administrative purposes and contributions to the Association became payable on securing a charter. The appropriate levels of contribution were based on gross freight rates or voyage charter rates. These were placed in a freight pool. The percentage of freight contributions to the pool of operating ships were on the following scales:

- 10% entered tonnage laid up, the remaining 90% contributed approximately 1.25% of their freights.
- 15% entered tonnage laid up, the remaining 85% contributed approximately 2% of their freight.
- 25% entered tonnage laid up, the remaining 75% contributed approximately 3.25% of their freights.

At the outset the Association provisionally estimated 75% of the world's eligible tramp tonnage would be essential should the scheme achieve any success. Such a level of co-operation was never achieved and the scheme was ended within two or three years.

In the dry cargo freight rate depression of the late 1970s the idea of a lay-up scheme re-emerged in the form of an organisation known as Intercargo, an association of international dry cargo shipowners and operators. A scheme was instituted to include all dry cargo motor ships, steam turbine vessels were not included. It also took into account the apparently recent development of combination carriers and such vessels of 10,000 dwt and over were included. Vessels on charter, laid up or operating the liner trade were not eligible to join. The principles on which the organisation was based were non-acceptance of a freight rate fixture that failed to cover operating costs. In line with other schemes it prohibited the sailing of vessels in ballast and unfixed, that is speculative voyages, to a loading region. The cancelling or postponing of new building contracts, unless they were tied to long-term charter contracts were also included in the scheme. The central feature of this scheme was the establishment of a new company whose only function was to charter laid up vessels at $1 per year with the duty to release them back on the market only with the return of a stable period of buoyant freight rates. Each owner was free to lay-up 20% to 30% of their dry cargo tonnage, that meant chartering it to the above company. The scheme did not succeed it has been suggested because of the freight rate improvement of the turn of the decade 1970 to 1980. Be this as it may the important difference was a general lack of support which meant it failed to possess comprehensive cover of this sector.

Returning to the earlier model Figure 10.13 the initial position is one of a low freight rate, operators are well below full capacity. Along the total supply curve the quantity of active tonnage is Q. The equilibrium freight rate is denoted by E. In return for financial inducements or compensation vessels, within the proximity of their lay-up points would be encouraged to become inactive, that is to lay-up. This is a method of collectively encouraging a contraction in quantities of tonnage supplied. In this way a new curve is created Q^1S^1 engendering a new equilibrium at E^1 and causing an increase in the freight rate to F^1. The major or central difference between this scheme and the ones previously discussed, that or minimum freight rate agreements, is that the present scheme does not stipulate minimum freight rate level rather it encourages a contraction in supply as a way of improving from the shipowners' point of view the level of freight rates. The model indicates that the shippers are paying a higher freight rate, F^1, and being offered less tonnage, OQ^1. For tramp shipowners operating tonnage the collective revenue has improved substantially from being area $OFEQ^1$ to area $OF^1E^1Q^1$ Whether they are collectively better or worse off financially is dependent primarily on the elasticity of demand from tramp shipping services. In the above figure, assuming the slope of the supply curve indicates elasticity, and the demand curve is inelastic as argued, and there will be an increased total revenue from decreased tonnage. Should the demand curve be elastic rather than inelastic the improved revenue situation would not follow. Any important change in supply elasticity would also raise the question of revenue levels.

Scrap and build schemes are merely mentioned here as being relevant to the present discussion. The figure indicates the contraction in total capacity TC to TC^1. The impact on the immediate situation would be dependent on the type of tonnage scrapped and built. Presumably such a policy would impact on the whole length of the supply curve to analyse this would require a considerably more detailed set of information, hence it is not being undertaken in the present context.

The discussion and the model serve to highlight the methods of operation and the problems confronting such schemes. The central objective has been to increase freight rates, create stability or a semblance of stability and in this way engender confidence within the freight market. Generally they have failed or at best had limited success in particularly favourable operating circumstances. There appears to be a number of insurmountable difficulties in establishing a successful cartel of this type. While there has been no consideration here of the demand side of the market, the shippers' opposition, tacit or otherwise, can be expected. It is doubtful whether they would support a venture whose general objective was to increase their freight burden. It has been suggested that they would be prepared to do so if assured of a medium or long-run freight stability but this has never as yet been achieved. On the other hand if they were denied any choice in the matter, that is to say there was no alternative supplies available these schemes would probably have more chance of success. Such a situation has never arisen as shippers have always been able to draw on non-participating tramp tonnage and those participating in the scheme who despite this have made offers secretly or otherwise. In addition there has always been the influence or influx of competing operators from other sectors, keen to secure cargoes in lean periods, for example cargo liners and tankers, the latter in the grain trade. There is a general sense running throughout any examination of stabilisation schemes in any form of the underlying idea of the movement towards a spirit of collective co-operation. This is a concept or philosophy in total contradiction to the aggressive individualistic entrepreneurial spirit of successful individual tramp shipowners. Slogans like 'gentleman's agreement' are concepts indicating the absence at the administrative centre of any disciplinary power over participants who contravene the rules established by the centre.

To create a hypothetical example the temptation presented to any individual owner with tonnage laid up seeing the improved freight rates secured by the cartel system to reactivate tonnage must be virtually irresistible. In this form of reaction lie the seeds of the destruction of the mechanism that defied the freight market and created the improvement in freight rates. This is the classic dilemma of all such schemes where there are numerous participants and no disciplinary power not even moral persuasion. The collective agreements are destroyed as the individual shipowners incentive to 'cheat' on such agreements increases as the number of participants to the agreement increase. History is thus strewn with attempts to fix the freight rates or control the tonnage supplied.

Comments in Conclusion

The central analysis in this chapter has been based on the presumption that the dry bulk cargo market is perfectly competitive, but in recent years this presumption has been questioned. This has been on the basis that by taking advantage of economies of scale, with increased specialisation of vessel type and service, the shipowner has encouraged the development of a growing diversity of charter terms both generally and in detail. In particular the movement towards long-term arrangements. During the 1960s long-term contracts became increasingly accepted as they gave security for the financing of the ship's construction. Such secure charter payments are sufficient to meet amortisation of loans from financial institutions. The arrangements usually meant that the shipowners operated at a negotiated charter rate with the charterer sharing in some measure in the risk of the venture. The extent of such ventures in the less favourable market conditions, from the shipowners' point of view, in the mid 1970s, is not clear. This began a long period of excess capacity and persistently low freight rates. This was a situation causing the demand side of the market to possess the upper hand which meant that charterers became increasingly selective about tonnage usually relating to costs. Some were accused of chartering often rather unsuitable tonnage simply on the basis of cost considerations. In this market depression shipowning firms became increasingly unwilling to contract for the building of specialised tonnage capable of operating only in limited and specific sectors of the market if they lacked the security of medium or long-term contracts. Despite this, a number of authorities have argued that, particularly in these years of depressed freight rate, the charterer has begun to possess a growing influence on the market. A number of reasons or methods are cited for this trend. The progressive use of medium and long-term charters, strength, the ability of larger cargo owners or charterers to influence the market especially where there are a small number of substantial charters. One suggestion is that such influences have often been strengthened by such substantial charterers operating their own tonnage in the expanding industrial carriers sector. Influences of this type,

261

along with that of certain governments, (the latter particularly in the grain trade) have raised the spectre of 'price discrimination'. This implies some level of monopoly of oligopoly power exerted either on the individual shipowner or within a section of the market. Such cases are difficult to substantiate as it is often a condition of the charter that its details and freight rates are confidential. This denies the perfect knowledge necessary in a competitive market. It is also not clear how far contracts of affreightment fit into this idea of a changing balance and level of influence within the market. Such an argument suggest that the substantial charterer exerts undue influence through tonnage ownership and type of charter. These and other factors, combined with the level of long-run expectations about the condition of the freight rate market serve to distort an otherwise competitive market.

The answer to this criticism is based on what is regarded as the central importance of the spot market freight rate, not only to the comparatively small tramp sector, but to the whole of the bulk trade. This approach is based on the assumption that both sides of the market, shipowners and charterers, are primarily concerned with the recent and current periods and the immediate future when making charter rate decisions. An argument of what has become known as 'short- termism', but here with long-term ramifications. long-term charter policies are concerned with the present or next freight rate period. This means that medium or long-term charters are constructed in all essentials on short-run perspectives. Time charter rates tend to be at a high level when the voyage charter spot rate is on a rising trend. In such market conditions shipowners demand high rates for the presumed disadvantage of committing their tonnage for an extended period. If the spot rate is declining charterers seek a lower long-term freight rate, a rate which shipowners with depressed expectations will accept to secure employment for their tonnage. Here lies the crux of the argument: the idea that time charter rates in all essentials are simply a reflection of the current spot rate at the time of negotiating the time charter.

This hypothesis has a number of implications. It dismisses expectation of the future to a minimal position at best, while not totally dismissing the earlier discussion of undue influence with the process of establishing a long-term charter rate again gives it limited importance. The curtailing of these two factors' level of importance is to reinforce the primacy given to the spot freight market is the formation of all other freight rates. It follows that long-term charters are ineffectual in preventing or distorting the freight market in any positive way because their central point of reference is the current spot rate.

There are undoubtedly certain respects in which the bulk shipping market does not function fully as a perfectly competitive market. However the core questions is: does the dry bulk cargo freight market, or any section of it, conform to the theoretical perfectly competitive model and if not to any degree, what relevance has the analysis to such a notion? The answer to the first part of the question is complex from any aspect, particularly on the supply side of the industrial sector approximate to perfect competition. As far as sectors of the market are concerned the answer is best put thus: tramp shipping is an industry that has a market which functions under conditions that are not dissimilar to the theoretical model of perfect competition.

The other part of the question is: does the notion of perfect competition assist in developing some measure of desirable performance applicable to the industry. To that extent it is relevant in an intelligent evaluation of economic performance. Interwoven in the above chapter was the notion of a perfectly competitive model creating the standard criteria by which activities of non-competitive market can be judged. Despite that necessity of oversimplification and construction of assumptions (and thus once removed from reality) it provides a relatively simple model of the general functioning of the freight market system. This gives some insights into pricing, entry and output decisions of use in understanding the operation of any less than perfect industrial model. The bulk dry cargo freight market is competitive enough to make the conclusions derived from the study of the perfect market practically relevant.

Summary

This chapter began by examining the dynamic changes that have taken place in the Dry Bulk Cargo market in recent years. This is best illustrated by the movement from what are now termed handy size tramp tonnage to bulk vessels, a process termed as 'bulkerisation' The general growth in the volume of trade and tonnage, has increased the extent of competition from other sectors. There is also considerable competition within this sector of industry, between shipping firms. The argument was put forward that this competitive market structure was similar to that of perfect competition. Much of the latter part of the chapter was based on the assumptions of such a competitive market. The effect of changes in demand, supply and these elasticities being considered. Both sides in the market it was argued, are (price) freight takers. The final section looks at stabilisation schemes which are attempts to influence the freight rate by restricting the supply of active tonnage.

Further Reading

Metaxas B.N. *The Economics of Tramp Shipping*
London. Athlone Press 1971.
Metaxas B.N. *The Future of the Tramp Shipping Industry*
Journal of Transport Economics & Policy, V1(3)
September 1972.
Norman V.D *Market Strategies in Bulk Shipping*
in Hope E. Studies in Shipping Economics.
Oslo, Bedriftsokonomens, Forlag A/S 1981.

Rogers P. Strange and Studd B. Shimojo T. *Coal Carriage by Sea*. 2nd Edition London.
Lloyds of London Press 1997.
Economic Analysis of Shipping Freights
Kobe, Research Institute for Economic and Business Administration, Kobe University,
1979.

[1] Gripaious, H. Tramp Shipping
London, Thomas Nelson and Son Ltd. 1959, p9
[2] For the details of crisis see Chapter 11
[3] Similar agreements also operate in the bulk tanker market
[4] Discussed in detail in Chapter 8
[5] Boulding K.E. Economic Analysis (4th Edition) Vol. 1
London, Harper & Brothers, 1966 para 409.
[6] See Chapters 3 and 6.
[7] See Chapter 11
[8] See Chapter 11 for cobweb theory and further discussion.
[9] See Metaxas. B.N. The Economics of Tramp Shipping
London, Athlone Press, 1971 - Chapter 10. pp229 - 249

Chapter Eleven

TANKER MARKET

Introduction

Tankers are the most highly specialised sector of the industry. They are vessels designed to carry liquid cargo in bulk. A tanker is at it simplest a group of tanks within a ship's hold, with an engine at the stern. The crude oil carrier is the least complicated vessel to build and operate. They concentrate on the movement in bulk of crude oil, although, occasionally, in particular freight market conditions, they will have ventured into the movement of grain. A sub-group in this market are the combination carriers. These have the facility to carry oil or bulk dry cargo. There are a number of combinations, the most common being O. B. O. which are Ore Bulk Oil carriers. Such flexibility allows tonnage to switch between markets, or often, of more importance, to reduce the time spent operating in ballast. Another specialised sub-section of the trade is the product or parcel tanker. There are a variety of these, carrying clean, refined or specialised products, like liquid gas. In addition, there are what can be termed fringe commodities, such as wine, orange juice, molasses, asphalt. These sub-sections are overshadowed by the vast majority of tonnage engaged in the conveyance of crude oil. In 1995, these carriers constituted 36% of the world fleet, while the

267

more sophisticated and expensive specialised tonnage constituted some 4% of the world fleet. Hence, the present discussion will concentrate wholly on the bulk crude tanker market.

The movement of bulk liquid requires a specific technology, with limited alternative uses, so the tankers represent a specialised industrial or tramp operation. Despite similarities with the dry bulk carrying market, they have to be considered as an individual sector. This is not only due to the enormous size of the sector, but directly to the economical impact of these specialisations, which causes their operational activities to differ in two essential ways. Firstly, they normally convey a full cargo in one direction, followed by a similar voyage in ballast. They have no alternative cargo. These technical imperatives mean that the vessel must return to its starting point, with the cost implications of a non-freight earning back haul. In economics this is termed a **"Joint Cost"** problem, that simply, the production of the freight-earning voyage entails the production of a non-earning voyage. No revenue is earned, but there are the costs of production.

The second feature is the length of time spent in port. Here the difference between dry cargo is stark. Tankers have, since their inception, taken a very short time to load and unload, an advantage achieved by complex gravity or cargo pumping systems. Such short periods in port have been the essential factor in the movement towards larger vessels, thus having an impact on the cost structure of the largest mobile construction in the world.

Developments Since the Second World War

In any consideration of the sea-borne trade in oil since the second world war, the predominant feature is its huge expansion at every level. Oil production growth was matched by a similar expansion in its international sea-borne trade, the size of the fleet serving that trade, and the size of the individual vessels in the fleet. This massive expansion is summarised in the following table:

Table 11. 1

**The Development in the International Sea-borne
Trade of Oil 1938-1995**

YEAR	1938	1955	1960	1965	1970	1975	1980	1985	1990	1995
World Production (M. Tons)	278	792	1,092	1,565	2,550	2,734	3,082	2,806	3,179	3,248
Seaborne Trade (M. Tons)	-	350	540	860	1,440	1,644	1,871	1,459	1,755	2050
World Tankers (M.D.W. T)	16. 6	41. 0	63. 0	88. 7	151. 7	291. 4	324. 8	246. 7	258. 1	267. 6
Tankers as % of World Fleet (GRT)	19	28	33	35	38	44	42	33	32	36
Tankers Average size (D.W.T 000)	-	15.0	21. 1	28. 8	46. 9	79. 3	97. 3	85. 8	84. 6	86. 6

Source: Various

Oil production more than doubled between 1945-1950 reaching approximately 500 million tons, and a decade later, in 1960, it had doubled again. During the next decade, there was a remarkable growth as production doubled once more and, by 1975, it stood at some 2,734 million tons. It has been estimated that, during the fifty years prior to the crisis of l973, the supply of oil grew at some 5.5% per annum. Following the high level of 1980, production had contracted to 2,800 million tons and, during the 1990s the production oscillated around the 3,000 million tons mark. In terms of oil production, there had been a fairly constant expansion until 1973, but, since then, output has been uneven. The crisis of 1973 destroyed the presumption of steady long-term growth. Sea-borne trade in oil followed, as would be expected, along a similar line to that of world oil production, and initially, a rapid growth in post-war decades followed by a slowdown in the 1970s. The turning point to serious decline was in 1979 and this change was confirmed during the 1980s, with a recovery in the 1990s.

The long-term trends in tanker tonnage, and the percentage of the world fleet, moved in a similar way. In terms of GRT, the percentage peak came in 1976, contracting rapidly to the mid 1990s. The average size (dwt) of vessels continued to rise until the 1980s. The movement in size broadly doubled each decade until the 1980s. Since then, there has been some contraction in the average size of vessels.

Early in the period under consideration, the growth in vessel size can be seen as a classical example of economies of scale, with the size of the vessel being responsible for the decline in transport costs particularly in the 1960s and 1970s. Later these were due to changes in a combination of factors. The average cost of transporting a barrel of oil, in a large vessel, over an average voyage decreased from approximately $2.25 in the mid 1950s to $1 two decades later. This decrease can be attributed mainly to geometry. If for example a tanker of 20,000 dwt is used as a base line, a tanker of 200,000 dwt is approximately twice its length, beam, and draft, but can carry ten times as much cargo. In addition, in building cost terms per dwt, the large vessel cost in the 1970s only one third that of the smaller vessel. Operating costs can also decline per dwt as the vessel's size increases. All these factors encouraged the trend towards larger vessels.

This growth in oil production and utilisation had been due to a combination of convenience and price. Some 90% of oil is used as an energy source. The remainder is used in lubricants, bitumen manufacture and other specialised products. As an energy source, it has always been in competition with coal and, during recent years, natural gas . In the generation of electricity, it has been in competition with minor producers like hydro and nuclear power. In energy use, there has, as yet, been no practical alternative for transport, in all its modes. In most applications, oil has certain technical and physical advantages over coal, although these are not quite so clear in relation to natural gas. The choice between oil and coal is usually made on the lower capital costs associated with burning oil and its conversion, but mainly on price, particularly long-run price. In the period from 1945 to 1973, it was the combination of convenience and comparative price which created the increased consumption of oil. During the late 1950s and early 1960s, oil became cheaper than coal for the first time. This, combined with the enormous increase in over-all demand for energy and the dramatic growth in all forms of transport particularly individual road transport in OECD countries, was the primary factor in the growth in demand for oil. Following this short summary, some of the underlying factors will be examined in more detail, before relating them to a micro-economic analysis. The first issue is the price of oil, which helps explain the experience of the sea-borne trade sector of the oil industry since 1950. The following figure shows the general trend in oil prices, using Arabian Light Crude Oil as the benchmark.

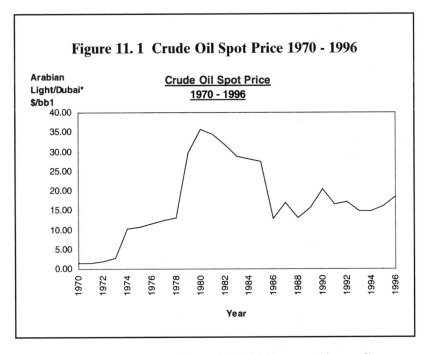

Figure 11. 1 Crude Oil Spot Price 1970 - 1996

Source: BP Statistical Review of World Energy (Annual)

Throughout the 1950s prices remained low, apart from, in retrospect, some minor movements around the Suez crisis in 1956. Such price levels were important in undermining competitive fuels and encouraging oil use. At these levels, prices exceeded the long-run supply price, hence the oil business, in all its stages, remained extremely profitable. With ease, price could be modified slightly to offset any additional supply cost and increase to secure profit levels. However, during the 1960s, the highly favourable positions of both producer countries and oil companies began to deteriorate, under the impact of a world surplus of oil production capacity. Under such pressure, price weakened to the very low level of $1. 60 in 1970. In analysing these price changes, the relationship which developed between the multi-nationals cannot be underestimated, mainly involving American oil companies and the governments of oil producing nations.

This was reinforced by the geographical structure of the industry's markets. The great increase in oil demand was predominantly from OECD countries, in particular Western Europe, Japan and the USA. The latter a substantial consumer of oil having changed from being a net exporter to a net importer in the late 1960s. The supply was drawn in the main from non-industrial developing nations, the Middle East, the Caribbean, North and West Africa and South-East Asia. The major oil companies had retained their flexibility by increasing the regions of production. Hence, the enthusiasm the major companies had for new oil exploration in Libya, in the late 1950s and the early 1960s, and, since then, for Alaska, and the North Sea etc. Such flexibility was a factor in enabling companies to withstand pressure exerted by governments of the long-standing production regions. This regional spread of oil production was not to the clear advantage of maritime transport, as many of the new oil producing regions were close to consumer markets.

The pressure on the oil price due to surplus production, was at a time when oil companies "posted" the crude oil price. The reductions of the 1960s meant the government revenues from their oil producing industries were contracting. This was based on some percentage calculation of the posted price. The results of finding their revenues falling due to low prices was instrumental in the formation of the Organisation of Petroleum Exporting Countries (OPEC) in 1960. This comprised 13 countries including Saudi Arabia, Iran, Kuwait, Venezuela and Nigeria. Its main object was to collectively increase their bargaining position vis-a-vis the oil multinationals. A key aim was to prevent the oil companies playing one country off against another. During the next decade, OPEC played a comparatively minor role, failing to develop any strategy in relation to controlling, regulating output, or in consolidating its relationship with the oil companies.

The lack of any consensus persisted until the winter of 1970 when, at a meeting in Caracas, OPEC declared its intention to take control of supply and, hence, price. By 1973, it had consolidated its price strategy, initially through the introduction of 'Net Book Prices' and, later, by production quotas.

In that year, against the background of the Middle East War (Yom Kippur), OPEC assumed complete control and doubled the price. Thus, after 20 years of low-cost oil it rose to just short of $5 a barrel. In less than three months, it doubled again to $10.70. The oil price advantage over alternative sources of energy, in particular coal had disappeared within less than 12 months. At the same time, the major industrial economies went into recession, an element of this being the sudden increase in oil prices after such a sustained period of low price stability. The Iranian revolution of 1979 caused the price to double again in that year. Prices remained high throughout the first half of the 1980s, and, by 1983, there were signs of some modification in price, with a substantial fall in 1986 to $13 a barrel. The low price was an important factor in the increase in demand from the OECD countries and, in particular, Europe, Japan and the United States. The latter was of particular importance for, while USA domestic production was declining, there had been a steady increase in the quantity imported, up to 40% of consumption. By the end of the decade, the price again increased, under the influence of the Kuwait War. It has since declined to movements around $15 a barrel.

These changes in crude oil prices also meant a change in **bunker costs**, that is, the cost of ships' fuel oil. Pre 1973, there were some minor variations to bunker prices, particularly in reaction to the first Suez closure of 1956, but prices were low, in the region of $20 a ton. There was also some differentiation between bunker visits in different ports. These low prices of bunker fuel meant that any saving through strategic buying was limited. Under such long-term low cost conditions, tanker owners were not very interested in fuel costs, hence the movement to high powered turbine-driven vessels, with the advantage of low maintenance costs, combined with the disadvantage of high fuel consumption

Using Rotterdam bunker prices for January of each year as an example, in 1970 it stood at $20 a ton, in 1973 at $30 and in 1974 at $75. Hence, in four years the price had increased threefold. It stabilised until 1979-1981, when another massive increase was experienced, taking the price to $186. Empirical research suggests that, in 1970, bunkers accounted for about a tenth of operating costs. By the early 1980s, it was a third, and that was despite modifications in vessel technology. Such a rapid change quickly concentrated the minds of shipowners towards a number of policies aimed at curtailing bunker costs. The collapse in freight rates (discussed below) was a further prompt. Apart from leaving the active market by laying up or scrapping, there was re-engineering to a lower fuel-cost-consuming means of propulsion, slow steaming, as well as using bunker price differentiation to good advantage by means of strategic purchasing policies.

From the tanker sector the importance of distance between location of consumer and crude oil producer has already been mentioned. An important relocation was the movement of refineries from the region of the well towards the market. There were a number of reasons for this. Primarily, it was to satisfy the massive increase in demand from the developed economies of the OECD. Secondly, the advance in refining techniques meant local market requirements could be satisfied. There was no longer excessive unusable waste, since crude oil cargoes were almost totally utilised. The economic and technological relocation was confirmed and encouraged by political events, for example, the Iranian nationalisation of the Anglo-Iranian companies oil refinery at Abadan in 1951. The most obvious impact on the industry was the development of large bulk crude oil tankers. In the interwar period, the majority of tankers were, comparatively small refined product carriers. The improvement in refining techniques and their relocation meant that, not only was there a growth in the number of tankers, but also the large homogeneous cargo-carrying tanker could be developed.

Expansion

Table 11.1 illustrated, in percentage terms, the growth in importance of the tanker fleet as a proportion of the world supply of merchant shipping. It stood at 21%, in 1950 peaking in the mid 1970s at 45% of GRT, followed by a contraction to 32% in 1990, with a small percentage increase since. The expansion and contraction in the tanker fleet and its level of activities is illustrated in table 11.2:

Table 11.2   Development of the Tanker Trade 1950-1990 (% variation per annum)

Section A

Section B

PERIOD	TONNAGE (GRT)	TONNAGE SHIPMENTS	TONNAGE TRANSPORT PERFORMANCE	AVERAGE VOYAGE DISTANCE	PERIOD
1950-1965	8. 0	9. 5	-	-	1950-65
1965-1970	9. 4	10. 5	16. 0	7,060	1965-73
1970-1975	11. 8	-	-	-	-
1975-1980	3. 1	0. 2	-0. 9	6,970	1973-80
1980-1985	-4. 6	-	-	-	-
1985-1990	1. 7	0	-2	4. 620	1980-90

Source: Maritime Transport OECD (Annual)

The table (section A) shows the growth rate in terms of GRT increasing in the decades before the 1970s. This was often in excess of 9%. In the period 1970 to 1975, it leapt to 11. 8 %. Much of this tonnage was ordered before the autumn of 1973 and delivered afterwards. This growth persisted until the 1980s. The second oil shock of 1979 created considerable pessimism. In the last five years of the table, there have been some improvements in terms of tonnage, but the heady days of the late 1960s and early 1970s are over.

In terms of shipping activity (section B) that is tonnage shipped and ton mileage (Tonnage Transport Performance), a similar trend can be seen. In the period 1950 to 1973 the steady increase in tonnage shipped is highlighted, with a 10% per annum growth. The impact of the 1973 crisis is clear here, with the decline to a low if positive level. Post the 1979 crisis, there is no growth at all. Ton mileage performance is even more dramatic in the period 1965-1973, and growth in ton miles is in the region of 16%. This is, of course, heavily influenced by the closure of the Suez Canal in 1967, not only increasing the length of voyages, but creating a shortage of tonnage. This encouraged the trend towards larger vessels which had already begun. The situation post 1973 illustrates not only the impact of the crisis but the loss of the hegemony of the Arabian Gulf.

Table 11. 3   Volume of Tankers Completed 1966 -1988 (+ 10000 Dwt)

Period	No. of Ships	Million DWT
1966-1979	2,359	299. 14
(VLCC)	(737)	(193. 88)
1980-1988	958	54. 06
(VLCC)	(41)	10. 63
Total	3,317	353. 20
(VLCC)	(778)	(204. 52)

Source: Jamri Report on Shipping & Ship Building 1990 P24.

The expansion in tanker tonnage, which had been gradual throughout the 1950s and early 1960s, gathered pace during the late 1960s and early 1970s, reaching a peak in terms of new completions in 1975. Table 11.3 illustrates the rate of change during the whole period.

The table shows that the total number of vessels newly built in the 22 year period 1966 to 1988 stood at 3,317. Of these, VLCCs, that is a very large crude carrier being vessels over 200,000 dwt, constituted some 778 or 23% of tanker tonnage. Some of these, later in the period, would be ULCCs, ultra large crude carriers, vessels over 350,000 D.W.T. In tonnage terms, during the same period, some 353. 2 million dwt were delivered, of which 204 million dwt were VLCCs or 58% of tanker tonnage. If the period is broken down into years, the tonnage peaks in the middle years of the 1970s. The year 1975 sees the highest level of completions. In that year 326 tankers of some 43. 34 million dwt entered the fleet, of which 108 vessels of some 29. 86 million dwt were VLCCs, or 68% of the total. In the fourteen years from the debut of the VLCC in 1966-1979, they consisted of some 65% of the total tonnage of 299. 14 million dwt. The annual average volume of tankers completed during the period was approximately 21. 36 million dwt. In the second period under consideration, 1980 - 1988, which were years of constant depression in the tanker freight market, the annual average completion fell to 6. 01 million dwt. The share of VLCCs collapsed to a mere 18%, that is, 10. 63 million dwt. Hence the days of substantial investment were over by the year of the Iranian Revolution, 1979. Still in the five year period from 1972-1976 some 478 VLCCs were built, a sum total of approximately 12. 9 million dwt.

In retrospect, it is difficult to understand why such an orgy of investment in shipping should have been embarked upon in the early 1970s. Much of the tonnage was delivered post the 1973 crisis, despite numerous cancellations of orders. It is suggested that the closure of the Suez Canal (1967), combined with the enthusiasm with which financial institutions engaged in shipping investment, is relevant here. What is clear is that expectations were extremely high. Such optimism can be illustrated by

277

quoting the annual report of the OECD "Maritime Transport" for 1970. This repeats a section of another report from the same institution:

"We possess [now] the experience of a quarter of a century of virtually uninterrupted growth - an unprecedented record in the economic history of modem times, as regards both the length and strength of the expansion. This record points to the existence of strong forces built into modern economies, favouring growth. Rapid technological progress, constantly rising expectations of consumers, dynamic attitudes of firms towards investment and innovation, the willingness to engineer and to absorb change have acquired a quasi-automatic or spontaneous character: these are all self-reproducing causes of, and have self- reinforcing effects on the growth process. Even government policies share these characteristics. "[2]

The Report does comment that this statement may convey undue optimism, but the quote used is of some interest, as its central idea is of some self-reproducing, re-inforcing, and easily absorbed mechanism for dynamic growth. This is not only indicative of this period, but is also an important influence in it. In such an economic atmosphere, it is hardly surprising that large amounts of surplus tonnage appeared quite rapidly. The same report for 1975 comments:

"Then during the last two years demand has ceased to grow, and even decline, while supply increased at a rate even faster than in the past. As a result, the world tanker market found itself, at the end of 1975, with an over-capacity in excess of 115 million dwt, equivalent to approximately 37% of the total fleet available to transport required quantities of crude and oil products, under full operation in 1975"[3]

What this highlights is the fundamental supply and demand imbalance, which becomes obvious with the crisis of 1973 and is confirmed with that of 1979. The level of capacity utilisation persists throughout the 1980s, and into the 1990s, although with differing degrees of intensity. An analysis of that over-supply is shown in Table 11.4:

TABLE 11. 4 Analysis of Tonnage Oversupply - Tankers 1980-1995
(Average year figures in million dwt)

	1980	1981	1982	1983	1984	1985	1986	1987	1988	1989	1990	1991	1992	1993	1994	1995
Supply of World tanker fleet	341. 8	341. 3	335. 0	319. 4	296. 7	273. 0	261. 7	255. 1	250. 6	253. 9	266. 2	273. 5	283. 4	284. 6	282. 9	277. 0
Total tanker surplus fleet of which:	74. 0 (21.6)	107. 7 (31.5)	130. 7 (39.0)	134. 0 (41.9)	111. 7 (37.6)	100. 9 (36.9)	68. 8 (26.2)	65. 8 (25.7)	54. 7 (21.8)	41. 0 (16.3)	40. 9 (15.3)	39. 8 (14.9)	41. 8 (14.7)	43. 5 (15.2)	39. 0 (13.7)	28. 8 (10.3)(2)
Laid up and idle	25. 3	41. 1	76. 7	89. 2	71. 3	68. 5	45. 1	40. 8	- (1)	-	-	-	-	-	-	-
Slow steaming	48. 3	66. 6	54. 0	71. 3	40. 4	32. 4	30. 6	34. 0	- (1)	-	-	-	-	-	-	-

Source: UNCTAD Review of Maritime Transport (Annual)
(1) Category not included in recent tables
(2) Surplus as % of total supply

Surplus tonnage is defined as not fully-utilised tonnage, which includes slow steaming, being laid up, or lying idle. It does not include other reasons, such as casualties, use as storage or under-going repair. Throughout the period, the tanker sector of the industry had the largest excess fleet and the majority of this was made up of VLCCs and ULCCs. As can be seen from the above table, a considerable amount of the estimated surplus is due to slow steaming. Initially, following the 1973 crisis, this was a method used by the oil majors in response to lower demand and increased bunker costs. Furthermore, it provided a form of in-transit storage easing pressure on shore storage capacity. It was a technique soon followed by the independents, as reducing speed lowers costs, particularly for bunkers, and influences the level of supply in a period of low freight rates. The importance of lay-up tonnage and slow steaming is reversed during the period. The latter was important at the beginning of the 1980s, the former later. What is most noticeable in the table is the steady growth of surplus tonnage during the early 1980s, reaching a peak in 1983, which, in real terms, was 134 million dwt or 42% of tanker tonnage. From this peak in over-supply, there has been a slow and, on these annual average figures, steady contraction, in both tonnage and percentage terms, to 10% by 1995. The other point of importance in the table is the reaction, not least to sub-optimal utilisation of total supply. This has been contracting through much of the decade and, in particular, the middle years. The stabilisation of tonnage at the end has not caused a return to the totals of the earlier years.

Tanker Freights

The tanker freight market operates with a high degree of instability, where changes in rates can occur suddenly and, on occasions, for reasons not immediately apparent. In general terms tanker rates are not dissimilar to those of the dry cargo market, but they are considerably more volatile. This volatility relates to a number of factors, two of which are central. Firstly the inelastic derived demand for tanker tonnage reacts rapidly to particular events, changes in climate, and levels of international and national business opportunism. Secondly, on occasions, the limited opportunities to increase or decrease short-run supply, particularlt in the region of full capacity, where total supply is active. The spot freight rate market can at times expose a combination of erratic demand with fixed supply in the short-run. The results bring a high fluctuating rate. As Figure 11.3 illustrates, there are periods of rapid increasing rates, following periods of comparative stability.

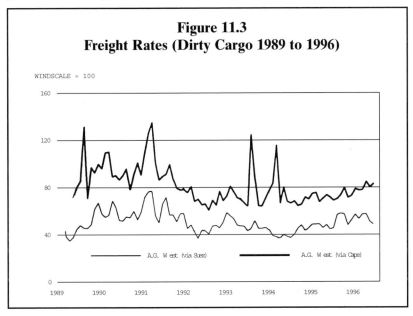

Figure 11.3
Freight Rates (Dirty Cargo 1989 to 1996)

As can be seen from the vertical axis, Tankers are 'fixed' chartered generally on **'World Scale'** rates. This is an index published in London, and based on the costs of operating a standard tanker over a specific route. In 1995 for example, the base of 100 was calculated on a tanker of 75,000 dwt, with operating costs taken into account.

The Economic Theory

This generalised empirical discussion will now be related to an economic analysis. As in previous chapters, this is a partial equilibrium analysis, in which one market, here the tanker market, is viewed in isolation, to discover and highlight the main effects of economic forces on the market. The central concern is with the tanker sector market and its movement in relation to some equilibrium position. The industry is, within a given level of technology, confronted by a dynamic demand situation and response comes from supply; and is continually adjusting to a new equilibrium. That is to say changes in economic and other conditions facing the industry will create changes in equilibrium levels.

Analysing these changes using the partial equilibrium method means an examination on two levels. Firstly, problems arising from economic disturbances, which are not of sufficient magnitude to move beyond the confines of the tanker sector. Secondly, the concern is with what is known as "first order effects" of economic or other disturbances outside the industry's confines. For example, as in the above discussion, major international calamities could increase the demand for crude oil and, hence, for tanker tonnage, suddenly and substantially. Partial equilibrium analysis of such an occurrence will provide answers to "first order" questions on the effect on the tanker market, discussing what will happen to demand for resources, the price, level of tonnage capacity, in relation to active supply and, of course, freight rates. These first order effects are the initial direct repercussions on the tanker sector. They are by no means the totality of effects; these will continue for a considerable time at a number of levels. They are not interwoven in the present level of analysis.

The earlier discussion concentrated on the major oil companies and their dominance of the oil market, which would suggest that it is an **oligopoly market**. That is a market structure with a few (more than two) firms supplying the product or service, each of which is conscious of the effect on it of any action on the part of its rivals[4]. All studies of the tanker industry contradict this view, claiming that it is a near perfect, or pure, competitive industry. The pioneer work on this was done by Koopmans (1939).[5] This was followed by Tinbergen (1959)[6] and perhaps the best known is Zannetos (1966)[7]. In the latter's seminal work on the tanker market, he highlighted this apparent paradox:

"Does the tankship market then operate under the impact of oligopolistic influences? The answer is no! Although logic as well as ownership composition could imply the contrary, the tankship market operates more like a perfectly competitive market".[8]

The tanker market operates in a similar way to the dry bulk cargo tramp market discussed in the previous chapter. Similarly, here the discussion concentrates on the importance and influence of the competitive spot market, despite its limited size, often accounting for only 10% of total tanker capacity. It is used by the major oil companies to balance regional supply and demand and, in this way, a freight rate is established, which strongly influences all other rates. Although the exact extent of this influence is open to question, the above authors examined the characteristics of the tanker market and concluded that they could be broadly subsumed within the assumptions of the neo-classical perfect competition model.

To examine this assertion the behaviour of the consumer, the oil companies and the entrepreneurs (shipowners) will be analysed in the light of the assumption that they are unable to affect the freight rate at which offers and charters are made. Shipowners face a given cost structure and decide to produce a service level at which profits will be maximised.

Collectively the individual actions of the oil companies and shipowners determine the freight rate, which is then considered as the parameter of each company's actions on either side of the market. In this way the industry's aggregate demand and supply function is used for the determination of the international freight rate market equilibria. Further, this is a market containing no barriers of entry or exit and in which capital requirements on the supply side are comparatively modest. The tanker market is thus placed in the area of a perfectly competitive market. There is some deliberate reiteration here which serves to relate the theoretical structures discussed in Chapter 8 to this sector of the industry. These general assumptions of the economic models of pure or perfect competition to the characteristics of the tanker spot freight rate market will be applied in more detail in the following section.

Supply

1. Large Number of Buyers' and Sellers

There are many buyers facing many sellers. Each firm is small, relative to the total market demand and supply, in the sense that they act as price takers, convinced of their inability to affect the price, that is, the market freight rate for tonnage. Zannetos relates this to the tanker market, by analysing tanker ownership in 1959. Finding the tonnage owned by oil companies, in total, to be 34% of world capacity, with no single company owning more than 6.-7%. Of this 34% of world capacity, 68% was owned by the then five largest oil companies. In other words, the big 5 owned 24% of world capacity, independent owners controlling the remaining 67%. Governments are excluded from this analysis. The five largest independents controlled 13% of the world fleet and 19% of the independent fleet. It follows that the five major oil companies and the five largest independents together owned some 33%. It was calculated that there were some 600 tanker owners. The combined five oil companies and five largest independents constituted 1.5% of all tanker owners, owning 33% of the total capacity, the remaining 98.5% of owners controlled the remaining 67% of world capacity, very thinly dispersed.

An UNCTAD study, undertaken in 1969, came to similar, if less detailed, conclusions. It first pointed out that 42% of world dwt capacity was in tankers, and then proceeded to divide ownership and operation of tankers into three groups as follows:

a) "Tonnage owned and operated by oil companies, which amounts to approximately 35%-40% in terms of dwt capacity of the total tanker fleet.

b) Vessels owned by private firms, but hired to oil companies for periods covering all or most of the ship's useful life; this tonnage is approximately 40% - 45% of the world's tanker dwt capacity;.

c)   Tankers owned by private shipping firms and owner operators in
     the spot market as tramps for single voyages or a few consecutive
     voyages, or time chartered to oil companies for a short period. ''[9]

This analysis is brought up to date with the following table which
considers the structure over the last two decades.

**TABLE 11. 5   Percentage Share of Tanker Ownership
and Total Tonnage
(Tanker 10,000 + D. W. T.)**

YEAR	OIL COMPANY OWNED	PRIVATE (INDEPENDENT) OWNED	GOVERNMENT VESSELS	MISCELLANEOUS TANKERS	TOTAL D. W. T
1965	32	68	-	-	90. 1*
1970	32	63	6	0. 1	155. 7
1975	33	64	4	0. 2	291. 4
1978	34	60	4	2	328. 5
1980	36	57	4	3. 6	324. 9
1983	35	58	-	7	282. 2
1985	38	62	-	-	239. 1
1988	38	61	-	-	233. 6
1990	36	60	1. 1	2. 8	246. 6
1993	26	63	9	3	280. 1
1995	29	66	1	3. 5	283. 7

Source: J. I. Jacobs - World Tank Review (Bi-annual)
*2000 + D. W. T.

The table illustrates the growth in tanker capacity until the late
1970s and the subsequent gradual decline until the 1990s. The
surprising conclusion of the table is the consistency of chartering
share against the changing background of total capacity. Oil
companies own between 26% and 38% of total capacity,
independents owning between 57% and 68%. The other
categories are important, because of tankers used for storage
purposes, mainly during Arabian Gulf conflicts. These are mainly
privately-owned tonnage and, as such, make the independent
charterers' percentage more consistent.   Put simply, oil
companies own one third and independent private companies

two thirds, with ownership in both groups being thinly distributed.

This thin spread of ownership implies that private tanker owning firms are small, in relation to the entire market, and are incapable of influencing the cost or resources utilised by their own purchasing actions. This situation serves to further strengthen the 'price taker' position, which means they adjust their purchasing of resources to the freight market situation.

The low level of ownership concentration is further emphasised by the imbalance in oil company structures. These companies tend to concentrate large parts of their resources on a particular stage in the productive process. Some being strongly committed to exploration, others to production, and yet others to refining or retailing. Not all of them own or operate tanker tonnage. Such structural imbalances are further heightened by geographic imbalances, where companies concentrate on particular regions for part of their industrial activity. Hence, there is no concentration of ownership or influence, (monopoly or oligopoly), within the productive process from exploitation to retailing. If such a concentration were envisaged for example, in the tanker sector, oil companies, seeing the prospect of commercial vulnerability, would invest in tonnage or encourage further expansion in independent capacity. The wide structure, and its imbalances, ensure the wide dispersion of companies owning, operating and chartering tanker tonnage, and confirms the first assumption of perfect competition.

2. Identical Service

The firms produce a homogeneous service. Put another way, there is an absence of product differentiation. It is important, here, that a homogeneous service is taken to mean, not only that the services are identical in physical terms, but also that they are perceived to be identical from the point of view of the consumer, in this case, the oil company charterer. Should such a charterer come to believe, however erroneously, that there were discernable differences between the quality of one or some tanker firms and others, the tanker operators providing the perceived superior service could influence the freight market. For perfect competition to exist within the industry, the homogeneity of the tanker owning firm and the consuming oil company as charterers must be assured. One tanker owning firm's service is indistinguishable from another, which means the charterer has no tangible reason to prefer to charter one owner to that of another. The uniformity in general chartering practice will mean that tanker companies will simply respond to the highest bidder, which will be the market freight rate. In other industries, the product or service offered may be homogeneous, but geographic influences present certain firms with advantages over their competitors, undermining the assumption of an individual service. Zannetos does not see this as a an inhibiting factor, as this is not the case in the oil industry. If, for example, freight rate differentiation existed in two markets, with a low and a high freight rate, a number of eager charterers would enter into the cheapest market and, therefore, freight rates in this market would rise. If, on the other hand, eager tanker owners and sellers, entered the expensive market, the freight rate would contract. The effect would be the elimination of freight rate differences. In this way, arbitrage forms an important part of the process by which movements towards equilibrium are created. Through the functioning of arbitrage on an international level in the tanker market, there is, presumably, perfect substitution, not only over all routes, but also sizes of tonnage.[10]

3. Free Entry and Exit

There are no impediments to the freight market which would serve to present difficulties for firms to enter or leave the market at will. It is practically feasible to see a tanker vessel as a firm. Tankers are individual units among different charterers and their freight rate offers. Thus there is flexibility within the freight rate market structure. The concept of mobility of capital is particularly obvious here, with each tanker firm providing only a small proportion of the total output of tanker services. The freedom of entry or exit by any of the tanker firms or chartering firms into or out of the freight market is possible and also means that such actions would have only a negligible effect on the total tanker freight rate market. Such extreme flexibility of capital in the shape of tanker tonnage makes movements from one geographical area to another normal practice, and entry into the international second-hand market for ships, equally simple.

The primary factor influencing the entrance to any market or industry is the amount of capital outlay required. In comparison with other industrial investments over recent decades, tankers have required relatively small amounts of capital from the tanker owners. In general they only need to raise a minor proportion of the capital the remainder of the security being raised from financial institutions, based on long-term contracts of affreightment and/or subsidies, mainly those of shipbuilding credits.

This concept of entry and exit ensures the unimpeded flow of all resources, not only capital, between alternative occupations in the long-run. The underlying presumption is that these mobile resources will involuntarily move into an occupation from which the greatest advantage is derived. Firms move into the market in which they can make profit, and leave where they incur losses. Resources are attracted to the markets that produce a service which is in the greatest demand. In this way, inefficient firms are eliminated from the market and are replaced by efficient ones.

4. Perfect Knowledge

Information or perfect knowledge. It is assumed that both the tanker owners and charterers have perfect information about the freight rate market. Tanker owners are aware of the opportunities for employment at the present freight rate. The rapid forms of communication mean that the freight market is fully informed. Since there are no uninformed charterers, tanker owners cannot attempt to change or modify the basic freight rate. Although there are, on occasions, fixtures that are not made public, these would appear to have only a limited impact on the market's operations.

These assumptions form the basis of the theory of the tanker market under perfect competition. This will be developed by examining the market demand within the industry and its recent development. This inelastic demand that is very close to zero, means that freight rate fluctuations have no or at most minimal influence of the level of tonnage demanded.

Demand

The demand for bulk tanker tonnage is as argued a function of the demand for crude oil and the sea distance between the producers and the final consumers. This demand for petroleum and its products underwent a profound change in response to the first and second oil crises of 1973 and 1979. The change was due to the long-term restructuring of petroleum use. Confronted with repeated price increases, conservation schemes and shifts to alternative energy sources, as substitutes for oil became increasingly necessary. The process of improving energy utilisation efficiency broke what appeared in OECD countries to be the perpetual unison between Gross Domestic Product (GDP) and the demand for petroleum. This caused, for the first time, the demand for petroleum to lag behind the growth in GDP. As the JAMRI Report published in 1984 states:

"Previously, the demand ratio of primary forms of energy against GDP coefficients of elasticity, as used by OECD, showed as a factor of 1 or higher up to the year 1973 and the First Oil Crisis. In other words, the demand for energy was in excess of the growth rate of the economy. Since 1973, this has undergone a decrease (elasticity of 0. 5), and, after 1979 or the Second Oil Crisis, the factors actually became negative. The link between economic growth and energy (petroleum) has disappeared".

This meant that, while oil consumption in the long-run continued to increase, it was no longer at the same level as economic growth in the major developed countries. The global decline in oil prices which began in the mid-1980s, removed the commercial emergency, slowing down the movement towards improved energy consumption efficiency. Such trends suggest that the conditions in which oil consumption and energy demand are closely linked with economic growth are being gradually re-established, following the restructuring of the late 1970s and early 1980s.

These changes, as has been argued, had a substantial effect on the level of demand in the sea-borne oil trade but not on the basic economic criteria of demand. The demand for transport services of tankers is created by the need to produce, from crude oil, products for sale. The demand is, therefore, a derived demand, the general assumption being that, usually, the demand for oil transportation is inelastic.

The following section examines the elasticity of derived demand (based on the Marshallian rules discussed in Chapter 6). The reasons for demand for oil, as a final consumer product in the short and intermediate run, are inelastic as follows:

Elasticity of Demand for Oil

1.   Lack of Substitutes

There are only a small number of sources of energy, hence substitution is extremely limited. In addition, conversion from the use of one type of energy. For example oil to coal, would be highly capital-intensive.

2.   Technical Substitutes

Substitution, on a technical base, can only occur in the extremely long-run and, in some cases, is problematic. The question of road transport vehicles is the obvious one. Even if electric vehicles became generally practicable, there is still the requirement to generate electricity, fuelled, presumably, by oil as other forms of generation are taking some considerable time to develop commercially.

3.   Small Proportion of Total Costs

The oil industry's structure and organisation allows at all levels the multi-national companies to pursue, in the short-run, production policies with little or no regard to the cost of a single-factor input.

4   Final Product Price

The operations of regulation and price influencing institutions, such as the State, serve to confirm the demand for oil as price inelastic, as they can, and do, instigate change, rather than it being demand led.

The Marshallian rules of derived demand serve to confirm the above discussion of demand and the inelasticity of the final consumer product. These have strong influences on the tanker industry as discussed in the following section.

Elasticity of Demand for Tankers

1   Final Product

The demand for tanker services will be inelastic, the more inelastic the demand for the final consumer petroleum product. The logic of this rule is that the more inelastic the demand for the product, output will accordingly rise for a given fall in freight rate.   The tankers are a central factor in the output of oil products, whose demand is inelastic.   In other words, the demand for oil products is inelastic, so that the final consumer will pay an increased price, before beginning to seriously curtail the amounts purchased. In such a case, the derived demand for tankers, which is an important factor in the production process, will also be inelastic.

2.   Substitutes

The demand for a service will be inelastic, the greater the lack of alternatives, or substitute services. Here the question is one of technical substitution. When such substitution of other factors is low, the derived demand for the factor will be inelastic. Oil and oil product transportation requires a specialised technology, the tanker for which substitution, particularly in the short-run, can be considered impossible.

3.   Proportion of the Total Cost

The smaller the productive service, as a percentage of total cost, the less elastic will be its demand. The cost of transporting oil is only a small proportion of the cost of the final product to the consumer. Freight rates are a small proportion of the value of the cargo of crude oil. It follows that a relatively large increase in the freight rate will make little difference to the final price. This rule is often referred to as "the importance of being unimportant". The smaller, as a proportion of total cost, the amount is spent on tanker services, the more inelastic the derived demand for it will be.

4.   Other Factor Inputs

The derived demand for a productive service will be more inelastic, the more inelastic is the supply of other productive services contributing to the final product. There are two ways to react to this. One is to increase the price of the consumer's final product, 'say' petrol. Alternatively, and of interest here, the increased cost can be borne by the supplier of the other product services. The more inelastic the supply of these other services, the more possible it is to increase their costs, while only marginally reducing their quantities. The larger the change induced in the cost of other factors necessary in the production of petrol, the more inelastic will the demand be for tankers whose freight rate changes initiated the cost structure reorganisation. Put another way, changes in the freight rate force other sectors of the productive process to react in such a way as to lessen or remove the impact on the final consumer. As one author put it:

"It shows that changes in transportation rates may induce changes in other factors but will not decrease or increase the quantities of transportation services demanded in the short-run"[11]

292

5. Long and Short-Run

The above discussion confirms the presumption that productive factors, for which substitutes are plentiful will have an elastic demand, whereas for other factors, like tankers, where there are no good substitutes, demand will be inelastic. Substitution is central to the logic of the rules, and it follows that the elasticity of demand for any input to the productive process will increasingly become more elastic in the long-run, as increased substitution becomes possible. This is often referred to as the fifth rule.

In the short-run the quantities of all resources are not readily variable, so that the proportions in which other factor inputs are used will be unaffected by changes in the freight rate. It is argued that there may be a need for at least two long-runs, or, perhaps, medium-runs, to take into account any basic change. The consumer industries purchasing the inputs whose price, freight rates, are changing, will need time to make a full substitution in favour of or against tankers. The final consumer will also require time to make full adjustments to the change in the freight rate.

Such arguments serve to confirm the traditional presumption that demand for tankers in the short-run is insensitive to changes in freight rate. This insensitivity persists, even in periods of boom in freight rates in the tanker sector, unlike the bulk dry cargo sector . Research showed that in the tanker trade, the result of a 10% increase in freight rates was to reduce demand by a mere 0.05%. As E. Erikson writes:

"The demand for the transportation of crude oil does not seem to be significantly dependent on tanker freight rates. The result is reasonable, given the dominant role of the Arabian Gulf as an exporting area of crude oil, which gives little room for changes in relative demand. In addition, tanker freight rates here are considerably less important, relative to the value of the cargo than for any other bulk commodity".[12]

The supply curve is similar to that of dry cargo markets, moving from elastic in the region where there is considerable spare capacity to inelastic where capacity becomes fully employed. The central difference is that while the bulk dry cargo market supply undergoes a gradual shift between elastic and inelastic, in the tanker market the shift is an extremely rapid one. The factors underlying this rapid change is the specialisation of bulk crude carriers, meaning they have no alternative use. No alternative trade or market in which they can become actively involved excepts, (limited gain market activity is being ignored here). A comparison can be made with the dry cargo market supply curve, where a multiplicity of cargoes can be lifted, and owners will endeavour to operate in those sectors with the higher freight rate, rather than those with the lower.

The Spot Market

The fact that the supply curve moves from being elastic to inelastic beyond some high level of active tonnage is further analysed in Figure 11.4.

The general situation for tonnage supplied can be seen from the lower part of the supply curve which is highly elastic. There is a substantial change in demand D to D^1 bringing a small increase in freight rate F to F^1. Such a minimal increase in freight rate brings forth a substantial increase in the quantity of tonnage supplied Q to Q^1. The supply of tonnage is dependent on the different lay-up points, which is occasionally in discussions on the tanker supply curve referred to as the refusal freight rate of the marginal vessel. An important point about the position of Q^1 is that supply is nearing full capacity. At Q2 full capacity is reached, at which point the only way quantity supplied can be increased is by raising the level of utilisation. This is done by increasing vessel speed, delaying repairs and classification surveys, and shortening time spent in port. All these actions add considerably to cost. Shipowners will be reluctant to accept such additional expenditure if freight rates fail to cover them. In the model a small increase in demand D^1 to D^2 has brought a substantial increase in freight rates F^1 to F^2 and only a small increase in quantity Q^1 to Q^2, which is full capacity as indicated

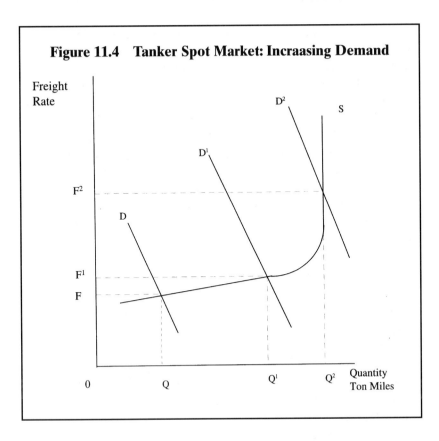

Figure 11.4   Tanker Spot Market: Incraasing Demand

by the inelasticity of the supply curve. In the short-run, once laid up tonnage has joined the active supply, only extremely marginal increases in capacity are possible. The supply curve has an L shape similar to that of the dry bulk tramp market but far more acute. Hence once at full capacity a small increase in demand has lead to a very large increase in tanker freight rates. In his analysis of this change, that is the move from elastic to inelastic, from Q^1 to Q^2 in the above figure, Zannetos argues it occurs to within less than 2 percentage points of full capacity. "Up to 92% of capacity the elasticity is infinite but the schedule suddenly becomes unit elastic around 93%. Between 93% and 94.1% the index of elasticity is approximately 0.656 it changes quickly to 0.02 between 94.1% and 95.6% and it remains at approximately 0.02 up to 97.2% from then on the elasticity is zero."[13]

Here is the central characteristic of the tanker spot freight market which is an important element in explaining the volatile booms and slumps in this sector, as illustrated in the earlier discussion of freight rate [14].

These are generally long recessions or slumps interspersed with short extremely hectic booms. In the latter inelastic demand interacting with a supply curve with properties of rapidly changing elasticity. What occurs are changes in supply from a horizontal to a vertical supply curve over an extremely small quantity range. "The change from elasticity to inelasticity occurs within less than 2 percentage points of total capacity, and indicates that a shift in demand by as little as 1 % around a critical area will be enough to create fortunes or disasters. With an elasticity of supply of 0. 02 immediately beyond full capacity a shift in oil demand of 1% and a consequent shift in transportation demand of 1. 66% will increase rates by no less than 83%."[15] Thus the effect of a small change in demand can have a considerably greater impact in the tanker than in the dry cargo spot freight rate market.

There is a situation where a change in demand will bring forth a different reaction from suppliers as illustrated in the following Figure 11.5.

The original equilibrium position is E on demand curve D and supply curve S. The freight rate stands at F with quantity Q. With an increase in demand from D to D^1, a new equilibrium is created at E^1, freight rate is F^1 and quantity Q^1. The tanker owners respond to this increase in demand by increasing tonnage from S to S^1, the supply curve moves to the right, bringing a new equilibrium at E^2 and causing freight rates to decline to F^2 with an increase in quantity Q^2. The expansion in supply has caused a contraction in freight rates, F^1 to F^2. B. Volk[16] uses this type of model to discuss a period of crisis in the tanker or wider shipping industry. In this case the two closures of the Suez Canal 1956 and 1967 which created circumstances where the supply response was less predictable. The suggestion is of a two fold effect. To begin at the original equilibrium E, tonnage is requisitioned or

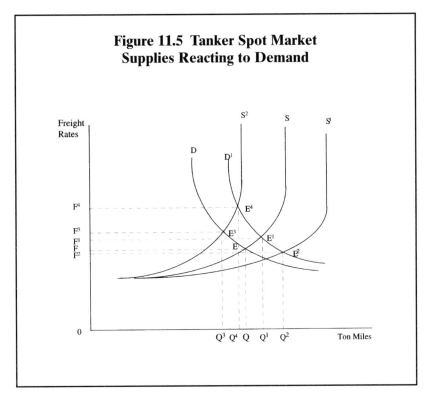

Figure 11.5 Tanker Spot Market Supplies Reacting to Demand

chartered for military rather than normal commercial purposes. The quantity decreases, the supply curve shifts to the left, a new supply curve is formed S². There is a new equilibrium E³, with freight rates at the high level of F³ and a contraction in the quantity to Q³. The second effect follows from a crisis increase in demand, the demand curve moves to the right D to D¹. This demand increase, bringing a response along one of two routes depending on circumstance and timing.   If the military requisition has already taken place a movement from E³ to E⁴ will increase freight rates to F⁴ and increase quantity from Q³ to Q⁴. If the demand increase precedes the military requisition the impact differs the movement being from E¹ to E⁴ causing the freight rate to increase from F¹ to F⁴ , but quantity moving in a different direction decreasing from Q¹ to Q⁴. What the figure illustrates is that crises affecting the tanker sector when analysed at a partial equilibrium level brings forth a complex set of responses.

The above discussion examined the way the spot freight rate market functions. Turning to examine the amount of tonnage operating in that market. This has expanded radically over recent decades. During the 1950s it was calculated that the spot market involved between 11% to 15% of the total tonnage capacity. An UNCTAD study suggested that during the 1960s the tonnage in this category fell to as low as 10% and at its highest rose to 30% of total world capacity. The amount is dependent on the condition of the industry as a whole. By 1978 independent tanker owners not securing long-term charters stood at approximately 30% of total capacity. This process of increasing the amount of independent tonnage on the spot rate market has continued with prolonged freight rate depression. By 1984, 48% of capacity was operating on the spot market, confirming the hypothesis that during periods of recession when demand is weak, oil companies are reluctant to secure tonnage on the expectation that the freight rate will continue to stagnate or decline. In periods of boom, when demand is strong the reverse is true, oil companies are eager to charter as much tonnage as possible long-term as a protection against their expectation of further increases in freight rates, due to shortages in available tonnage.

Cobweb Theorem

The concept of expectations and actual outcome has a version in what is known as the cobweb theorem. It analyses a market situation in which the amount currently supplied is dependent on the level of price, freight rate, set in some previous period. As Hicks points out, "The current supply of a commodity depends not so much upon what the current price is as upon what entrepreneurs have expected it to be in the past. It will be those past expectations, whether right or wrong, which mainly govern current output; the actual current price has a relatively small influence".[17]

The Cobweb theorem was originally devised to explain the relationship between agricultural prices for such things as pigs, cocoa and coffee and their supply and has more recently been used in the context of capital goods. The theorem differs from the original static model, because an essential element in the static approach explaining market equilibrium, is that the mutual adjustment of demand and supply will occur instantaneously. The cobweb theorem's method of establishing an equilibrium following a change in demand, is that a change in supply does not occur instantaneously, because supply can only partially adapt to the new situation. The change in demand establishes a new equilibrium to which supply has to adjust. In the case of agricultural products, this may require a season and so there is a 'time-lag'. What happens to the supply of a commodity in any time period is dependent on the equilibrium price of the previous period expectation. For example, when responding to a change in demand, the shipowner will increase, or decrease, the tonnage offered depending upon the expectation of freight changes, as

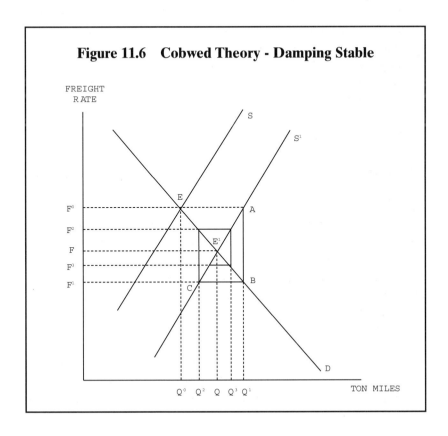

Figure 11.6   Cobwed Theory - Damping Stable

based on previous experience. The time-lag makes accurate adjustment to change a complex operation. A change in supply (or demand) may lead to a succession of reactions in quantity demanded and supplied, thus creating a cyclical or oscillating movement in freight rates and tonnages, known as the cobweb effect. Such oscillations are of three types, (1) dampening or stable oscillations, which eventually lead to the securing of a new, comparatively stable, equilibrium, and (2) a dynamic, explosive or anti-dampening oscillation causing increasing distance from an equilibrium, inevitably ending with some basic change in demand or supply, (3) the uniform oscillation, a position where equilibrium is never achieved, the cycle or oscillation simply repeating itself. The following figure examines in detail the cobweb theory form of oscillation showing the reaction to changes in the quantity supplied.

D and S represent the current demand and the previous supply curve. The original equilibrium was E at freight rate F^0 and quantity of tonnage Q^0, the current supply curve being S. With the movement in supply to the right to S^1, the freight rate F^0 dictates the quantity of tonnage supplied as Q^1. At this quantity, the freight rate is F^1, with reference to the demand curve is at point (B). At freight rate F^1, shipowning firms decide to supply Q^2 point (C). This process is repeated until the new equilibrium E^1 at freight rate F and quantity Q is established.

The explosive unstable equilibrium situation is illustrated in Figure 11.7.

This model assumes an increase in the supply of tonnage, as indicated by the shift in the industry's supply curve from S to S^1. At the original equilibrium, E, freight rate F is expected to prevail. The shipowner increases the offer of tonnage from Q to Q^1, point A on the supply curve. But that quantity of tonnage will only be chartered at the freight rate F^1, according to the demand curve, point B. At this level of freight rate, shipowners offer only to supply Q^2, point C on the supply curve. With this new limited quantity of tonnage supplied, freight rate rises to F^2, point G on the demand curve. Here is a boom level of freight rates, to which

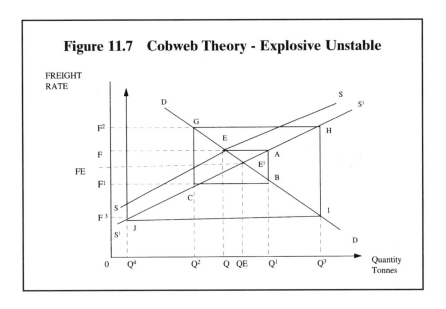

Figure 11.7 Cobweb Theory - Explosive Unstable

ship owners respond by offering quantity Q^3 point H on their supply curve. There is a surplus of tonnage and the charterer would only accept a freight rate of F^3 point I on the demand curve. At such a low level of freight rate, shipowners withdraw tonnage, offering quantity Q^4 point J on their supply curve. The process will continue in this explosive way until one of the basic criteria, and, particularly, the elasticity of either curve, is modified. As can be seen, there is no movement towards the stable equilibrium E^1 at freight rate FE and quantity QE. The usual equilibrium solution is inoperable in this case.

In the case where the elasticities of demand and supply were the same, uniform oscillations would occur at points equidistant from the original equilibrium. Therefore, no stable equilibrium is ever achieved. Whether the freight rate will approach an equilibrium level or not will be dependent on elasticity. Here, it is assumed to be the relative slope of the demand and supply curve. Adapting to modifications in supply and demand requires a certain period of time. This time period will vary, but it is of importance, where inelastic supply obviously relates to substantial capital goods, like tankers.

301

The theorem entails two basic adjustment processes. The first is the adjustment by shipowners of the tonnage offered, in the light of the previously established freight rate. The second is the adjustment of freight rates to this new level of tonnage. This conversion of the static analysis into a dynamic one is concerned with the behaviour, over time, and attempting to take into account the complications of expectation and uncertainty, is useful in analysing the tanker sector. The cobweb theory goes some way to explain what is happening during periods when there are a limited range of freight rate oscillations around some stable equilibrium.

The theorem illustrates the logic of having a freight rate movement around each stable short-run equilibrium. This is a situation where freight rates may change without setting in motion dynamic freight rate changes. This concept is of an area, within which range there are limited movements of the freight rate, which has been termed the price or freight rate range of **Strict Static Relevance**, that is, a set of freight rates about a static equilibrium, such that dynamic freight movements are absent.

In any discussion of the cobweb theorem, it is presumed that a stable equilibrium exists and can possibly be established by market forces. There will be deviation from the equilibrium freight rate, so long as there is no alteration in the underlying demand and supply conditions. For example, if a rumour of a shortage in tanker tonnage drove the freight rate above the equilibrium rate, the fact that the quantity of tonnage supplied exceeded that demanded will drive the freight rate back towards an equilibrium. If, at some freight rates the quantity of tonnage demanded exceeded the quantity supplied, freight rates are increased. Conversely, if the quantity of tonnage demanded is less than that supplied a process operates to lower freight rates.

Unstable Equilibrium

The equilibrium is stable, so long as demand curve cuts the supply curve from above, for, here, excess demand drives freight rates up, while excess supply, which can be termed negative excess demand, will drive freight rates down. Equilibrium is unstable if the demand curve cuts the supply curve from below, for now, rather than excess supply being above the equilibrium and excess demand below, the positions are reversed, the law of supply is inverted as in the following figure:

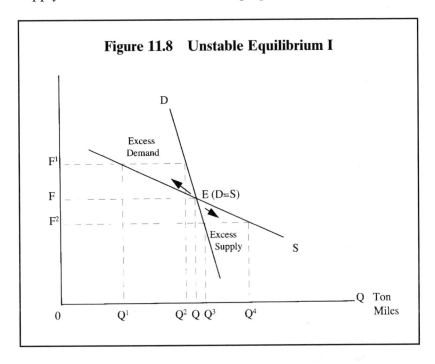

Figure 11.8   Unstable Equilibrium I

In this figure, the slope of the supply curve is reversed from positive to negative, inverting the relationship asserted in the law of supply between price and quantity. The quantity supplied therefore increases at a lower freight rate. The supply curve is less steep than the demand curve, meaning that the slightest movement away from E, the equilibrium, is not capable of producing forces to restore the equilibrium, rather the opposite. If, for example, freight rates rose from F to F^1, the amount demanded is Q^2, which is in excess of the amount of tonnage offered, Q^1, a position of excess demand. Charterers attempt to outbid each other for this limited tonnage, Q^1 forcing the freight rate even higher and moving further away from the equilibrium freight rate at E. If the freight rate declined from F to F^2, demand

303

will stand at Q^3 and supply at Q^4 and there is an excess of supply (Q^3 to Q^4). Should demand increase to take up some of this surplus, supply will respond by also increasing as freight rates decline, a movement away from the equilibrium freight rate F and quantity Q. This is a system where the forces of demand and supply push the freight rate in the "wrong" direction, that is, away from a stable freight rate. In the following figure, a similar form of unstable equilibrium is illustrated, on in which the law of demand is inverted.

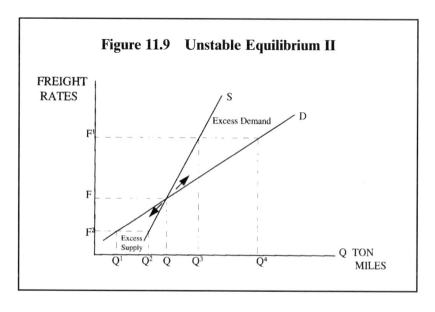

Figure 11.9   Unstable Equilibrium II

The supply curve has its usual positive slope, a direct relationship between freight rate and the quantity supplied, as per the law of supply. The demand curve, however, has a positive, rather than the usual negative, relationship between freight rate and quantity, that is, more being demanded with rising prices. The same logic exists in this as in the previous figure. A movement away from equilibrium E will create considerable instability. Here, should the freight rate rise from F to F^1 the amount demanded would be Q^4 in excess of that offered, Q^3. The charterer would attempt to secure tonnage by bidding up the freight rate, in this way exacerbating the situation by moving even further away from the equilibrium E, lowering of the freight rate to F², a situation of excess supply of tonnage. Shipowners will tend to reduce the freight rate even further, in the hope of securing employment and eliminating the excess supply. In this way, the situation deteriorates, as freight rate reductions follow one on another.

What the above figure highlights is the mere existence of an equilibrium is no guarantee of its attainment. Unstable equilibria exist if the demand curve cuts the supply curve from below. In this situation, where excess demand drives the freight

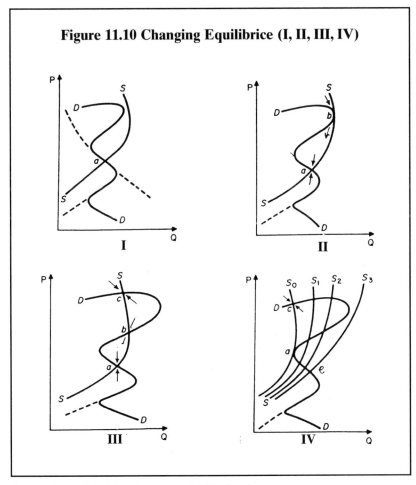

Figure 11.10 Changing Equilibrice (I, II, III, IV)

(Based on Op.Cit. Zannetos Z.S. p230)

rate down, the stability of an equilibrium is dependent on the slope of the demand and supply curves. A model with lagged adjustments demonstrates that the tanker freight rate market, which is stable according to a static analysis, may be dynamically unstable. Particular dynamic problems arise in a freight rate market because, as pointed out, supply reactions are lagged. The tanker market, with its supply rigidity, fits well into the concept of lagged reactions. The following set of figures illustrates the shift in the demand function, with lagged response from the supply function. These differ from previous models, and it is assumed to be a long-run situation, precisely because of the changes in the inelastic supply curves, which indicates the industry or sector is working in the region of full capacity and, assuming, as previously, that all other things are equal.

Figure 11.11 illustrates four situations. First, (I) the usual demand and supply position, the equilibrium at point a. This is a stable equilibrium, as defined earlier, where demand cuts the supply curve from above and market pressure will restore it. The supply curve has the usual positive slope throughout the discussion. This is due to the length of the period taken for supply to react to any dynamic change in demand. The curve maintains its slope and, therefore, supply reactions are assumed not to be instantaneous, the original demand curve being indicated by the dotted line as a normal negative sloping curve. Wherever the demand curve cuts or joins the supply curve from above, a normal equilibrium is ensured. Whenever the demand curve is positively sloped and cuts the supply curve from below, an unstable equilibrium is created.

The situation is changed when the demand curve moves to the right, because of the generation of dynamic expectations due to the initial impact of some external event, such as the Gulf Crisis (II). The force is so intense as to force the freight rate to increase above point (b), where equilibrium will be stable. This is not the case from below. If the freight rate either does not get above (b) or declines only slightly below it, demand will contract rapidly in a wide oscillation until returning to the stable equilibrium at (a). If it is assumed that some event, for example, a series of Gulf crises, there is not simply one shock to the tanker freight rate markets, but a series of such shocks is illustrated in figures (III) and (IV). These show the demand curve further to the right because of the expectations generated by the second shock of the crisis. In (III) there are three equilibria: two stable, a and c and one unstable, b. Assuming the impact is so great as to force the freight rate up to c from below, this will be a stable equilibrium. If, on the other hand the rise was limited to b, an unstable equilibrium, a move above the positive slope of demand, entailing excess demand, the freight rate is forced rapidly upwards to c. If the freight rate was marginally below b it would drop, because the demand curve remains positive, causing excess supply or negative excess demand to the original equilibrium a. Assuming a further shock generates even more dynamic expectations, pushing the demand curve further to the right as shown in (IV). The original equilibrium a is found, which remains stable from below, but not from above. It follows that any pressure would push the freight rate upwards, because of excess demand oscillating demand upwards, the freight rate increasing until it reached a stable equilibrium at c. The series of figures, thus far, have illustrated the virtually instantaneous effect of external pressure on the demand curve. In the main, it has been assumed this would force the freight rate rapidly upwards at an accelerating pace, to the high equilibrium c. Such a high freight encourages the ship-owner to acquire and offer additional tonnage. This additional capacity shifts the supply curve to the right, through S, S1, S2 and S3 in figure (IV), a situation, it is assumed, which puts the demand curve into reverse beyond S2, and it declines rapidly to a new equilibrium at E.

The above dynamic model with lagged adjustments in supply demonstrate that a freight rate market that is stable according to the earlier static analysis may be dynamically unstable. Such dynamic models with continuous adjustment enlarge and strengthen the static model by assisting in explaining the dynamic and often volatile path tanker freight rates follow over time and particularly in their reactions to exogenous disturbances.

It has been argued above that the demand for tankers is extremely inelastic. Tankers are primarily engaged in the movement of a raw material, oil. The transport demand is, therefore, derived in the main from international demand and supply of that fuel. Crude oil and its products have an inelastic demand because of a number of factors, such as the high capital cost of conversion to the use of substitutes and in some areas of activity technical substitution is impossible, transport being an example. The oil industry's structure follows short-run production policies with little regard for modification of the costs of a single input.

All these factors in the production process are confirmed by the inelastic demand of the final consumer. All this has an importance in creating the inelasticity of demand for tanker services for these are an essential element in the production of oil whose demand is inelastic. Freight rates play a minor cost role in the total production process hence it is easy to adjust changes in these rates. The important point to make here is that such inelasticity is only secured in the 'region of strict static relevance'. Above or below such a region elasticity can take many forms. On the supply side at levels of less than full capacity the supply of tonnage is nearly completely elastic being dependent on the differences in single vessel lay-up points. Supply in the region of fully employed capacity becomes completely inelastic. At the lower elastic part of the supply schedule, this is the region of static relevance where shifts in rates oscillate around some equilibrium in some form of cobweb cycle. Such fluctuations mean that there is an absence of any dynamic price expectation and tonnage demanded will be virtually unaffected by minor modifications in the freight rate. The most sensitive area of the supply curve will be that of change from an elastic curve with its mild changes in freight rates, to inelastic with its accompanying volatile changes. As has been pointed out this area is extremely small. "The capacity that separates the elastic from the inelastic part of the short-term supply schedule is not greater than 2% of the total".[18] these are static supply curves but are dependent on the type of response individual shipowners make to the changes in demand and freight rates, once all sector tonnage has become active, supply, service speed, port turnaround times, will be indicative of this response.

The interaction of demand and inelastic supply has been the reason for widening the analysis to include a dynamic element since in the tanker market a substantial movement in freight rate away from some 'normal' equilibrium rate creates expectations of future freight rate increases which are proportionately larger than present increases. Such freight rate expectations causes the demand curve to move upwards and to the right over a range of freight rates. The upper limit of this spiral being the budget or income effect. The budget or income effect can be defined in this case simply as the effect of change in freight rate on the quantity demanded. It arises from the consumer (charterer) being worse off as a result of the increases in the freight rate. Such a substantial budget effect forces the charterer to withdraw from the freight market. Zannetos suggests it may have wider implications:

"The withdrawal of the buyer, because of this budget effect, may be taken by the sellers as an indication of reversal in expectation."[19]

Such an increase in expectation causes inter-period substitution to occur. This is because it will be cheaper for oil companies to charter as quickly as possible rather than wait, as expectations dictate that charters in the near future will be at even higher freight rates shipowners will procrastinate by attempting to delay or postpone fixing their tonnage as long as commercially possible, a situation serving to drive the freight rates even higher. Simply, the model is dependent on autonomous and dynamic shifts in demand occurring, when the supply is fixed or can only respond to a limited extent. The above discussion can be illustrated by the following Figure 11.11.

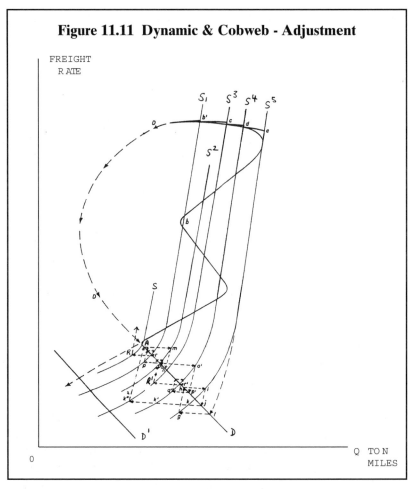

Figure 11.11 Dynamic & Cobweb - Adjustment

This combines the cobweb theorem with that of dynamic expectations. Prior to examining this in detail some general points will be made. First, in the lower half of the figure where the supply curve is becoming elastic, the area where, in the short-run, spot market freight rates are moving over a limited range, the cobweb theorem functions within the region of static relevance around some normal equilibrium rate. The spot freight rate fluctuates, tenuously around such a long-run medium rate, both below and above, but not so far above as to set in motion violent movements outside the region of static relevance. This volatile area is illustrated in the upper section of the figure. Here there are rapid spirals in the area of extremely inelastic supply the fluctuations being associated or instigated by the increase in the expectations creating substantial oscillations in the demand curve.

Examining the figure in more detail, the lower portion is where the cobweb theorem is functioning a situation of perfectly competitive spot rate market in the short-run. The present position is one following a period of high demands and the responding growth in capacity supply stands at S^5. The budget income effect and contracting demand has brought the freight rate down to point (f). This is a fall to below the lowest point on the supply curve S^5 which, because of the low freight rate offered, will cause some tonnage to be withdrawn. There is still a substantial surplus in the market as compared with the initial supply structure illustrated by S^1. At demand level (f) the quantity of tonnage offered contracts to (g). At this limited quantity a shortage emerges causing the offer to be bid up to (h). This freight rate brings forth quantity (i) causing freight rates to compress to (j). At such a low freight, many owners decide to withdraw tonnage, to lay-up or scrap, lowering supply. The extent of the curtailment of supply is indicated by the contraction moving beyond point (k) of some other level K^1 or K^2. Here the presumption is of K^2 on supply curve S^3. The freight rate begins to gravitate steadily upwards, due to this contraction in supply. This suggests a movement through l,m,n,o,p perhaps to r. Should this steady rise in freight rates continue it will encourage tanker owners to increase the amount supplied, and vessels will resume trading. This suggests a change beginning at 0 creating a movement through o^1 p^1 q^1 r^1 t^1 entering another unstable cobweb. In this section of the figure freight rates oscillate around unstable equilibria, these oscillations remaining within the lower level limitations so long as excess capacity exists and demand remains undynamic.

In the upper half of the figure here there has been a series of substantial disturbances. The initial one moves the demand curve from D^1 to D. This creates high expectation, causing the oil companies to rush to the market and charter tonnage causing inter-period substitution. The spot market becomes excited exaggerating the impact of the demand change. Assuming the movement begins at q the impact implies the demand curve followed by the freight rate is impelled upwards to b or b¹ depending on the extent of the disturbance. Assuming the freight rate attains the high level b¹ a number of possibilities are open. First the withdrawal of charterers, because of the high rates, would cause an immediate contraction of the freight rate. This trend becomes irreversible with demand rolling forward and downwards on the path marked D-D for simplicity returning to the demand curve at the lower level of its initial equilibrium q. An alternative is, on attaining the level 'b¹' it remains there and gives the shipowner time to offer additional tonnage as it comes on stream. The supply curve moves to the right S^3 at point 'c' creating a new equilibrium, similarly the supply curve moves to S^4 at point 'd'. These movements of the supply curve to the right increase the amount of supply, causing a marginal lowering in the freight rate. The following equilibrium 'e' on supply curve S^5 is created and like the previous equilibrium it is stable from above but unstable from below with excess supply that is negative excess demand. Any movement beyond 'e' will mean rates will slide downwards to 'f' the point at which re-establishment of a series of equilibria and eventually a region of static relevance possessing no dynamic demand elements, a return to the cobweb area.

The figure was dealing with spot rates in the short and medium or long-run. The latter was indicated by the movement in the quantity supplied particularly at full capacity. It gave some indication that in the short-run both spot and long-run rates appear to be influenced by expectations and costs to a greater or lesser extent. Both freight rates move in the same broad direction even when spot rates oscillate around some freight equilibrium in the range of static relevance. The reason for this close interrelationship is that spot rates incorporate many of the valid structural relationships between demand and supply reflected in the operations of the tanker market. As Koopmans pointed out "A striking characteristic of the tanker freight market is the manner in which rates of both types of charter fluctuate over a wide range. These fluctuations are very extensive and spasmodic and sometimes take place within rather short periods; they generally show a considerable degree of similarity between the movement of voyage charter rates and time charter rates".[20]

The short and long-term freight rate markets are intimately related on the rather obvious grounds that both shipowners and charterers have the alternatives of short-term spot agreement or a long-term charter. The spot rate market is a substitute for operating the other medium and long-term markets. During different levels of activity within the freight market the level of bargaining or choice between the two alternatives will change sometimes to the advantage of the shipowner and other times, the oil company charterers.

Some authorities claim the time charter rates are determined almost exclusively by the spot freight rate with a time lag between the two. The spot freight rate sector possesses the ability to give an immediate indication of any changes or modifications within the freight rate market as a whole. Oil companies demand for spot rate freight tonnage is the difference between the total demand for all independent tonnage and the time charter demand. A similar statement can be made from the supply side, adding the important element of idleness, broadly defined as non-active or potential supply. The spot rate market, therefore, has a primary influence on the medium and long-term freight levels and on the expectations of independent owners and the oil companies who are not only charterers that use independent tonnage but are often owners and operators of their own tonnage. At times when freight rates are at boom levels, oil companies increase their demand, to secure long-term charter tonnage. Meanwhile shipowners press for higher charter rates. This process is put into reverse when spot freight rates are low. Hence the proportion of independent operators in the spot market has increased consistently over the last decade or more, with vessels on long-term charter coming to the end of their charters and being redelivered. The ordering of new tonnage brings a broadly similar reaction from both shipowners and oil companies. As with any sophisticated industry, attempts to forecast spot freight rates are an important element in decision on medium and long-term rates.

Long-term agreements hold advantages for both sides of the market. For shipowners and charterers, the most important of these are security and stability. This has been termed the subjective value of certainty. Tanker owners forego the chance of high levels of profits, if and when freight booms occur, but equally insulate themselves against losses when there is a slump. There are relative differences in the cost levels of time charters and the spot freight rate. The monetary differences are perceived as risk premiums., For the tanker owners the risk of operating in the spot freight rate market, is one of under or unemployment. The risk of under employment is at times put down to the increased size of vessels, bringing not only the advantages of economies of scale, but also the disadvantages of immediate or short-run inflexibility. These vessels require not only adequate port facilities but deep water throughout the voyage, particularly when carrying cargo. Also ashore there is need for adequate storage, processing and distribution facilities for the immediate disposal of a huge amount of cargo. Hence such vessels only operate at full efficiency when fitted into a scheduled system, to avoid under employment of tonnage and of distribution on the shore side of the process, the short-run unemployment risks inherent in the spot freight rate market are removed by most long-term charters. There are not only the risks of frictional unemployment due to the completion of a charter but also risks relating to the tanker market in general. Primarily there is the unemployment related to surplus tonnage at times of freight rate recession, as discussed above. Secondly there is the seasonal cycle of demand for petroleum products, which is extremely sensitive to the winter demand of North America and particularly Northern Europe and Scandinavia. It has been calculated that this seasonal peak requires some 9-10% extra tonnage capacity than the average over the whole year. That is to say if demand was evenly distributed over the whole period some 90% of capacity would be required. Occasionally extremely short lived booms have been initiated, simply due to the demands of the northern winter, in particular if a severe

Northern European winter is forecast. Such a system implies that a certain amount of tonnage becomes only partially employed or under utilised taking part cargoes or remaining idle, that is to say tied-up, or waiting offers off some loading region, in operational readiness. In this way extended periods of idleness or semi-idleness, as in slow steaming, are part of the market structure. Such risks of under or unemployment in the medium or long-term charters are shifted from the tanker owner to the chartering oil company. The latter gaining the security of their transport needs into the future.

A further advantage from the view point of the tanker owner of long-term agreements is management requirements for a chartered vessel are minimal. Presumably brokerage fees will also contract as there will obviously be less need to revert to the spot market over the period of long-term charters.

Another advantage to tanker owners or prospective owners is the ability to obtain financial credit on the basis of long-term charters, what has been termed the loan value of the charter. That is to obtain a mortgage for the building and perhaps operating of tonnage from banks and other financial institutions using as collateral a long-term charter agreement.

A further element in long-term charter rates or costs is that, all other things being equal, these will be lower and fluctuate less violently than spot freight rates. In the main, the chartering oil companies are also owners and operators of tonnage. They are, therefore, perfectly equipped to make precise calculations of the costs of operating and profits accruing to independent owners at any level of charter rate. A further point here which should not be overlooked is that oil companies have the option of increasing their own tanker fleet committment rather than employing independents on long-term contracts. This, of course, presumes that tonnage is not required for prompt delivery. If the long-term market was such that chartering independent tonnage was calculated to be more expensive than operating their own tonnage, oil companies would opt for increasing investment in their own fleet. These will be elements present in any negotiations or bargaining of a long-term contract. Hence while the importance of the spot freight rate should not be under estimated, neither should the cost of operating tonnage, in the construction of long-term contract rates.

Underlying the above discussion was the idea of the long-term and spot freight rates moving broadly in the same direction. During any long-term contract there is an expectation, or presumption, that they move towards what has been termed the 'normal rate'. This is seen as a hypothetical rate, usually based on static long-run costs. The curve of this hypothetical rate is mildly sloping due to technical and technological developments.

As well as the premium risk removal, or the subjective value of certainty, empirical evidence shows that over time, long-term freight rates will approach the 'normal rate', from above in periods of generally high freight rates, and from below when the general freight rate market has been depressed. It follows that long-term freight rates, ultimately, will generally be gradually contracting in real terms. This suggests that in the long-run expectations and the freight rate market are marginalised and with long-term rates are determined on a cost basis.

As an UNCTAD report points out "The longer the period of chartering the smaller is the effect of transient market conditions on the charter rate. Really long-term agreements are made at rates which cover the shipowners long-term costs and provide him with a satisfactory rate of profit. Clearly, the respective bargaining positions of the parties to a long-term agreement are affected by the current market situation, so that the extent to which allowances for inflation can be built into long-term costs which are covered. The level of profit each side will regard as satisfactory are influenced by the market conditions at the time the charter is made".[21]

Concluding Comments

The analysis in some parts of this chapter have been questioned on a number of grounds. The most obvious being the questioning

316

of the relevance of the concept of pure or perfect competition, in particular in relation to the changes the industry has undergone since much of the basic analysis was made.

The idea of the tanker sector of the industry complying broadly with the precepts of perfect or pure competition is questioned because of the presence of large industrial operators, particularly on the demand side, contradicting the assumption of numerous buyers and sellers, of a homogeneous product, and the freedom of entry and exit. The presence of numerous sellers, owners and operators, despite tonnage owned by oil companies is not questioned, nor is the lack of those oil companies participation in the spot freight rate market, and of more importance oil companies as shipowners and operators, cargo owners and charterers. In the latter role being capable of some undue influence on the demand side of the market. Such suggestions of undue influence upon the functioning of the freight rate market are clearly tied to the assumptions of the perfectly competitive model. In particular, the assumption of perfect knowledge and a homogeneous product. As to perfect knowledge or transparency within the industrial sector it would appear that while there are secret, or semi-secret transactions taking place, these are not yet of such magnitude, to seriously interfere with the market's operations. It is argued that the presence of shipbrokers, tanker agents, and the amount of published information generally assist the market process.

On the question of the homogeneity of tanker services. The early discussion in this chapter was predicated on the dynamic shifts in demand in relation to a fixed supply, which was dependent on the tanker tonnage laid up, until full capacity was reached. The ability to substitute or even perfectly substitute size and class of tonnage and routes served, that is to generate arbitrage, within the tanker sector, was central to this assumption. Here lies the creation of a single homogenous service with aggregate supply reaction within a single spot freight rate tanker market. This assumption has been questioned by the development of combination carriers and their ability to switch between the bulk dry and wet freight markets reducing the specificity of the

317

markets and the potential supply. In addition to this and of primary importance is the element of the growth in vessel size. As has been argued, there was not only a growth in the trading of oil but the size of the tonnage unit engaged in the trade. The taking of advantage of economies of scale was of particular importance in the expansion of the Arabian Gulf trade. Here during the late 1960s and 1970s significant changes came about in the size distribution of oil tankers. The crisis of the 1970s and other developments reduced the importance of the Gulf and meant that VLCCs and ULCCs specifically built for that route were deployed on other, shorter, routes. A trend illustrated by the decline in the average voyage length of tankers and the declining productivity. Problems with ports or terminal capacity in terms of draft or storage limitations, meant larger vessels if they could be employed at all, suffered the disadvantages of transhipment or under-utilisation. All part of a process meaning that routes and size substitutability became increasingly difficult and the marginal vessel in a specific trade was protected from competition from larger tonnage. Glen argues "These developments, called into question the economist's assumption of a perfectly substitutable market across sizes and routes. Both size and routes differentiation have emerged. Size differentiation has emerged because of the limited flexibility of the largest oil tankers. This has developed for two reasons. Firstly, the supply of the largest tankers outstripped the growth in demand on the routes for which they were best suited, leading to an increased risk of unemployment. Secondly the growth in port capacity was less than the growth in large tanker capacity, creating severe constraints on ports availability, and hence route flexibility. Large vessels became riskier assets to own for these reasons".[22]

Such inflexibility it has been further argued could have important implications for entry and exit to and from the tanker market. These potential market imperfections, creating potential monopoly influences, have been successfully opposed by shipowners, shipbuilding and ordering policy, for the entrance of new tonnage serves to modify the impact of these market changes. The traditional perfectly competitive market model with perfect substitutability and in the case of the tanker sector a world-wide single homogeneous market, has been seriously questioned. A questioning based on vessel size and route changes, which have been an important influence in recent years on the spot market. The outcome has been the creation of a number of closely related but differentiated markets, at least in the short-run. An adequate analysis of what occurs in the long-run for example a disaggregation of markets has yet to be made. The differentiation within the spot market has not, so far as can be observed, affected the central importance of the spot market in the determination of freight rates in the short and long-run.

Summary

The last half century has seen a massive expansion in the oil industry and a concomitant growth in the level of its seaborne trade. An increase sustained by growth in the total size of the tanker fleet and the average size of individual vessels in it. This rapid expansion suffered two severe set backs with the twin crises of the 1970s, and the recovery has been a comparatively modest one. Against this background of industrial expression, the basic economic analysis has remained largely unchanged. That is despite superficial indicators to the contrary, this is a good approximation of the neo classical perfectly competitive market. The assumption is of such a market being largely satisfied, particular the two basic criteria of a large number of buyers and sellers, and freedom of entry and exit. Freight market activity is considerably more volatile than other markets. This is due to the interaction of inelastic demand and supply, elasticity changes rapidly when approaching full capacity utilisation, outside what was termed the region of static relevance This analysis was based on the Cobweb theorem, and dynamic disequilibrium, and can be deemed to relate economic analysis to the empirical imperatives of the tanker freight market.

Further Reading

Tusiai M. *The Petroleum Shipping Industry (Volume I & II)*
Tulsa, Oklahoma, USA PenWell Publishing Co. 1996.

Zannetos Z. S. *The Theory of Oil Tankship Rates*,
Cambridge, Massachusetts, the MIT Press, 1966.

Zannetos Z. S *Persistent Economic Misconceptions in the
Transportation of Oil by Sea.* Maritime Studies and
Management 1 (2) 1973.

Glen D R . *The Emergence of Differentiation in Oil Tanker
Markets.* 1970-1978. Maritime Policy and Management 17, (4)
(1990).

Hale C. and Vanags A. *The Market for Second-hand Ships:
Some Results on Efficiency Using Co-integration.* Maritime
Policy and Management 19 (1), 1992.

---

[1] See for detailed discussion Chapter 7
[2] Maritime Transport 1970, OECD. Page 71
[3] Maritime Transport 1975 Para 197
[4] See Chapter 8.
[5] Koopmans T.C. Tanker Freight Rates and Tankship Building. Garlem
Netherlands. 1939
[6] Tinbergen. J. Selected Papers, L.H. Klaasen et al Editor
North Holland Publishing Company, Amsterdam, Netherlands. 1959
[7] Zannetos Z.S. The Theory of Oil Tankship rates, the MIT Press 1966
[8] IBID. pp 175-176
[9] UNCTAD Freight Markets and the Level and Structure of Freight Rates.
UN New York 1969 p24
[10] See below for further discussion.
[11] Opt Cit. Zannetos. Page 37
[12] Ibid. Erikson. The Demand for Bulk Ship Services
in E. Hope. Studies in Shipping Economics. Norwegian School of
Economics and Business. Bergen 1982, page 60.

[13] Op. Cit. Zannetos. p17
[14] See Figure 11.3
[15] Op. Cit. Zannetos. p186
[16] Volk B. Shipping Investment in Recession
Bremen Institute of Shipping Economics, No.38 Bremen 1984
[17] Hicks J.R. Value and Capital (2nd Edition)
London Oxford University Press. 1953 p 117.
[18] Op. Cit. Zannetos p243.
[19] Ibid p.25
[20] Op. Cit. Koopmans. p13
[21] Op. Cit. UNCTAD 1969 p16
[22] D. Glen The Emergence of Differentiation in Oil Tanker Markets.
1970-1978. Maritime Policy & Management
[17] 17 (4) (1990) pp 289-312

Chapter Twelve

LINER SHIPPING

Introduction

Liner shipping is the leading sector in the shipping industry, not as with other sectors, because of the amount of tonnage, but because of the quality of that tonnage and the high-value cargoes conveyed. Thus, of the total freight revenues earned by the industry, over half accrue to this sector. Further average freight rate per ton mile for a liner is some ten times higher than for other sectors.[1]

Liners differ radically from other sectors of the industry. Accordingly, it cannot be defined on the basis of the individual specialised technology of the vessel, as, for example tankers. Liners, rather, consist of a group of widely differing vessel types. It is, therefore, more appropriate to seek a definition in terms of their operational characteristics, rather than technology used. The cardinal feature distinguishing liners from other sectors, is that they are engaged in the provision of scheduled services between specific ports. Scheduled services are those operating at a regular frequency on a particular trade route, according to a published timetable. Liner companies will deploy the same vessel or vessels along a specific trade route. They will load and or discharge cargo at the same pre-arranged port of each trip.

They convey general cargo on behalf of a multiplicity of individual shippers. The size of these consignments will differ widely, but they will only consist of a proportion of the vessel's cargo space, that is each consignment is small in relation to the cargo capacity of the liner vessel. Here the concentration is on conventional cargo tonnage, rather than containerised vessels. The latter, which will be discussed later, fit much of the criteria mentioned, with the obvious exception of the element of loading break bulk cargo. Shippers demanding the total capacity of a vessel would use bulk tonnage. The break bulk will cover a wide range of commodities, few requiring special treatment. What is essential is expert stevedores to load each diverse cargo efficiently in order to gain the highest level of utilisation of cargo space. Such operational structures mean that liners are referred to as 'Common Carriers'. These are vessels that will offer to transport goods for any shipper on the liner route and such shippers may also designate the vessel.

All liner operators have to provide this regular service, even if the vessel sails only in part cargo. Operating such a complex system requires a far more extensive administration and its associated costs, not only at head office, but in the establishment of offices and appointment of agents in the main ports of the trading route. Briefly, liner companies operate a regular quality service as a common carrier both of high-value break bulk cargoes and, occasionally, passengers. There is an important difference between the movement of the freight and passengers. The transportation of freight is part of the cost of production, as opposed to the movement of passengers, particularly tourists, who pay for the entire voyage themselves. They are the final consumers, a position making passengers fairly responsive to price changes (an elastic demand). Freight movement has no such elasticity. For this reason, and because passengers are now insignificant in deep sea liners' commercial activity, this discussion will concentrate on the movement of cargo. Individuals on sea cruises are seen as holiday makers not passengers.

Liners provide quite a different transport service from that provided by the bulk and neo-bulk trades, in two distinctive ways. The most important economic difference is the method of establishing the freight rates. Bulk freight rates emanate from competitive market activities. Liners freights are determined by a complex method of rate fixing, that is by Liner Conference, a form of price discrimination or the practice of charging different rates to different shippers. Such conferences prescribe, in considerable detail, the rate to be charged for each category of service. There is no "open market" price which liner companies can adopt. The structure within which they operate is one where the conference is the freight rate 'maker', as opposed to the bulk carrier market, where the ship owner is a freight rate 'taker'.

Secondly, liner vessels are available as common carriers at regular intervals, with little short-run regard as to whether the service is utilised or not. Vessels will depart with full, part or no cargo at a specific time in accordance with a pre-determined schedule. Operating such schedule services generally creates problems for capacity utilisation.

Development and Structure of Liners

This chapter, as has been made clear, is concerned with freight movement, not with the movement of passengers, but to understand the liner trade, it is important to examine the elements in its genesis. One of the most important of these was the movement of passengers, not only the general run of travellers, but immigrants and, on some routes, pilgrims. The primary passenger liner trade was across the North Atlantic, with what can be termed the Great Liners, operating such famous names as the Mauritania, France, Queen Mary and Queen Elizabeth. These ran regularly between Europe and North America across the North Atlantic, where it would be unusual to have a completely comfortable voyage, and where, in winter, extreme weather conditions could be expected. These liners were seen as setting the standards of opulence, such standards only achieved by carrying extremely large crews, the majority in the catering department. A general calculation is that the ratio of crew to passengers stood at 1 to 2.5, with this, during the winter, being in the region of 1 to 1 or lower. Thus, for the passenger crossing, the North Atlantic in a liner was an often unpleasant method of travel. For the shipowner this was combined with very high costs, particularly, labour costs. Hence, in the winter months the passenger liner sector was vulnerable to competition from any quarter.

One of the underlying contributory factors in the development of the large liner was long-term mail contracts. These were the most obvious methods used by governments to subsidise the development and stability of rapid trans-ocean communication. It was in this area of activity that serious competition began. Airmail developed and prospered in the inter-war period and, by the early 1950s, virtually all long-distance mail was conveyed by commercial aircraft. There have been some inroads made into passenger movement, but, during the 1950's the long range jet aircraft came into service.

This had a disastrous impact on the North Atlantic passenger trade, as the following table shows:

Table 12.1   Development of Air and Sea Passenger Traffic Between North America and Europe 1955-1970

YEAR	TOTAL	BY SEA			BY AIR		
	THOUSAND PASSENGERS (000)	THOUSAND PASSENGERS (000)	PER CENT INCREASE/ DECREASE OVER PREVIOUS YEAR		THOUSAND PASSENGERS (000)	PER CENT INCREASE/ DECREASE OVER PREVIOUS YEAR	AIR TRAFFIC AS PERCENTAGE OF TOTAL TRAFFIC
1955	1,616	964	3		652	16	40
1956	1,803	1,018	6		785	20	44
1957	2,004	1,036	2		968	23	48
1958	2,150	957	- 8		1,193	23	55
1959	2,247	880	- 8		1,367	15	61
1960	2,625	865	- 2		1,760	29	67
1961	2,701	782	- 10		1,919	9	71
1962	3,086	814	4		2,272	18	74
1963	3,210	788	- 3		2,422	7	75
1964	3,781	712	- 10		3,069	27	81
1965	4,260	649	- 9		3,611	18	85
1966	4,804	606	- 7		4,198	16	87
1967	5,493	506	- 17		4,987	19	91
1968	5,633	375	- 26		5,258	5	93
1969	6,331	335	- 11		5,996	14	95
1970	7,451	249	- 26		7,202	20	97

Source: OECD Maritime Transport 1970 p.53-54 and p.125

The first and obvious point of the above table is the massive growth in transatlantic passenger movement some sevenfold in the period. In the early years of the period 1955-1957, this was a combined growth, enjoyed by both sea and air, but, in 1958, air overtook sea and went on to grow at an astonishing rate, whereas liner shipping with the odd exception of 1962 declined year-on-year. Air increased rapidly, both in real and percentage terms, from 40% of the traffic in 1955 to 100% of a considerably larger whole a decade and a half later. The North Atlantic can be seen as the progenitor of other ocean passenger routes. These, of course, reacted to different time scales and events, the prime example being the closure of the Suez Canal and its effect on Eastern trades. Thus, by the 1970s, the primary method of moving large numbers of people, which had prospered for a century or more had been completely replaced by a totally different transport technology. Within the present context, two points need to be made. Firstly, this rapid change was bought about by external technology developments having nothing to do with shipping. Secondly, the eradication of the best known and most expensive sector investment had little or no effect on most other sectors of the shipping industry.

This served to verify the earlier definition of the shipping industry as a group of loosely associated industries.

The definition of liners emphasises that it is a group of technologically different vessels serving different commercial requirements. Table 12.2 looks at recent trends in this sector under three very broad headings; General Cargo and Passenger Cargo, Containerships, and Ferries and Passengers. The latter was added for information, as much of this tonnage will obviously be engaged in the short sea trade. Another point that should be made is that the table is based on dead-weight tonnage, which, in terms of liner vessels an is under-estimation of the value of such tonnage.

The table highlights the major restructuring of the liner fleet since the base year of 1980. The General Cargo and Passenger Cargo category has seen a decline in tonnage of some 12%. This

Table 12.2   Basic Liner Tonnage 1980-1995
(+ 1,00 DWT - of World Tonnage)

		1980	1981	1982	1983	1984	1985	1986	1987	1988	1989	1990	1991	1992*	1993*	1994*	1995*	Change
General Cargo & Passenger Cargo	DWT	117.8	116.4	116.3	114.6	111.3	108.3	103.6	100.6	98.1	104.2	105.4	106.1	104.9	106.1	103.7	104.1	88%
	%	(17.1)	(16.7)	(16.5)	(16.5)	(16.5)	(16.1)	(16.0)	(15.7)	(15.4)	(16.1)	(15.8)	(15.3)	(15.1)	(15.0)	(14.2)	(14.2)	–
Container Ships (Full & Lighter Carriers)	DWT	11.2	12.4	14.2	15.7	18.0	19.9	21.5	23.1	24.2	24.6	26.1	29.6	32.4	34.8	39.0	43.8	390%
	%	(1.6)	(1.8)	(2.1)	(2.2)	(2.6)	(3.0)	(3.3)	(3.6)	(3.8)	(3.8)	(3.9)	(4.3)	(4.7)	(4.9)	(5.4)	(6.0)	–
Freight & Passengers	DWT	2.4	2.4	2.5	2.5	2.5	2.6	2.7	2.8	2.8	2.9	3.2	3.4	3.7	3.8	3.9	4.3	180%
	%	(0.4)	(0.4)	(0.3)	(0.4)	(0.4)	(0.4)	(0.4)	(0.4)	(0.4)	(0.5)	(0.5)	(0.5)	(0.5)	(0.5)	(0.6)	(0.6)	–

Source: UNCTAD Review of Maritime Transport (Respective Years) (1980 = 100)
* = Category Change from 1992 to General Cargo and Container Ship

was almost totally concentrated in the 1980s. From 1989 onwards, tonnage has stabilised, with only marginal changes. In percentage terms, the decline has been continuous with the single exception of 1989. Accepting this, this category still constitutes some 40% of world dead-weight tonnage. Containerships have experienced a massive increase in terms of tonnage, in the region of four-fold. This has been a steady uninterrupted growth. Similarly, in percentage of world tonnage, it has increased to 6%. This is, as argued, being in tonnage terms rather underestimates the importance in economic and commercial terms and the impact on not only liners but the industry as a whole.

These basic growth figures gives some broad indication of liners' development over the period. Their weakness is they indicate only tonnage. Some clearly not within the sector, as they would be small vessels operating in the short sea trade. In an attempt to rectify this problem and widen the area of examination, table 12.3 has been constructed for vessels over 6000 g.r.t. and the number of categories has been expanded.

This table serves to confirm the earlier one, with contractions in some sectors being more than matched by expansions in others, this despite the table being on a different basis (that is dealing only with larger vessels). General cargo vessels have seen a 40% fall in a number of vessels and a 25% decline in tonnage, suggesting some movement to larger vessels. The average age profile is one of an ageing fleet, presumably related to minimal investment in the tonnage. The passenger and general cargo has experienced what can only be termed a collapse, with some 60% decline in the number of vessels and in tonnage, the average age remaining remarkably and consistently high throughout the period.

Containers on the other hand, have, in the period, experienced a massive expansion, the number of vessels increasing threefold. The increase in total tonnage is even greater. The average age is consistent, with a high level of new investment, as it is particularly low when compared with other sectors.

329

Table 12.3 Development of Ship Types in the Liner Trades

		1980	1981	1982	1983	1984	1985	1986	1987	1988	1989	1990	1991	1992	1993	1994	1995	1996
General Cargo	No	4857	4755	4751	4632	4431	4123	3854	3588	3433	3351	3323	3303	3256	3166	3104	3050	3025
	GRT	4767	4710	4738	4677	4546	4337	4141	3909	3772	3708	3686	3678	3652	3570	3519	3476	3468
	Age	13	13	14	14	14	14	13	14	14	14	15	16	16	17	17	18	18
Passenger/ General Cargo	No	74	62	61	54	51	41	39	38	36	29	28	28	28	28	28	26	27
	GRT	787	632	622	540	497	399	368	350	336	273	261	268	273	273	273	263	275
	Age	25	26	25	25	24	24	25	24	24	24	24	24	24	25	26	25	25
Container	No	575	602	645	712	770	935	882	891	909	939	998	1066	1142	1225	1348	1478	1635
	GRT	1275	1339	1428	1575	1741	1902	2060	2127	2237	2345	2494	2690	2896	3113	3415	3771	4199
	Age	8	8	9	9	9	8	9	9	9	9	9	10	10	10	10	10	10
Refrigerated Cargo	No	336	337	349	379	408	407	410	414	429	447	473	490	522	560	554	536	529
	GRT	2998	3028	3125	3366	3687	3720	3767	3807	3937	4100	4345	4512	4817	5168	5135	4989	4925
	Age	9	9	10	10	9	7	7	7	7	7	7	7	7	7	7	7	7
Ro-Ro Cargo/ Container	No																	
	GRT					171	348	348	348	348	348	348	348	348	348	348	348	348
	Age					3	7	7	7	7	7	7	7	7	7	7	7	7
Passenger(Cruise)	No	232	231	232	232	236	237	239	242	247	254	264	277	284	291	293	298	307
	GRT	2557	2620	2718	2741	2855	2877	2973	3073	3164	3288	3622	3946	4192	4469	4608	4985	5551
	Age	22	23	23	23	24	24	24	25	24	24	24	23	23	23	24	24	24

Source: Lloyds Register of Shipping
Notes: Average Age. GRT is in 000's

Refrigerated cargoes have expanded in a similar way. There has been a steady expansion in vessel numbers and in tonnage. The difference is that this peaked early in the 1990s, and in recent years there has been a mild contraction. The average age was steady throughout the 1980s and, in the 1990s, has begun to increase.

Large RO RO (Roll-on Roll-off) cargo/container vessels are designed to load and discharge containers and other cargo on wheels, using trailers, small tractors or fork-lift trucks. They have an interesting development during the period. There was a remarkable burst of investment 1984-1985, creating several vessels of 3,480,000 g.r.t. in total. Since that date, there appears to have been no further investment in this class and size of tonnage. The age profile regularly increases on an annual basis, confirming this.

Passenger and cruise liners have been added to broaden the picture, but, of course, are not included in the freight analysis. Here, the numbers of vessels and tonnage have increased substantially and there is a suggestion of larger vessels operating in the trade. What is of interest is, despite the increase in both measure of numbers and tonnage, the age structure is remarkably and consistently high in both passenger carrying sectors. This higher-than-average age of tonnage indicates that there is a considerable number of vintage vessels operating in this trade.

The description of the development and present aggregate position should not be allowed to cloud the spectrum of firms within the liner sector. In addition to the few extremely large and well established companies, there are a number of small or medium-sized firms owning from 2 to 20 liner vessels, operating within both the conference and the independent sector of liner services.

Liners' Cost Structure

The liner section cost structure has much in common with other sectors in the industry, in that capital costs are a large proportion of total costs.

The significance of fixed costs (FC) is that, from the time vessels are committed to maintaining a schedule of service, a high proportion of costs become fixed for a considerable period of time. It has been suggested that for the conventional cargo liner, these fixed costs range from 80 to 90 percent of total costs[2]. These fixed costs (FC), it will be recalled, are costs which, in the short-run do not vary with output. Total costs are FC added to the variable costs. Variable costs (VC) will be those related directly to production.

It follows that average total costs (AC) will be actual cost of production, per individual units of output, and marginal costs (MC) are the total costs involved in producing an extra single unit of that output.

Relating these costs to a single liner vessel in the short-run, fixed costs, sometimes referred to as overhead or direct costs, will be a large percentage of total costs. These are substantially covered, once the vessel is in a position to load cargo. With such a high level of fixed costs, once output begins, average costs will decline rapidly. This decline in average cost (AC) relates largely to a lower level of marginal cost (MC).

The average cost curve (AC) for a single cargo liner is illustrated in the following model[3]:

The model assumes the cost of handling is constant per unit of output. The flow of trade constitutes a stable demand. The high level of fixed costs (FC) means that, as the volume of output increases average costs (AC) decline rapidly at quantity OQ. This will mean fixed costs (FC) are being spread over an increasing output. MC will be lower than AC, until they are equal at output Q, at the lowest average cost. From there, both these costs (AC and MC) will be identical and rise vertically. OP marks the lowest price level at which the vessel would continue to operate. In the above model the AC curve turns vertical when

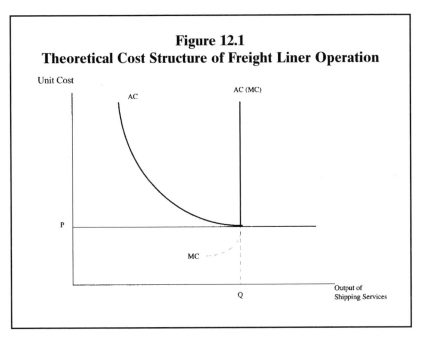

Figure 12.1
Theoretical Cost Structure of Freight Liner Operation

Source: Deakin, B.M. with Seward, T. Shipping Conferences. A
Study of their Origins. Development and Economic Practices.
University of Cambridge Press 1973. p91

the vessel reaches full capacity, a 100% utilisation. It should be
made clear that, for conventional liners loading break bulk cargo,
such a level of utilisation will be extremely difficult to achieve.
This is due to the difficulty in stowing and discharging such
heterogeneous cargoes. In reality, average costs (AC) would
begin to rise before quantity OQ was reached, it is suggested
some 10% short of full capacity. This makes little difference to
the general thrust of the argument. Deakin describes briefly
what he terms the theoretical cost structure of a single vessel,
thus:-

"In the short-run, therefore, the costs which have to be met
before any output can be achieved account for a very large
proportion of total costs and are, in fact, total costs, less only
selling, the cargo handling, and a proportion of ship's time costs;
and these are the only costs which will vary with output in the

short-run. So, once a vessel has been put "on the berth", a large proportion of total costs is fixed and inescapable in the short-run. Average total costs will, therefore, fall steeply as a large proportional fixed cost is spread over an increasing output. This characteristic of a ship's cost structure puts a premium on a high level of the ship's capacity at any level of price[4], the latter point of utilisation at any freight rate will be returned to".

A characteristic of this cost structure will occur not only in liner shipping, but in other modes of transport, in that, once the capacity of the vessel (or vehicle) is reached, as in this case, the vertical AC line at OQ, further capacity can only be furnished by providing another vessel with a similar cost structure. This cost structure will change, in the short-run, in relation to larger vessels only to the extent that variable costs will increase in proportion to total costs and average costs fall more rapidly and further with the vessels increased size. In the case of a smaller vessel, the process would be reversed.

This single ship cost structure is the short-run, that is, where freight earnings only begin after a large proportion of costs have already been covered in putting the vessel in a position to earn freight revenue.

The earlier model can be converted into a cost structure for a number of such vessels. Deakin argues that:

"Such a structure will create constant average costs and marginal costs in both the short and the long-run. Unlike the railways, sea freight transport has no track costs and very little long-run fixity in terminal costs. The output of freight shipping services, the flow of cargo, and the total cost of sea transport will therefore vary directly with each other and by approximately the same proportion over an extended range of output in the long-run, in other words the liner trade is likely to experience approximately constant marginal and average real costs in the long-run."[5]

A model is constructed to prove this assertion, using similar assumptions to the one above. Cost of handling is homogenous and common per unit of output. The flow of trade consists of a long-run stable demand. There are no economies of scale present.

The obvious distinction for other forms of transport, as the above quote makes explicit, is that there are no additional costs in the form of track or terminal costs, hence the cost of an additional unit of production is an additional "sailing" (that is, the distinctive cost structure of a single vessel already discussed), additional sailings logically adding further vessels to the model as illustrated below:

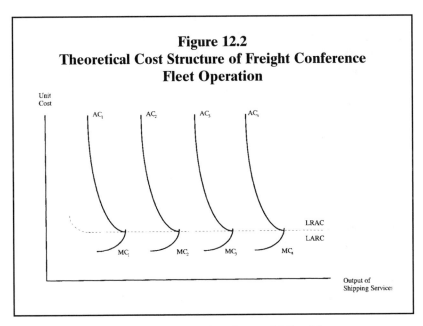

Figure 12.2
Theoretical Cost Structure of Freight Conference Fleet Operation

Source: op. cit. Deakin B. M. with Seward T p. 93

The model relates to vessels as members of conferences. There are, therefore, no discontinuities due to widely differing vessel types or efficiencies. This was largely covered by assuming no economies or diseconomies of scale. Sailings will also match the flow of transport, since demand is assumed to be stable. As to the question of capacity or utilisation, it is argued that, if this is a closed conference, the questions will not arise, as vessels in this system habitually achieve levels of 80-90 percent. In such circumstances it is reasonable to suggest that the rapid decline in the AC^6 to the juncture with the MC is followed by a vertical rising cost at the point of full capacity. It follows that the long-run average cost curve (LRAC) and long-run marginal cost curve (LRMC) come into contact at each level of full capacity.

This long-run curve is known as an envelope cost curve, because it includes all the average costs from below. It further indicates that no cost point below long-run average costs can be achieved with the present technology (that is, the present vessels operating in conference). The central thrust of the above discussion is that liners produce a broadly homogenous service, which will operate on a horizontal long-run average cost curve. On this basis, a comparison with the other dry cargo sector can be made.

Cost Competition Between Conventional Liners and Tramps

Dry bulk or neo-bulk carriers will for convenience be referred to here under the broad heading of "Tramps". These respond to different market demands for ocean transport liner shipping. But there can be substitution of this sector at the margin, that is to say, there is competition between them.

Tramp shipping's function is to convey commodities in bulk (that is, the movement of homogenous cargoes, of relatively low value, easy to store commodities moved in large quantities i.e. iron ore, steam coal or wheat). Such cargoes travel the world's main seaborne trade routes. In such trades, arrival dates and promise of delivery will be of relatively minor importance. Conventional liner shipping, in contrast, aims to lift cargoes of assorted merchandise of intrinsically higher value in relation to weight. These are break bulk cargoes, each consignment belonging to a different shipper. Being heterogeneous cargoes, each consignment will be separately packed, without uniform pattern or style. There will, for example, be manufactured or semi-manufactured products, bailed, bagged or boxed commodities

336

like electrical goods, cotton, rubber or tea. They will require skilled stevedores to efficiently stow such cargoes so as to utilise fully the vessels' capacity. Such conventional liners are specifically designed to effectively convey heterogeneous cargoes. The essential difference, then, lies not only in the different qualities of vessel use, but in the markets in which they trade (that is, one of homogeneous low-value cargoes, the other of heterogeneous high-quality cargoes). This will reflect on the cost structure of both sectors. Briefly, transport costs will be higher for smaller volumes of cargo in conventional liners.

Such a diverse structure appears to suggest individual and clearly separated markets, with no competitive interaction between them, but no such sharp division of mutual exclusivity exists. Conventional liners will, at times, load part cargoes of the type used in tramp tonnage. This can be done for a number of reasons, including trade revenues in excess of the incremental cost of the extra loading and discharging cargo at port time. This fits into the earlier argument of a premium on high level of utilisation of the ship's capacity at any level of freight, rather than operating a service in part cargo or completely empty, because of the lack of suitable cargoes. It may also be due to the need for a particular cargo configuration in the vessel, with fragile or delicate cargoes requiring to be stowed in the upper section of the hold, or the need to have the vessel sitting lower in the water.

Tramp owners may, on occasions, find it advantageous to lift liner cargoes, particularly if the port of discharge is one with a high probability of being offered another full bulk cargo. What is being argued as the prime reason for the difference in cost between liners and tramp owners is in the type and volume of the commodities shipped. Tramp technology and economic function is to convey large quantities of relatively low value goods, whereas the liner business is to convey comparatively small parcels of high value commodities. This should not be seen as implying there is no competition between the sectors for, at the margin, there can be active competition, as the following model illustrates. It is constructed on costs per year with high values of traffic.

337

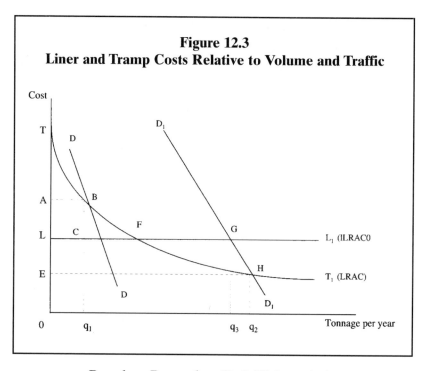

Figure 12.3
Liner and Tramp Costs Relative to Volume and Traffic

Based on Bennathan E. & Walters A.A.
The Economics of the Ocean Freight Rates F.A. Peager. LTD
London 1969 p14

The model is constructed on a number of assumptions; liner costs are constant per ton and the horizontal long-run average cost curve and long-run marginal cost curve L to L^1. These costs relate to the operation of a regular schedule service. Tramp costs will indicate this decline rapidly with the increase in the volume of cargo T-T^1 (long-run average cost). The demand curves DD and& D^1D^1 are inelastic and there are no economies of scale present.

The model is based on the relative costs, in relation to the volume in traffic. At the above point F, tramp costs TF increase rapidly (from L to T). Below F, tramp costs decline from F to T^1. It follows on a simple basis that, above F, liners have the competitive edge; below, tramps have the advantage.

338

Consider now the inelastic demand curve DD. This demand curve is for a small quantity of tonnage ($0q^1$). Should the liner rate make a fixed rate above A, that is, above the tramp costs B, it would be profitable for the tramps to enter the trade, despite there being no obvious freight rate and only a small quantity of cargo. If the freight rate was fixed at a level of A or marginally below it, the traffic would be lifted by liners at the quantity $0q^1$. Profits would be AL tons a year. The revenue is given by the rectangle $0ABq^1$, the costs $0LCq^1$. Profits are therefore shown by the area ALBC.

Examining now the other inelastic demand curve D^1D^1. There is demand for a much larger quantity at this level. Liners would theoretically offer to lift q^3 on their cost curve G, which is less than q^2. It is safe to presume they will make no such offer. They are not interested in lifting such large quantities of cargoes. Tramp costs at this quantity q^2 are clearly well below those of liners (the distance E to L). This would be the type of cargo to interest tramp owners. Their cost would be $OEHq^2$. This would secure them normal profits, which is, of course included in average cost (LRAC).

In this simple model, a demand curve in the region of F has been carefully avoided. To place a demand curve there would present particular difficulties with accurately assessing the elasticity. Demand curves DD and D^1D^1 are inelastic but, obviously, in the region of F there is a possibility of close substitution between liners and tramp tonnage. This would entail, by definition, a highly elastic demand curve. To avoid this complication, no demand curve has been added. What the model highlights in the behaviour of both sectors is related to the volume of cargo offered. In the small volumes, liners have the advantage, large volumes are advantageous to tramp tonnage. The model also shows the competition or potential competition with liners comes from tramp tonnage, particularly at the high cost levels in the area LFT. In addition tramps would be an important restraint on conference rates. [7]

Liner Revenue

The revenue or pricing policy of the liner conference is based upon the principles of "Charging What Traffic Will Bear" or a similar concept "Value for the Service", what in economics terms is price or freight rate discrimination. This is the practice of charging different rates to different users of a single service, when such rate differentiation is not justified by cost differences. Such a policy is only feasible when some markets are capable of being isolated and the service must, of necessity, be consumed on the spot, rather than elsewhere, or stored. Of central importance is the inability to re-sell the service in another market (that is, the prevention of lower price services being re-sold at a profit in a higher priced market). This is sometimes referred to as arbitrage. Such criteria assumes some oligopolistic collusion and means that freight discrimination is a wide-spread phenomenon in the transport industry, not only in liner shipping, but in civil aviation and railways. In transport, there is clearly a segmentation in the market. Such criteria sits comfortably within the liner sector, but this rather strict definition of price discrimination has the underlying presumption that all services will be sold at or above the level of average cost. This, as has been seen, does not necessarily follow in the liner sector, where cargo will be lifted at levels of freight which do not cover long-run average cost (or long-run marginal cost), such operational decisions implying or necessitating cross-subsidisation between different groups of cargo. This argument has been confirmed in a number of studies in the structure of liner conference pricing. They conclude that some commodities are charged substantially higher freights than the long-run marginal cost, while other commodities are charged considerably less. Further, at both ends of the spectrum, freight rates become susceptible to competition, commodities with high freight rates per tonne being bid for by civil air transport, and low freight rated commodities, particularly those capable of being moved in bulk, being bid for by what had been termed "Tramps".

The aim is to have a freight structure which creates some balance between the profit gained in the higher rate section against the losses of the lower, and, hence, some cross-subsidisation between them. In any estimation of freight rates, there are two important elements; firstly, the value of the commodity being shipped and, secondly, the stowage factor. This is the quantity of freight tons of a commodity that can be loaded in a vessel. It is measured in cubic feet per metric ton and there will be considerable variations between the space required. Take a few examples; one ton of metal ingots or iron ore would occupy a volume range between 10-15 cubic feet; the same amount of coal, 50 cubic feet; the same quantity of baled wool, some 200 cubic feet. A number of studies have confirmed that there is a strong correlation between the stowage factor and liner freight rates. There is some disagreement as to which element is the most important, that of value of the commodity or stowage factor, in the establishment of the freight rate. This will presumably relate to the particular trade in which the conference operates.

One of the most important investigations into the structure of shipowners' average revenue curve was completed in the 1970's and concerned commodities shipped on conference vessels between Australia and Europe. There were over 1000 commodities shipped and these were arranged in seven broad homogeneous groups, on the basis of shippers associations related to the particular commodity groupings. The following model 12.4 illustrates the researcher's outcome. The model estimates average revenue function from Australia to Europe 1973-74[8].

Here, the long-run average cost curve (LRAC) is shown to be at $55. The average value per ton is showed under the commodity and the approximate stowing factor in cubic feet per long tonne within the brackets. As for the example, wool valued at $2,086 per ton with a stowage factor of 120, the commodities categorised are in blocks, as with wool 0ABC, a total revenue block. The average revenue (or demand curve) has been indicated by the theoretical curve, the thick line A-AR. This is based on the descending average value and stowage factor for the seven commodities. The model points out two main elements in freight rate discrimination: Firstly, that there is a strong correlation between freight rates and the stowage factor, the particular example being wool, which is considerably more expensive, in freight terms, than iron ore or metal. Secondly, it presents a cross subsidisation situation. Wool and sheepskins can be referred to as the "donors" while metal, ingots and ores are 'recipients'. It could be argued that this is an over-simplification, but the point is still well made.

Figure 12.4   Estimated Average Revenue Function for Australia-to-Europe Conference, 1973-74

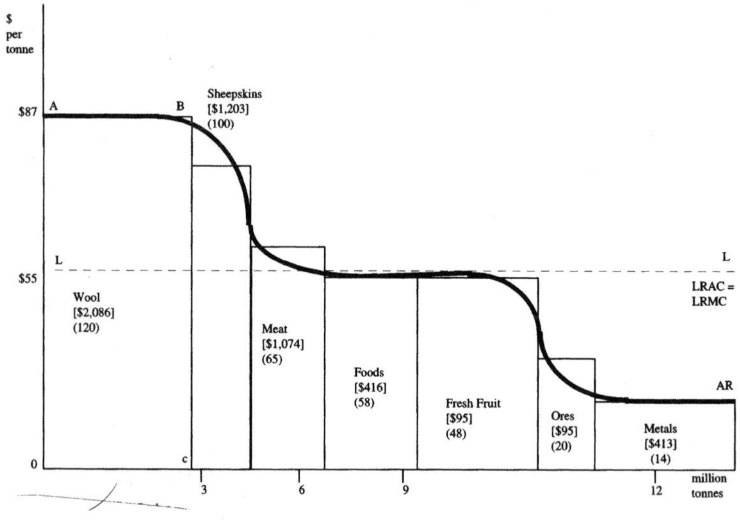

Source: Zerby and Conlon

The above revenue model explains the system of freight rate differentiation and long-run constant costs. Deakin constructs a similar revenue model 12.5, but with additional cost criteria added. This relates to a particular conference and a number of assumptions were made to assist in clarifying the data;

i)   Costs are homogeneous per unit of cargo, the long-run (LRAC and LRMC) being the horizontal line (LL). This stood at £16.07 (0B).

342

ii) The average incremental cost (AIC) is the cost of loading, stowing and discharging units of cargo, plus other costs, for example, rebates, but makes no allowances for ship time costs or differences in port efficiencies. These costs stand at (P1-A1C) £4.42.

iii) Perfect freight differentiation, rather than a block revenue system, is used. This ensures a smooth average cost curve A-AR (D).

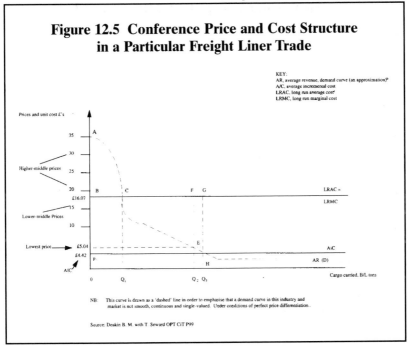

Figure 12.5 Conference Price and Cost Structure in a Particular Freight Liner Trade

The Deakin model suggests a balance between profit and loss sectors. The profit or "donor" sector is the area ABC at output 0Q1. These are consignments carried at a profitable freight rate and are in the high or middle freight rate traffic. The loss or "recipient" sector is CFE at output Q^2. These are consignments carried at a loss below LRAC cost line and at a lower/middle freight rate.

The lowest freight charged is £5.04 which is just above AIC. In the model, output stops at Q^2E on (FEQ^2). It could increase further to Q^3 at H (GHQ^3). Any cargo lifted beyond would be conveyed at a serious loss, for it would fail to cover incremental costs (AIC). The balance between the areas ABC and CFE, or, in the complete case CGH, is of importance to profit levels. In such an arrangement, the position of LRAC is essential. As Zerby and Conlon point out, the policy of differential freight rates "...makes it possible for shipowners to cover losses from all sources". For example, an increase in fuel costs will raise the long-run average cost curve. An above percentage increase in all rates will move the entire average revenue curve upwards, and thus eliminate the loss (the effect of any increasing unutilised capacity can be offset in the same way, assuming demand is not affected). If the general increase in rates leads to a substantial decline in value of certain commodities at either end, then exemptions can be made and compensated for, raising the rate even higher for commodities in groups.

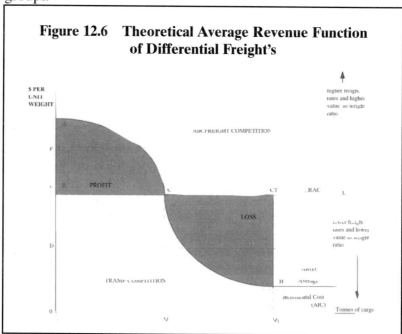

Figure 12.6 Theoretical Average Revenue Function of Differential Freight's

Source: Compilation of Figures

Thus one pricing system serves all purposes,[9] to summarise the above discussion of freight differentiation within a simple model figure 12.6.

Holding the assumptions already stated above, that there is a horizontal long-run average revenue curve and perfect freight differentiation, illustrated by the smooth average cost curve (A-H), freight differentiation, or charging what the traffic will bear, is constructed on two main pillars. Firstly, that the freight charges will not be so high as to stop the cargo moving; secondly, not to charge freight rates so low as not to cover the additional costs (AIC) to which moving the cargo gives rise. Such freight differentiation can be achieved by conferences, because of the extreme fragmentation of the shippers (buyers). They have precious little knowledge of the freight rate beyond their own consignments and, perhaps, that of their direct competitors. The importance of the two curves AR (D) and LRAC (LL) has been emphasised. The AR (D) curve follows from left to right as will a normal demand curve. The area above the LRAC (LL) (that is ABC at production 0Q) is of the high freight rate, the high value-to-rate ratio commodities. There are a number of arguments put forward for the position of A, the presence of air competition being the most important. This is considered to be most prevalent at rates between F and A.

The areas CCTH at product 0Q1 is the loss-making area, where lower freight rates and lower value-to-weight cargoes are carried. The base rate is shown as IH, this is just above AIC curve, the point where revenue would just fail to cover incremental costs. The other element here is presence of competition from what has been turned tramp tonnage. In the bulk trades, this would operate in the area below D. The model also suggests a perfect balance between loss and profit areas of commercial activity.

Deakin comments on the above:

"We have seen earlier that there is a strong motivation by operators towards a high degree of utilisation of ships capacity, due in most part to short-run factors governing ships' economics. There is also a desire on the part of shipowners to attract some bulk or "base" cargo, as it is called, to each voyage for technical reasons associated with the handling of the vessel at sea, and also in order to deny such cargo to actual or potential competitors, who wish to attract such cargo for similar reasons. From conversations we have had with shipowners and operators within conference, we understood that basic cargo is so called for both physical and financial reasons. It is loaded into the hold first and, so, is the base upon which the smaller "parcels"[10] of manufactured goods are then loaded. The freight revenue for basic cargoes is also deemed to cover a substantial part of the basic cost of the voyage, and therefore, it is regarded as the base upon which the usually small, individual consignments of high-value and high-rated cargo then provide the profit. The shipowner is, therefore, regarding economically marginal cargo as being non-marginal, in fact as "base" cargo, and this may lead to financial losses on the voyage concerned, but, if the competition is warded off by these pricing tactics, then there is some commercial advantage to individual conference member and to all conference members."[11]

Conferences

Liner conferences are one of the most enduring of the industry's institutions. They are an informal association of independent liner operators which act collectively to limit competition among participant lines, by instituting a uniform freight rate structure for a diversity of commodities over particular routes. This is combined with policies to limit external competition from non-members. There are also various methods used for the sharing of trade among members and a common policy towards shippers and their associations.

The United Nations offers the following definition:

"The word 'conference' denotes, not a single system, but a generic term covering a whole variety of common services and common obligations undertaken by shipowners serving particular trades. Broadly speaking, the term denotes a meeting of lines, serving any particular route, aimed at agreements on uniform and stable rates of freight and the provision of services under stated working conditions in that trade. It ranges from a very informal association to a well developed organisation, with a permanent secretariat behind it. The obligations the parties to such agreements undertake towards one another will vary as widely as do the agreements themselves." [12]

After making the point that there was no such thing as a typical conference, they added a further description, as follows:

"A shipping conference is an unincorporated association of mutually competitive liner operators, maintained for the purpose of (1) controlling competition among its members; and (2) strengthening the members through co-operative action in their competitive fight against non-member carriers." ([13])

Conferences have traditionally been seen as a classic example of cartel operations. A cartel is an agreement made by a number of independent suppliers for the co-ordination of a common production or selling policy. The aim is to secure some level of monopoly profit. The principal problem is, if such profits are to be made it is essential to restrict the member companies activities, which may interfere with the conference management, while avoiding the possibility of some members breaking away. Conventional liner markets are organised on the basis of conferences, which combine a number of interlocking cartels with substantial monopoly pricing. Participants argued that the power was extremely limited and their object was to stabilise trade conditions. This description is of the general "closed" type conferences (that is, where new members join only with the consent of the existing membership). Because of the peculiarities of the United States government regulation, closed conferences are not allowed in their trade, within that trade "open" conferences function which allow any line operator to become a member. The economic question that persists in all conference operation is the level of monopoly power. It is generally agreed that, in recent decades, it has been seriously

347

weakened by the rapid development of containerisation. The impact of this, it has been argued, transformed conferences from cartels to oligopolistic producers. An oligopoly occurs when there are just a few firms sharing a large proportion of the industry's production and each firm is concerned with the effects of its actions upon the behaviour of the other firms. One authority points out "oligopolistic tendencies to liner shipping are strengthened also by the existence within many conferences of pooling agreements, designed to reduce or eliminate in-service competition among the participating lines. There is no information on a world-wide basis to indicate the extent of such practices".[14]

To examine the development of conferences, in an attempt to determine the type of economic analysis best suited to their activities. Conferences originated as a reaction to the expansion in fleet capacity, which outstripped the growth in the volume of international seaborne trade. The original conference, it is generally agreed, was the Calcutta/UK tea trade established in 1875. The growth in supply on that route resulted in serious over-tonnaging, the reasons for this were technological developments of the steam ship, with faster average speeds and greater cargo stowage capacity. This was combined with a massive increase of supply brought about by the opening of the Suez Canal, which shortened sea distances dramatically. Conferences soon developed into a group of shipowners, operating independently, but co-operating to control competition among themselves and present a united front to prevent non-conference vessels interloping in their trade. The problem, or need for oversupply, has persisted. "The conferences also had consciously maintained some measure of excess capacity on the grounds that this cushion is needed in order to maintain frequent schedules sailings during good years and bad. Coupled with relatively high fixed costs, this excess capacity creates a condition in which affirmative protective action is required to maintain tariffs at compensatory levels".[15] The central plank of the organisation was a deferred rebate system, a method of retaining the loyalty of shippers. This insisted on the shippers sent all their cargoes to destinations covered by the conference only in conference vessels. In return shippers would receive a rebate, a proportion of previously paid freight rates, typically between 5% and 20%. Should the shipper despatch cargo by non-conference operators, this was failure to abide by the agreement and the rebate for the whole period was forfeited. Various forms of rebate systems were developed.

The United States Shipping Act of 1916 specifically forbid such agreements in their country's trade. To avoid this, a Dual Rate Contract was introduced. Here, in return for shippers undertaking to direct all their cargoes exclusively to conference vessels, they would receive, immediately, the discount removing the requirement to wait the deferred period of time.

Another element in the economic development of conferences was pooling of trades or revenue. Put simply, this consisted of each member being allotted a given share of cargo on offer. Such sharing was calculated on a variety of bases, for example, the average lift of cargo by member companies over the number of years. What conferences extensively offered their loyal shippers was a regular service at comparatively stable freight rates, as against the volatility of competitive bulk trade markets. The price of such stability was shippers' loyalty to the conference.

While criticism of the conference system concentrated on the level of freight rates, this was rarely an internal question, for conference agreements removed competition between shipowners, based on the level of freight rates. What competition did exist was on the quality on the service individual companies provided. In this way, conferences succeeded as organisations on regional break bulk cargo operators. They have two basic aims to regulating trade and fixing freight rates, entailing combined opposition to any interloping company trespassing on conferences trade.

An enquiry undertaken by UNCTAD constructed an interesting and illuminating model of the different forms of conference trading on what was termed "way port conferences". Such conferences were defined as "trade from or to a port which was served by conference lines as part of a longer route [16]. The

349

central point emerging from the model being the variety of conferences with no specific pattern. The model was illustrated by a schematic diagram, upon which some generalisations on conference trade methods can be made.

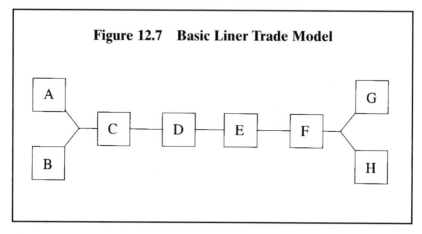

Figure 12.7   Basic Liner Trade Model

Source: UNCTAD The Liner Conference System.
New York 1970 p.61

A number of assumptions and clarifications are required:

(1) A and B were at one end of the route, an area, region or country, for example, the UK and Europe. Both engaged in owning and operating liner tonnage.

(2) G and H, similarly, are at the opposite end of the route and are countries, for example Japan and the Philippines, also operating and owning liner tonnage. Thus A, B, and G and H are the key elements in the system.

(3) C, D, E, and F are a port or ports in different countries along the conference route.

The model serves to explain three types and some sub-types of classes or conference, also the way in which specific conferences may serve to restrict the activities of other conference lines. That is to say that the conference system produces an individual

350

service, by organising trade with a number of ports in a diversity of countries.

The first type is simply a conference whose vessels operate between A and B at one end of the route, and G and H at the opposite end, including C, D, E and F as 'way ports' on the conference route.

The second type serves to identify two sub-classes of the first type. Here, the service is bifurcate, that is, divided into two branches. The 'way ports' are unaffected. In this, trade moves from A through the way ports to G and H, or on the same route, with a single source B. The progress can also be reversed, with a single trading source being either G or H. Often this form of service was organised in an agreement based on the national lines of the originating country.

The third type is where various sections of the whole trade model is broken down and covered by individual conferences. A complex of structures can easily be built, with trade from either end and forming into conferences, for example A and B to D and E or C and G. Any number of combinations can be found. Further, if A or B are considered the home base, separate conferences can be formed to operate service from A or B to D and E outward and for the homeward legs. If the assumption that the key elements own and operate tonnage is dropped another system can be drawn up on the separate conference trades of homeward and outward.

Three generalised types can be tentatively suggested; where the conference main trade covers all interim ports on the route; where a single origin similarly covers all the intermediate ports and, finally, a situation where a separate conference or conferences cover individual key ports and some specific intermediate ports. As stated this is an extremely simple structure, but, for all that, it serves to emphasise the wide diversity in conference trading activity.

Conference structure, while expanding considerably, remains, in all its essential elements, unchanged from the turn of the nineteenth century. They merely consolidated and strengthened their position, broadening their spheres of influence. The exception is passenger liner conferences whose operations were never as efficient or resilient as that of cargo liners. They have, with the short sea conferences, largely ceased to function in the inter-war period. In the decade following the second world war, the liner sector found not only external competition, but also competition directly from technological change and the development of shippers organisations. The latter despite it being recommended at the turn of the century, created the first Shipper's Council in the United Kingdom in 1955. Others in Europe and elsewhere followed. Hence, for the first time, the customer, the shipper, began to speak with a uniform and authoritative voice to the conferences.

Conference members operated traditional or conventional break bulk vessels, designed to carry heterogeneous cargoes, generally finished goods or semi-manufactured, in compartments on separate decks, with, on some vessels, refrigeration space or tanks for conveying edible oil and the like. Depending on the trade they were engaged in, such vessels were, by the mid 20th century, ranging in size between 6,000 and 15,000 g.r.t.

These vessels had the basic problem of all vehicles providing a regular transport service, that of optimum capacity utilisation. Services attempt to optimise the level of capacity from high and low cargo routes, a trade structure complicated by surges in demand, on particular legs of any conference route. By the 1950s, the massive increase in demand was still being served by a technology which had not been radically altered since the early part of the century.

As Rochdale points out:

"Given the decline in the profitability of liner operations during the last decade, and the trend of costs incurred by operators in providing a service, this suggests that the overall economic efficiency of liner services did not improve in the two decades following the second world war".[17]

This lack of improvement in economic efficiency can be attributed to the break bulk system being largely incapable, at this time, of taking advantage of the economies of scale, unlike the other bulk sectors in the industry. The cargo liners problem was the length of time required in port, loading or discharging cargo. Data for the year 1966 estimates, for liners, 175 days at sea, matched by 175 days in port, with 78% of cubic capacity utilised at sea. This can be compared unfavourably with other sectors. Taking the extreme case of tankers, they operated 290 days at sea, 60 days in port, and at a 98% cubic capacity at sea [18]. The liner's time required in port was simply exacerbated with any increase in the size of the vessel. The port time is one of the economic criteria of which the size of the vessel largely rests. To increase vessel size beyond some optimum related broadly to the length of trade route, speed and, of course, time in port. To attempt to move beyond such an optimum would be disfunctional, necessitating the lengthening of cargo operations and increasing costs which would outstrip any marginal increase in revenue. A utilisation problem relates to the labour intensive loading, stowing and discharging of small heterogeneous parcels and cargo, a situation where it was argued that a typical cargo liner spent half its time in port and half at sea. While dock labour in most of the developed countries was cheap, the perception was of an adequate system, but, during the 1960s labour costs began to increase rapidly, becoming an increasing percentage of total operating costs. It was estimated that approximately 25% of costs were due to traditional labour-intensive cargo handling methods and the total round voyage costs. Some 60-65% were incurred while the vessel was in port, much of the time spent not moving any cargo.[19] The solution was seen in unitisation, on the classic economic criteria of a labour-intensive port operation being replaced by capital-intensive one, the presumption being that such investment in a capital-intensive system of cargo handling and moving would be more than compensated for by increased efficiency and economies of scale.

Unitisation was to be achieved in three main ways; palletisation, roll-on roll-off and containerisation. Palletisation is a comparatively inexpensive modification of cargo- handling methods, binding small packages into large ones. These are handled by fork- lift trucks, removing the need for manhandling. This standardisation of consignment size serves to simplify storage. Roll-on roll-off vessels, which quickly became known as 'Ro-Ros', were a variation on the container theme. These vessels loaded vehicles carrying containers, losing between 30 - 40% of the cubic capacity, largely because of the axle space. However, they gained in loading and discharging speed generally using the vessel's own ramps, in this way moving much of the heavy capital expenditure of equipment and parking areas.

Containerisation was the prime engine of change. It enabled large initial expenditures, mainly in port infrastructure (that is, handling equipment, unloading and distribution areas).
The advantage to liner shipping was highlighted in the 1970s:

"Containerisation affects the economic structure of the industry in three ways. It brings economies of scale to the stevedoring process, by making the process capital-intensive rather than labour-intensive, drastically increasing vessel utilisation by reducing port-to-sea ratios from 1:1 to 1:4, and making possible the development of intermodal services by facilitating the interface between carriers. Because of the high fixed capital costs, unit costs decreased drastically as volumes increased. Vessel costs per tonne may be lowered to one half of break bulk operations, assuming volume operations are achieved, and, more significantly, translating increased capacity into annual revenue. The high-productivity ship may achieve as much as five times the revenue of a break bulk type vessel." [20]

Containers initially operated on coasting and short sea trades, where only limited amounts of capital were required. The standardisation of the containers was an important factor in its further development. They began to be built to the specifications of the international standards office (ISO containers). The definition of a container as "an article of transportation equipment intended to facilitate the carriage of goods by one or more modes of transport without intermediate reloading." The generally accepted dimensions are 8 feet wide by 8 feet high (or

8 feet 6 inches) and 20 feet in length. A double container is 40 feet in length. The standard unit of measure is the 20 foot box as a TEU. These have become the current measure of our ship's capacity or a port throughput. Hence a container vessel will be defined as having the capacity of 2,500 TEU for example.

The institution of a new standard container ensured the development of deep-sea routes. Initially, large individual companies from traditional liner fleets began the process. The first stage was to replace the existing general cargo vessels with fully cellular containerised tonnage, a process where it quickly became obvious that the level of risk and the amount of capital required meant that it was beyond the capacity of these not insubstantial companies. The answer was to establish consortia. The original examples of such, were OCL, which were made up of P& O, Ocean Fleets, British and Commonwealth, and ACT(A) which was a combination of Blue Star and Cunard Lines. This group participated in the container trade between Europe and Australia. They were the base of an even larger consortium of OCL and ACT(A), as well as constituting the first operational consortium of the Australia-New Zealand container service (ANZECS). At the inception, it was assumed to be a temporary organisational method, which would function until a considerably larger Far East trade was containerised. Despite this, it lasted in its original form until the 1990s and still operates with some modifications. The requirements to establish very early in the deep-sea container's developments such a highly sophisticated consortium, often with pooling agreements and financial and operational co-operation, served to emphasise the level of capital investment required. Here, for obvious reasons, port infrastructure is ignored, simply to concentrate on shipping where the level of investment is extremely large. The general growth in containerised vessels was discussed earlier in this chapter, looking at them in terms of tonnage. Turning to examine the recent development in terms of TEU, there have been two inter-related developments, first, the simple growth in the number of TEU transported and, secondly, the increasing capacity of individual vessels. These trends are highlighted in the following tables. It should be noted it deals with vessels with a capacity of over 2,500 TEUs.

355

**TABLE 12.4: Containerships 1972 -1990 to 1996
(2,500 TEU Plus)**

	2500-3249	3250-4249	4250 Plus+	Total	Cumulative Total	
1972 - 1990		169	63	5	237	237
	(71)	(27)	(2)			
1991		20	5	3	28	265
1992		12	13	9	34	299
1993		9	20	1	30	329
1994		7	27	4	38	367
1995		5	23	21	49	416
1996		11	13	22	46	462
Total in Operation		233	164	65	462	
(%)		(50)	(36)	(14)	(+97)	

Source: Lloyd's Shipping Economists (LSE) December 1996.

The broad trends between 1972 and 1990 are covered, with detailed developments since 1990. The total number of vessels operated in 1996 is approximately double that of 1990. In terms of capacity, the total of 1.6 million TEUs in 1996 is double that of 1990 (not in the table). The number capacity of 2,500 to 3,249 constituted, in 1990, a rise of 71%. By 1996, it had declined to 50%. At the opposite end of the scale, the larger vessels' (4,250 TEUs plus) share of the increased total moved from 2% to 14%. Very large container vessels have, by the mid 1990s, begun to operate with a capacity ranging between 5,250 to 6,000 TEUs and the tonnage range at between 68,000 and 84,000 DWT (Dead-Weight Tonnes). These are post-Panamax, the large panamax vessels being in the range of 1,000 to 4,500.

The investment is such a substantial amount of capital in large. Often post-Panamax tonnage has been combined with the process of rationalisation and restructuring of the world liner trade routes. By the early 1990s, three major lines employed some 60% of TEU capacity. These were Europe-United States, Europe-Far East and Far East- United States. It was on these high volume trades, combined with the around the world service that these large vessels were being increasingly concentrated, as can be seen from the following table:

TABLE 12.5 : Containerships by Trade Route 1996 (2,5000 TEU +)

Route	2500-3249	3250-4249	4250+	Total TEU
Round World	94	42	3	139
Asia/North America	68	42	25	135
Asia/Europe	35	69	36	140
Europe/North America	12	9	--	21
Other (including Vessels in dry-dock or between services)	24	2	1	27
Total in Operation	**233**	**164**	**65**	**462**

Source: LSE December 1996.

Round the world service is reducing the total number of ports at call, increasing vessel speed and there is a trend to larger TEU capacity. The inhibiting factor is a requirement to transit the Panama canal. Hence, vessels in the range 3,250 - 4,429 TEUs are the central type in this trade. The very large vessels are concentrated in the two Asian trades. The developments have created a position where vessels looked upon as large during the initial development of the container trades (that is, in the range 2,000 TEU) are increasingly operated as feederships, in this way, serving what has been termed as "The Global" or "The Mega" carriers or the plus-Panamax tonnage.

What has occurred in the last quarter of the century is a metamorphosis of the liner industry, from the established conventional cargo line, with all its limitations, which has operated successfully since the beginning of the century, to the larger and expanding container trades with the liner sector having responded to, as well as being a prime element in, its creation. In addition, this innovation has enabled the liner sector to withstand competition from bulk and neo-bulk shipping and land transport.

Such dynamic developments have only come about with very

large capital investment. This is being achieved in two ways; firstly, rationalisation, co-operation and strategic partnerships and, secondly, mergers and acquisitions of competitors. Rationalisation has already been discussed in the first and second generation of containers, the response being the creation of OCL and ACT(A). Strategic partnerships seek to operate on an improved service, but, to avoid danger of aggressive expansion which has, at times, created situations which have lead to a considerable over-capacity, such relationships imply operating co-operation, combined with equipment purchased and sharing in an attempt at cost-efficiency. The extensive mergers and acquisitions are evidenced by the increasing international concentration. In 1982, for example, the twenty leading carriers controlled some 32% of the trade. A decade later, they control 42% of a considerably expanded trade. This has created a situation where:

"Half of the worlds first twenty container operators are now setting-up "global partnerships" on the European-Far East and the trans-pacific trades (the transatlantic routes are being served by the vessel sharing agreements). Such alliances differ from the classic consortia in many ways, and, individually, none of them are constructed in the same way. shipowners are adapting their strategy to specifics of the trade. The normal linked conference-minded shipowner of similar size (global carriers) generally operate a long time in the trade. They are not part of an integrated financial or marketing scheme, as they were in the classic consortium. The new co-operative agreements are more flexible, their main concern being to maximise their ability to increase their market share and to extend their market, via space sharing. Financial, integration, however, is not ruled out, as there are general agreements including joint operating of container ports and terminals. It is even likely to improve in the near future and some partners of global partnerships are likely to decide to join in joint vessel ownership".[21]

The Question of Maximisation

What has been put forward is that liner shipping differs radically from other sectors of the industry and this can be attributed to the individual characteristics of this sector. The prime reason is the obligation to provide a scheduled service. This means a vessel will sail, virtually regardless of the amount of cargo loaded and the level of capital utilisation. This is combined with the fluctuating demand from a multiplicity of shippers, the unit of this demand being generally relatively small in relation to the supply (that is, the carrying capacity of the vessel on a given service voyage).

Such radical differences underline the following discussion, which suggests different theoretical criteria are appropriate to liner shipping. This is essentially that liner conferences will produce a level and quality of service exceeding that of the individual profit- maximising firm. Previously, the discussion has concentrated on the theory of the firm in relation to bulk markets and has been based on the presumption that these firms are generally motivated by the desire to maximise profit (that is, the standard motivation of a pure desire to maximise profit in a competitive firm in the short-run, by applying the marginal tools of MC = MR, which will also be the minimising loss production position). This, as suggested, is appropriate to bulk freight markets, which are akin to perfectly competitive market situation. As pointed out, the conference liner's function in a structure of a cartel. In such a structure, the suggestion is high-value commodities will be shipped at high freight rates and large quantity low-value commodities will be shipped at low rates, with the stowage factor taken into account in all cases. Such criteria, which is based on price discrimination, will not fulfil the profit-maximisation goal; the goal will be different. The suggestion here is that it is some form of sales or revenue maximisation, a criteria which falls well within that already stated as the aims of maximising capacity utilisation and concern about potential competition.

A number of authors have contended that liner conferences objectives differ from that of the rest of the industry. S.G. Sturmey argues that:-

"Conferences both fix price and regulate capacity, but they do not, in the technical sense of economic theory, maximise the profits of the member lines considered as a group."[22]

They do not profit-maximise because of apprehension about new entrants, attracted by the high levels of profit in the short-run, which would probably encourage competition. Rather they maximise the present value of the flow of the revenue from the trade. This maximisation, Sturmey points out, must not be confused with maximising sales revenue. The argument may be summarised thus:

"It has been that conferences do not attempt to maximise short-run profit. A perfectly sensible explanation is that, if they pitch all freight trades to levels necessary to do this, in the long--run, they would attract competitors who could cut rates to such an extent that the traditional weapons of the conference for retaining its customers would be ineffective. Pricing is, therefore, determined on a basis which will yield reasonable profits to lines in the trade, but will not attract extra competition. The following model illustrates this argument:

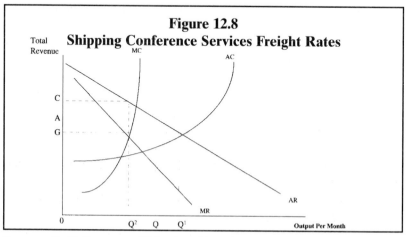

Figure 12.8
Shipping Conference Services Freight Rates

Source: S. G. Sturmey Shipping Econics: Collected Papers. Macmillan Press 1975 p125

The assumptions underlying the model are that conference sees the long-run and the relative policy in a particular way. The scale of productive enterprise remains the same and any additional capital equipment supplied simply duplicates that which already exists. Thus the long-run is not the one used in pure economics theory, because all factors are not variable. The model illustrates freight rates that will encourage or deter entry. At freight rate level C, output Q^2 profits will be maximised (MC=MR). This indicates cartel or monopoly profits, a profit level encouraging new entrants to compete, and, if successful, decrease the level of profits in the short-run. The average cost curve (not included in Sturmey's model) indicates a freight rate of G and a quantity Q^1. Here, normal profits will be secured, as average costs include normal profits. This will constitute a deterrent position, as there would be no pressure to enter the trade. The conclusion is that conferences would look beyond the short-run, to be assured of their long-run position, in this way creating the freight rate A at quantity Q somewhere between the two extremities, a position which does not aim for normal or maximum profits, but maximises the present of the flow of revenue from the trade.

In the above discussion, it is pointed out that "Maximum present value of the flow of revenue from the market is not the same as the maximum sales revenue". The latter revenue-maximisation objective was developed by W. Baumol and other economists. What the theory postulates is that contemporary firms seek to maximise revenue in relation to some level of profit constraint, a fundamental change in name due, it is argued, to the majority of large shipping companies being organised on a clear division between ownership and control. Ownership is spread among the shareholders, whilst day-to-day control is left to management, a separation giving management wide discretion, underlying encouraging them to pursue their own goals. Baumol argues this causes management to be pre-occupied with maximisation, not of profit, but of sales revenue, an assertion based on the salary and status of management being closely linked to the growth in sales, not to profitability. It is not claimed that there is no need for profit, but the profit is recognised as acting as a constraint. This minimum profit-constraint is the appropriate profit rate that

361

has to be secured to satisfy shareholders. In a company aiming to maximise sales revenue, it will necessarily mean lower profit levels. To quote Baumol:

"To generalise from these observations and assert that the typical oligopolist's objectives can usefully be characterised, approximately, as sales maximisation, subject to a minimum profit constraint. Doubtless this premise over-specifies a rather vague set of attitudes, but I believe it is not too far from the truth. So long as the profits are high enough to keep stockholders satisfied and contribute adequately to the financing of company growth, management will bend its efforts to the augmentation of sales revenue rather than to further increases in profits."[23].

We look at this analysis in the following model, which is based on a number of assumptions:

i)   During the period, the firm attempts to maximise revenue, subject to profit constraints.

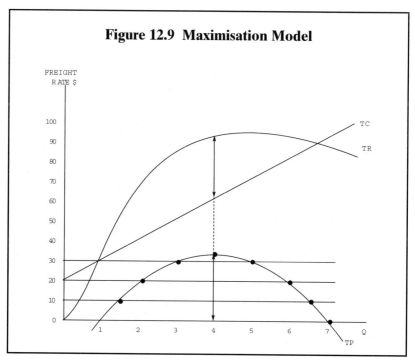

Figure 12.9 Maximisation Model

ii) Such profit constraints are determined by the expectations of a wide range of shareholders.

iii) The total cost-curve of the conference is linear, for reasons already discussed.

TR = total revenue, TC = total cost and TP = total profit. The profit maximisation output can be determined by the use of these total concepts as follows:-

$$TP=TR-TC$$

If the objective were to profit-maximise, production would be at **(4)** level of output, a position where the positive distance between TC and TR is greatest (that is, where the slope of the two curves is equal). TR is at **(95)** and TC is at **(60).** Therefore, total profit TP will be at **(35).** This position will coincide with the maximum point on the total profit curve TP (which, in previous models would be at MC=MR output.) However, the model is directed at examining revenue-maximisation with minimum profit-constraints. This can be expressed as a return on investment, or, as in the present example, as the rate of profit. If the minimal acceptable level of profit is at **(10)**, which is revenue maximisation level of output **(7)**. If the level of output were **(5)**, profits would stand at **(3)**, which is greater than the minimum required to satisfy shareholders. In other words the minimum profit-constraint is not operating. The maximum revenue will be dependent on the minimal acceptable level of profits. This can, therefore, act as a constraint on conference activities. Should the minimum profit be above **(35)**, no output or revenue would satisfy the profit-constraints, although management might, or will, attempt to achieve it. Thus, not only would profit-maximisation output and revenue-maximisation output coincide, but profit-constraint would be set at the same point as profit-maximisation. Therefore, the profit- maximisation model is the specific case within the revenue-maximisation model and output achieved by the revenue-maximisation model will be that assumed under profit- maximisation.

The underlying rationale for the revenue-maximisation model, in relation to liner conferences, is that the latter aims to increase trade, accept collective decisions and create a balance between profit-maximisation and trade-expansion. As has been pointed out:

"While extreme actions are not predicated on the basis of economic theory, the inability of conferences to act as profit-maximising cartels is expected. The presence of numerous cost levels and product differentiation among firms precludes joint profit- maximising agreements. The conditions and inertia within the conference system has led individual firms to play the role of price-takers rather than price-setters. (sic) It may be concluded, then, that attempts to explain conference actions in terms of profit maximisation goals will encounter significant inconsistencies. More likely, adequate explanations lie in the application of conference rule-of-thumb within a revenue-maximising goal, subject to minimum profit-constraints." [24] This should be tempered by making it clear, in general, and specifically for liner conferences, the empirical evidence of revenue-maximisation is both mixed and inconclusive.

Summary

Liners are the most sophisticated sector of the shipping industry, and one which has undergone profound changes in the last two or three decades. Still, many of the basic problems remain, particularly those inherent in running a regular schedule service. This creates a cost structure with a large element of fixed costs. Conferences, were in part, a response to this problem and that of over supply. The structure of conferences causes the aims of the Liner operator to be less explicit than those operating in other sectors. The introduction and rapid expansion of the container trade has created the need for large increases in the size of capital investment in the liner trades. This trend is still very much in evidence.

Further Reading

Bennathan E. and Walters A.A.
The Economics of Ocean Freight Rates, London, F.A. Peager Ltd, 1996.

Deakin B.M. with Seward T. Shipping Conferences. A Study of Their Origins. Development and Economic Practices,.Cambridge, University of Cambridge Press 1973.

Jansson J.O. and Schneerson D.
Liner Shipping Economics: London, Chapman and Hall 1987.

Pearson R.
Container Ships and Shipping: London, Fairplay Publications. 1988.

Sletmo G.K. and Williams E.W.
Liner Conferences in the Container Age: US Policy at Sea. New York, Macmillan 1981.

Sturmey S.G.
Shipping Economic: Collected Papers, London, Macmillan 1975.

Evans J.J. Concerning the Levels of Liner Freight Rates: Maritime Policy and Management. Vol. 9 (2) 1982.

---

[1] Jansson J.O. and Schneerson D.'Liner Shipping Economics', Chapman and Hall 1987.

[2] SG Sturmey - British Shipping and World Competition p.246. London, Athlone Press 1962

[3] This model and much else in this section is based on BM Deakin with T Seward - Shipping Conferences Fig. 1 . London, Cambridge University Press 1970

[4] ibid. page 91

[5] op cit. page 92

[6] op. cit. Deakin B.M. with Seward T.

[7] The high reaches of costs say ATB will also be open to commercial airline freight competition discussed later.

[8] Source: Zerby J.A. and Conlon R.M. An analysis of capacity utilisation in Liner Shipping. Journal of Transport Economics and Policy XII (i) 1978 p.33

[9] Source: Zerby J.A. and Conlon R.M. An analysis of capacity utilisation in ibid. page 33

[10] The discussion here predates containerisation.

[11] opt cit. Deakin with Steward p. 100-101.

[12] UNCTAD Liner Conference System New York 1970 p.3

[13] ibid.

[14] Lawrence SA International Sea Transport: Lexicon Books Toronto 1972 p.100

[15] ibid.

[16] UNCTAD The Liner Conference System New York 1970. Chapter 10 from which much of the following discussion comes.

[17] op cit. Rochdale

[18] op cit. Rochdale para. 412

[19] ibid. para. 616 Table 11.1

[20] Barker J.R. and Brandwein R. The United States Merchant Marine in National Perspective, Massachusetts, Lexicon Books, DH Chese & Co. 1970 p.6

[21] Maritime Transport OECD 1994 p.91

[22] Sturmey S.G. Shipping Economic Collected Papers, London, Macmillan 1975 p.76

[23] W. J. Baumol Business Behaviour, Value, Growth - Revised edition London Harcourt Brace and World 1967 p. 49

[24] Heaver T.D. A Theory of Shipping Conference Pricing and Policies, Maritime Studies and Management Volume 1 (1) 1973 p.26/27

Chapter Thirteen

PORTS

Introduction

Ports have, for the last half-a-century, responded to the demands placed upon them by the extraordinary growth in sea-borne trades[1]. This dynamic economic process has evoked technological responses from both ports and the shipping they serve, underpinning the reduction in the relative cost of maritime transport.

Ports are the essential components of the maritime industry, as there is an economic interdependence between shipping and the ports they use. A sea-port can be defined in terms of its function, which is the transfer of passengers and goods regularly between land and sea transport. The port performs, for sea transports, the crucial role of a terminal. In this way it differs from a "haven" or "harbour", which are geographical areas where the vessels may shelter from foul weather, revictualling or undergoing necessary repairs. Although the activities of ports and harbours are often combined, they can also be carried out separately. Terminal activities can take place regularly, out of sight of land, (for example, loading crude oil in tankers from a sea-bed pipeline). Another type of port is a naval one, which concentrates on the necessary measures required by military and defence operations. Here again, it is not unusual for both commercial and naval activities to occur in the same port complex.

In the maritime industry, the dynamic economic changes that take place are regarded as specific to sectors of the industry, These are exogenous factors, outside the sector's influence. It follows that port owners and operators see developments in shipping as externally determined factors, over which they have little control, but to which they must react. Similarly, individual shipping companies will modify their commercial activities, having taken account of port activities and developments. To illustrate this with a simple example, the operator of a gearless container vessel will not trade in a port lacking the necessary unloading facilities for containers. Within the maritime industry, the shipping sector and port operatives will see each others' activities as largely outside their sphere of influence. Although operating independently, there is a recognition that the activities of the other sectors have an impact on the others. Attempts are therefore made to predict long-run changes. Hence, changes initiated by one side are, in general, to be reacted to by the other.

A port can also be seen as a gateway, through which exports and imports move on their way to the next stage of production, or the final consumer. In this descriptive definition, the phrase "gateway" is used to represent a complex of physical facilities and services which provide an interchange between sea and domestic transport. The essential characteristics of such facilities are their ability to accommodate the needs of inland transport and that of sea-going vessels. The fundamental element of this multiple-stage process is the capability of the port's cargo-handling techniques. Simple technological capability defines any port's operation, activity and, on occasions, its ownership. Facilities designed specifically to efficiently load iron ore are generally incapable of any other function and, hence, designate that port's or jetty's central function. Often ferry ports, or bulk loading or unloading ports, are owned by the ship's operators. Petroleum ports are the obvious example of this type of industrial port. Here there is a "closed system", where shipowners, port owners and operatives are one and the same entity. In the movement of these bulk commodities, shipping and ports are perceived simply as part of the production process from the oil well to the retail outlet.

The following discussion will concentrate on the economic factors influencing a general port, with industrial ports receiving only limited attention. The chapter begins with an examination of capacity and performance, then a consideration of the philosophies of port management, factors influencing the investment decision, port costs and finally queuing and congestion.

Capacity

Industrial ports have a relatively short history. General ports, on the other hand, have an extremely long and complex one. At the outset, they were often simply places for the loading and unloading of goods. Further developments related to a number of factors, the most important being their geographical position and characteristics, both seaward and landward. These factors included the proximity to active sealinks, and ease of cargo movement into the hinterland of the ports. Jansson and Shneerson [2] suggest the following equation as a useful means of illustrating the technological development of a general port:-

---

Equation 13.1

$Q = \emptyset.n.u.$

where Q = Total Port throughput

$\emptyset$ = Expected berth occupation rate.

n = The number of berths (most adequately measured by the total

length of quayside).

u = Expected throughput, capacity of the berth.

They point out that the development of most general ports can be divided broadly into two periods.

Firstly, the long period of expanding capacity, achieved by increasing the number of berths. This was a period in which the introduction of some mechanisation, particularly cranes, improved berth capacity. In this situation, short-run, often second-cycle increases in demand were addressed by increased berth occupation, until full capacity was achieved, with its ensuing congestion and queuing. In the long-run, such congestion was avoided, either by investing in construction of additional berths (n), or by increasing berth capacity (u). This increase in berth capacity represents the second stage of development, with berth occupation improvements related to unitisation, specifically for containers.

The question of capacity throughput (Q) is based on the concept of some optimum level of activity, both from the sea and the hinterland. The aim is to suffer neither from unnecessary congestion and its costs, nor the problems associated with over-capacity. A model can be constructed, based on the problems of port throughput over a particular period of time, which is shown in Figure 13.1.

Throughput in tons per shift is shown on the vertical axis (Y), and the time period on the horizontal axis (X). The two measures used are the intrinsic capacity and slack. Intrinsic capacity is not full capacity, but the uninterrupted working at a high rate for a whole shift. The actual performance falls short of this rate and brings the idea of "slack" into the system. "Slack" exists for the reason that resources are not being used to the full and there are interruptions from external sources. The relationship between capacity, "slack", and actual performance is not a static one, since some excess capacity is necessary for seasonal and unexpected peaks in demands. As the model indicates, the object of port investment and operation is to limit the amount of such "slack". In such a system, increased demands will easily be met, even when occasional peaks occur. Should demand increase and stabilise, the slack will be reduced, but, if

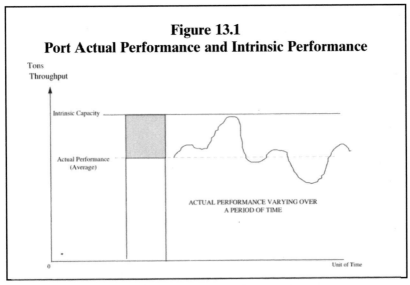

Figure 13.1
Port Actual Performance and Intrinsic Performance

Source: UNCTAD Berth Throughput United Nations 1973 p4

the seasonal peak demand can no longer be satisfied, it will be necessary to improve the performance of the system, leading to an increase in the intrinsic capacity.

Managing Philosophies

The general aim of limiting what has been termed the slack in the system can be identified in relation to specific managing philosophies. Such philosophies underpin the attitude, both to investment and pricing policies. The two most common and extreme managerial ideologies are the European or Continental, and the Anglo-Saxon or Peninsular. European and Continental philosophies see the ports as an important part of the regional infrastructure, beyond the parameters of the port's economic and social activities. Ports are a public service, a philosophy which is reflected in management ethos, institutional and regulatory factors. The value of the port is perceived in terms of the development and progress of industry and trade within its region of influence. Port management will support this, and, consequently, there will be a comprehensive Port Authority influencing the whole operation (that is, the organisation of the port areas and structure). In European countries, like Greece, and Latin nations, this would be the typical approach.

The Anglo-Saxon or Peninsular approach sees the port simply as a commercial activity, like any other commercial activity. Management control of the port is a private undertaking. The objective should be to earn appropriate profits or avoid unnecessary commercial losses. According to this approach, public intervention by any form of state administration has to be severely curtailed, limited to general duties such as land planning permission, safety, environmental problems, pilotage and navigation. This is also a measure to assure fair and competitive practices. Such a formulation of commercial services being in private hands operates in the United States and in Northern Europe, particularly in the United Kingdom, Denmark and Ireland. While both the European and Anglo-Saxon are useful models, what must be emphasised is that they are an over-simplification. In reality, there are no pure examples of these philosophies to be found, but groups of ports situated near both ends of the spectrum. These ideologies can be summarised by the amount of consideration given to the impact of any policy or action beyond the ports immediate perimeter.

An examination of the position of port services was undertaken by UNCTAD in the mid 1970s[3]. It showed that, not only did ports operate with different ideological aims, but there were considerable differences between developing and developed countries:

"Broadly speaking, the ports of developing countries mainly seem to be characterised by the existence of port authorities with far reaching powers, and by a public monopoly of the main services. In developed countries, the responsibilities of port authorities are generally less extensive, being limited to the construction and maintenance of facilities and, sometimes, official or unofficial supervision of other services. Other port activities of a public-service nature (police, fire-fighting, etc.) are often the responsibility of the State enterprise, while commercial activities are mainly the provision of the private sector, and often give rise to competition."[4]

During the 1980s, there were some modifications to these objectives of ports or port systems in some countries and much talk of privatisation. Much of this appeared largely to have simply confirmed the country's adherence to what has been termed the Anglo-Saxon ideology. Broadly, this has been seen as an increase in the autonomy of ports outside central government control increasing the role of the private commercial sector. Where such changes have taken place, they have varied from country to country, taking different forms, from privatisation, commercialisation, or co-operation, to some forms of de-regulation or reform of regulation. It was this de-regulation that was one of the necessary criteria to give ports' management the ability to function in a liberalised environment.

Though not always made explicit, the main purpose of these changes has often been to radically reduce the cost to the State. The State sometimes gained limited resources from the sale of port assets but, most importantly, it relieved itself of either the actual or potential need to invest in substantial long-term port infrastructural improvements. The immediate consideration was often combined with a belief in the importance of ownership, and that commercial ownership is superior to other forms.

These changes in ideology have evoked a wide variety of responses. In some countries, such substantial commercial investment proved impractical, simply because the private sector lacked the required resources or the necessary organisational structure for such a large undertaking. There was also the short-run temptation to take profit, rather than engage in long-term investment. The most significant risk in what was initially perceived as a market or competitive liberalisation has been the swift movement towards oligopoly or monopoly structures, removing any competitive element. This trend is particularly prevalent in countries where port commercialisation has been taken the furthest. To prevent these excesses, regulatory laws and legal restraints have had to be instituted, often in contradiction to the earlier dedication to commercialisation. The extent of the trend is difficult to assess. Not surprisingly, it was strong where the Anglo-Saxon ideology was firmly established, in the United Kingdom, some parts of Northern Europe, Australia and New Zealand. At the other extreme, it does not appear to have any marked impact on Africa.

There is also the question of how far public power has been transferred to the commercial sector, which, again, varies widely. In some areas, commercial operators have taken over virtually the whole of the port industries, apart from some minor public-services (for example, pilotage). In specialised terminals, particularly in the bulk commodities and commercial ownership, this is evident. In some commercial operations, there have been movements into super-structure and equipment, with the public sector retaining infrastructural investment. In others, the State still remains in total control of all port and hinterland activities. The lack of a dominant position for either of the ideologies underlying port policy is not unexpected. In such a dynamic industry the influence, particularly, of economic factors and the continuing change in national perspectives will create policy modifications, over time. What must be made clear is that national perspectives and policies are sometimes seen as international imperatives. This analysis was confirmed by a European Parliamentary study which stated:

"The performed comparative analysis showed that Europe does not escape the general rule that applies at a world level and provides for the existence of different types of port organisations. Authoritative experts point out that countries with similar geographical environments and compatible cultural traditions take exactly opposite philosophies regarding the operations of their ports. Moreover, it is well known that very efficient port administrations are to be found in countries which apply opposite principles and philosophies."[5]

Port Investment

It has already been established that ports are a grouping of facilities, designed specifically to ensure, as far as possible, the efficient interchange between sea and land transport. These fixed, highly-specialised investments are extremely expensive and have accrued in the long-term, using enormous amounts of scarce productive resources. In most cases they represent a large part of a nation's inherited economic assets. The maritime industry has similar economic characteristics to other transport modes, in that the mobile unit, the ship, has a comparatively short economic life and is inexpensive, compared to the industry's main infrastructural investment, the port. These terminals often have extremely long economic lives and only extremely limited alternative uses. The ancient ports of Shanghai and Alexandria confirm this.

Within these characteristics, the most important economic aim or benefit of investment in ports is to reduce ships' turn-around time. In such investments, economic principles will embrace technical ones, in the sense that the minimum amount of productive resources should be used to fulfil the purpose of the investment. In other words, limited resources are used to achieve maximum results. A technical example is the use of minimum-cost level bunker fuel to gain the highest vessel speed. Such investment is combined with the removal of what has been termed "slack" in the system, by seeking to secure some acceptable economic optimum. Before embarking on such investment, the question must be asked "What are the specific costs required in terms of factors of production in order to produce a particular quality and quantity of port services?" The cost of resources is the cost of the highest and most attractive alternative use. This is generally termed the **opportunity cost** [6], and is the amount sacrificed or foregone, should the resources be used in another project. In this way, the measure of cost of port investment is the value of the next most useful investment that could have been created with the same factor of production. For example, rather than port investment, investment in a quantity of railway track or an airport runway. This is the essence of the concept of opportunity or alternative cost.

As with much other transport investment, investment in ports is in highly specialised equipment that has a single efficient purpose or function, that of assisting in the transfer of cargo between land and sea. It has no alternative use. Once such an investment is made, there is no opportunity cost; the equipment is valueless. The obvious simple example here is a railway tunnel, which, when it ceases to be used, is generally a valueless hole in the ground, because it cannot be used for any other purpose. Similarly, with ports, an old enclosed dock would have no alternative use and, therefore, no value. There are some exceptions to this situation, where, for example, conversion has taken place into leisure and housing as with Albert Dock in Liverpool. However, this must not be allowed to cloud the general idea of no alternative use meaning no value.

Port investment is embarked upon to promote and develop the port itself, or its facilities. It is an attempt to make it more efficient by, for example, removing or lessening the amount of queuing and congestion on both the land and sea approaches to the facilities.

The basic criteria for such investment is as follows:

1. To choose between a range of projects proposed.

2. To decide the most appropriate time to embark on and complete such a project.

3. To decide whether to renew the old equipment, to continue to use it, or expand the facilities with totally new equipment.

The immediate benefits of such investment are felt immediately by the port users, which, in some cases, could be foreign-based shipping companies. Positive returns for the investor, however, are subject to a time-lag, emerging when the revenues start to exceed the costs. Numerous approaches may be adopted, in order to assess investment potential. Of these, the most frequently used is called the "pay-back" approach. This is a basic method where the annual returns are assumed to be constant, and other factors, such as interest rates and inflation, are not formally considered. Figure 13.2 assists in the explanation of this approach.

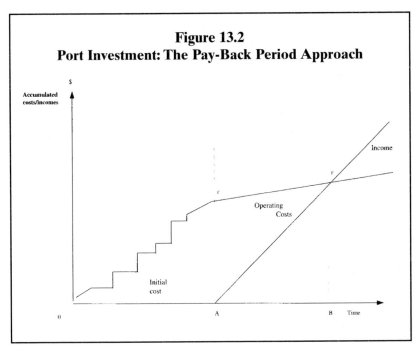

Figure 13.2
Port Investment: The Pay-Back Period Approach

Source: UNCTAD Port Development United Nations 1985
Figure B p13

The capital installation period is 0 to A. The steps in the diagram
serve to illustrate the 'lumpiness' of the investment costs over
this period. The investment becomes operational at point A, with
operating cost AC . The revenue increases, reaching point F,
where the income is equal to costs. This period AB is the pay-
back period. It can be defined as the number of years that has to
elapse before the operation sees a net return equal to the
investment capital expenditure. Different methods used in the
projects would ensure the same aim, but will be capable of
defining or moving point B. This would modify the length of the
pay-back period. The difficulty is to accurately estimate future
returns, since there is uncertainty as to when they will begin, how
long they will continue, and at what level. This is made
particularly difficult, as this method takes only limited notice of
external economic factors. Despite being commonly used, this
method is fairly crude. Its main defects are that it takes no

account of the time value of money or of the profit over the whole life of the port investment.

Port Costs

The level of investment is bound up with revenue or potential revenue (that is, port charges). Such charges are of importance when calculating freight rates. Research suggests that port charges at each end of a commercial voyage represent some 20-30 % of the costs included in the freight. An UNCTAD report on Port Pricing[7] produced a simple rule, which is still broadly accepted. Known as the "One-Third" rule, it suggests that in terms of freight costs the sea-leg consists of one-third, and the ports at each end one-third each. The study was "Valid for a medium sized cargo liner for a deep-sea route of average length".[8] Figure 13.3 is based on the UNCTAD study, combined with that drawn by Jansson and Shneerson. [9]

This shows the magnitude of various costs in relation to total sea freight. It has to be pointed out that, in this particular case, it is a break bulk vessel, trading between ports of developing countries. Shipowners costs in-port are ships lay time costs and the combined charges of the port and stevedoring. These each constitute an equal one-third of the total freight rate or costs. Costs at sea constitute the remaining one-third. Other cargo handling charges are those of the consignee. Consignees port charges are not part of the shipping freight costs.

The above discussion relates to a single voyage, and its freight costs in relation to port charges at either end. There also has to be a consideration of costs from the point of view of the supplier, the port, those demanding or consuming the services, the shipowner, and to combine these to give the total costs of the whole operation is the next stage of this discussion.

One of the core problems for all port operators is that ships arrive virtually at random, this applying equally to bulk tonnage and even, it is argued, liner vessels. In addition, time taken loading and discharging can vary widely, for a multitude of

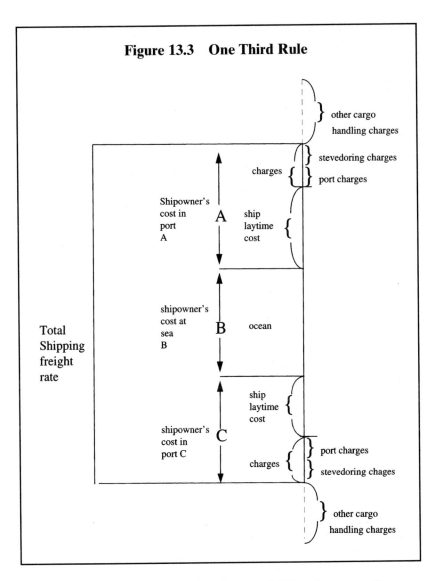

Figure 13.3   One Third Rule

reasons. Due to these and other factors, full berth occupation can only be achieved at the expense of vessels queuing and, perhaps, congestion in port approaches for longer periods. To ensure that no such congestion and queuing exists would require under-use of berths, i.e. the cost of lowering average occupation. Hence the optimum point has to lie between these two extreme positions. Examining the port costs, the standard economic cost structure is used, that of fixed and variable costs. Fixed costs, or overhead costs, are those which are independent of traffic volume or, put another way, tonnage throughput. They are costs that exist, even without any throughput. A large proportion of these costs will be related to capital. Variable costs are those related directly to the amount of production (that is, traffic volume or tonnage throughput). They consist of operating costs, such as power, labour and maintenance costs. These two cost-components are illustrated in Figure 13.4. This, and the two figures that follow (figures 13.5 and 13.6), are all constructed on two general assumptions:

1.   There is a given number of berths, which does not change.

2.   The working methods do not change during the period under consideration.

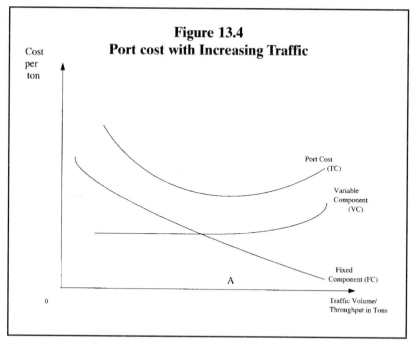

Figure 13.4
Port cost with Increasing Traffic

Source: UNCTAD Berth Throughput United Nations 1973 p9

The vertical axis (Y) shows the cost per ton, and the horizontal axis (X) the tonnage throughput or traffic volume. As tonnage throughput increases, the fixed costs (FC) decrease, and continue to do so. Variable costs (VC) remain stable, in the initial stages, until curving upwards under the pressure of higher levels of tonnage throughput, when it begins to rise steeply. This is related to the use of more costly methods of cargo handling (for example, the use of less efficient equipment). Total Port Costs (TC = FC+ VC) fall with the level of throughput. This is directly related to the contraction in the fixed costs element and stability of variable costs, until the minimum point A is reached. Just prior to this, variable costs begin to increase, an increase which soon outweighs the decline in fixed costs, causing the total costs to rise rapidly. From the port operator's stand-point, the minimum costs are achieved at a throughput indicated by point A, the lowest point of the total cost-curve.

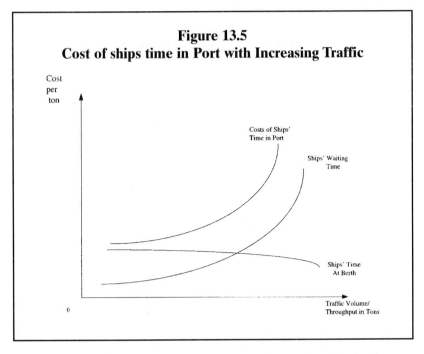

Figure 13.5
Cost of ships time in Port with Increasing Traffic

Source: UNCTAD Berth Throughput United Nations 1973 p9

Turning to ships' costs in port, the costs are examined in relation to non-productive time costs, that of time spent in port or related activities. This situation is illustrated in Figure 13.5, using the same assumptions laid out above:

Costs, in terms of ships' time in port, consist of two elements. Firstly, time spent alongside the berth, presumably working cargo or employed in another related activity, and, secondly, spent waiting in a queue for a berth to become available. The important variable element here is the level of traffic volume or tonnage throughput, a higher throughput creating increased costs. As costs per ton increase, the time vessels spend at the berth will move in the opposite direction, owing to the increased intensity of cargo working, causing the curve to gradually decline. The opposite effect is evident in ships' waiting time, which increases as volume increases. This waiting time has an important cost influence on shipowners, as can be seen from the total cost of port activities, which rises rapidly at the higher level of throughput. In other words the higher levels of berth occupation and working are the direct cause of the rapid rise in cost per ton.

In order to gain some understanding of the total costs incurred by shipping in-port, in relation to traffic volumes or throughput, it is necessary to bring together the total costs, the total ship's and port-time costs (that is, to combine the two previous Figures 13.4 and 13.5 into Figure 13.6).

The total cost-curve is a summation of port costs and ships' time. The total cost declines to a point where the two costs are equal at point B. It then increases rapidly, creating the classic economic U-shaped cost-curve. The rise relates solely, in its initial stages, to the increase in ships' port-time, as port costs are still contracting. This highlights the important point in this figure, the difference between point "B", minimum total costs, and point "A", minimum port costs. Both these points are dependent on the relationship between ships' waiting time and the level of occupation. What this combined figure emphasises is that the port authorities minimise their cost at larger throughputs than

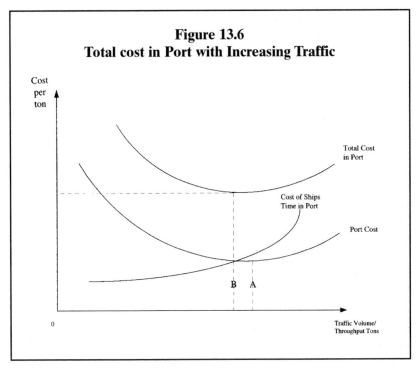

Figure 13.6
Total cost in Port with Increasing Traffic

Source: UNCTAD Berth Throughput United Nations 1973 p10

shipowners. In other words, port costs are improved only at the expense of the consumer of the service, the shipowner. Such high levels of throughput could also imply a tendency towards longer waiting times, queuing and congestion for vessels using the port facilities. In the above model, the port's authority or owners possess a valuable scarce resource. One of the indicators of this scarcity is the level of demand, shown by the length of queues and degree of congestion, which is discussed in the following section.

Congestion

Demand for port facilities, both from inland traffic and sea-borne movement, is erratic and random, making congestion a central feature of the economic activities of any port. Congestion can broadly be defined as a delay caused by waiting for other vessels to be worked. A particular feature of congestion is that it commonly affects the activities, not only of the supplier of the port facilities, but also of the consumer, for the vessel owners and shippers supply an important variable factor, that is, time. The period of delay for a shipowner is waiting for the vessel to arrive at its berth, or, for the shipper, the arrival of the cargo. In the short-run, there is no possibility of expanding, or, for that matter, contracting the size of the port to cater immediately for the random variations in the level of demand. In the immediate and short-run, port infrastructure has a finite capacity. Congestion begins at the point where users of the port facilities begin to inhibit the activities of other port users and there is evidence of limitations in berth capacity.

As argued, the major difficulties for port authorities is the random and volatile movement in demand. This causes uncertainty about the rate at which port services are required and creates, at one extreme, queuing and congestion and, at the other, low berth occupation. Congestion is created by the function of two variables, the volume of traffic, and time. As the number of vessels arriving at a port increases, the time taken in port activity also increases. In simple terms, queuing and congestion occur when too many vessels wish to use the limited amount of sea-ways or port space available. Such congestion slows the working of all vessels and, most importantly, each additional vessel imposes costs on all other vessels in the port, by increasing the length of queues or the level of congestion. Such increases in time are generally non-linear, in that the length of waiting time involved may increase dramatically, with only a small addition to the existing traffic.

Queues are caused by uncertainty about the rate and length of time which port facilities require, i.e. peaking in demand. Queuing increases, and its costs become particularly noticeable when the entry to a port exceeds the capacity of port facilities for the same unit of time. The total cost of such queuing can be expressed in terms of ships' queuing costs and port costs, as in Equation 13.2:

Equation 13.2

Total costs = (Ship's cost per × Cumulative total) + (Port costs × Port throughput)
unit of time of vessels in queue per shipload shipload per unit
and port of time

Simply, it consists of the ships' queuing costs and the port costs.

Another method of examining queuing is to compare the number of vessels arriving and departing from a port facility, and the length of time this takes. Wohli and Hendrickson [10] construct the following model, to illustrate what is termed the "Cumulative arrivals and departures at the transport facility", in this case modified to cover a port . This is illustrated in Figure 13.7.

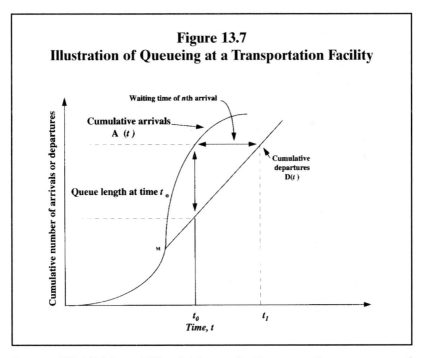

Figure 13.7
Illustration of Queueing at a Transportation Facility

Source: Wohli M. and Hendrickson C., Transport Investment and Pricing Principles, Chester, John Wiley and Son, 1984, p263

In this model, it is assumed that the arrivals are served in turn (that is, on a "first come first served" basis). The use of the term "cumulative" should be noted, as it serves to emphasise the importance of additional arrivals, and the subtraction of departing vessels, in the cumulative total. The (Y) axis is the cumulative number of vessels arriving and departing. The (X) axis indicates the units of time. Up to point M, there is no queuing, as arrivals and departures are served immediately by the port facility. Beyond that point, the cumulative arrivals begin to exceed the cumulative number of vessels departing the port. Here the distance queue (D) indicates the length of the queue (that is, the number of vessels waiting for the berth). This is matched by the length of waiting time t0 to t1. The number of vessels queuing will relate distinctly to the length of waiting time and lowering the former will obviously have an impact on the latter.

Initially, congestion will be examined, not in terms of a port, but in terms of some hypothetical sea-way. This is an imaginary navigational sea-way, passing through a single country, which will be the called the sea-gap. It is 50 nautical miles long and 4 nautical miles wide, and subject, at times, to high levels of congestion. This imaginary example will be used to confirm the empirical relationship as expressed in Equation 13.3 where the average transit time is a function of traffic volumes and the capacity of the sea-gap as follows[11]:

Equation 13.3 Congestion relationship

$T = f[N/K]$

where   T = the average transit time of the sea-gap

N = traffic volumes or density of traffic

K = the capacity of the sea-gap, i.e. the maximum number of

vessels it can accommodate in some period or unit of time

To convert the relationship to vessel movements, the sea-gap, like all such transits, will have a full capacity, which means that the vessel will pass through only until some maximum level is reached. Further, the law of diminishing returns will hold. Vessels crossing the sea-gap increase the congestion, by increasing the pressures imposed on other vessels. Each additional vessel is a 'vulnerable' input, increasing the transit times at all levels of traffic volumes beyond some maximum. This means that the number of additional vessels transiting the sea-gap increases proportionally to the number of additional hours required to produce an additional transit. This is illustrated inTable 13.1.

Table 13.1 Average and Marginal Transit Time per Vessel : sea-gap at Alternative Volume-Capacity Ratio

Volume-Capacity Ratio	Travel Time Average	Marginal
0	2.51	2.51
0.1	2.51	2.68
0.2	2.68	3.04
0.3	2.87	3.45
0.4	3.07	3.90
0.5	3.28	4.42
0.6	3.52	5.05
0.7	3.80	5.85
0.8	4.12	6.98
0.95	4.93	12.02

Source: H. Mohring[12]

The central point here is that the time taken increases as the number of vessels transiting the sea- gap increases. Also, the difference between the average and marginal transit times becomes greater. Thus, given a greater volume-capacity ratio, the marginal transit time will exceed the average, because the additional vessels will impose a time constraint on all other vessels transiting the sea-gap.

The information in Table 13.1 can be converted into a diagram as in Figure 13.8.[13]

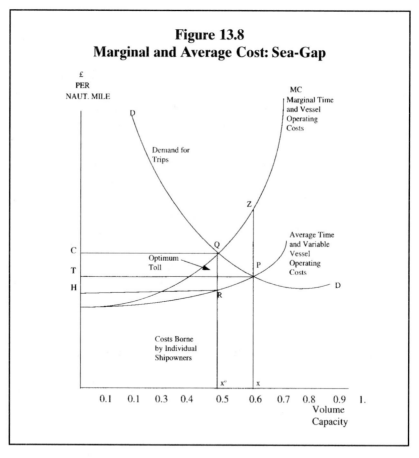

Figure 13.8
Marginal and Average Cost: Sea-Gap

Source: H. Mohring 13

The demand for transist DD is a normal downward-sloping curve. Average costs or time costs (AC) are essential to understanding the model. It shows that, when making the transist, vessel owners only consider their individual cost (that is, cost directly attributed to their transist bunkers, maintenance time and other costs). The marginal cost (time costs MC), indicate, at any transist level, the increase in the total cost for all vessels resulting from the marginal costs of the last vessel to join the flow.

As the number of vessels transisting the sea-gap increases, the volume-capacity ratio increases above zero. Congestion is apparent, and, as it increases, so does the divergence between AC and MC. Thus MC is equal to AC plus the congestion cost. For the transist flow X , the AC is P. It is argued that this is an inefficient or non-optimum use of the sea-ways, because of the fact that the costs imposed by the marginal vessel are P to Z. The argument is that the flow at X is excessive, and the aim should be to limit it to X0, an optimum flow. This optimum flow is where the demand-curve dissects the marginal cost-curve at Q. To achieve this, the government should place a toll on all vessels transisting the "sea-gap". The position of the toll is at X0. The toll is QR or (THQR). The optimum flow is where the demand-curve intersects the marginal cost-curve. At X0, each ship owner would recognise the cost of making the transit as AC, plus the toll (QR). Shipowners who value this transit at less than this would choose an alternative route or method. This means that the marginal journey would be cost plus toll. This would lessen the congestion X to X0. What should be noted is that congestion has been lowered (X0). It has not been eliminated completely, as, in resource terms, this would be too expensive an objective.

Taking a similar, if more complex, analysis of a port, the assumptions are:

1.   There is a more competitive shipping market.
2.   The port has only the usual regional or geographic monopoly power.

The marginal cost of loading vessels (that is, the last individual ship) is made up of port costs plus the time costs queuing and working and the delay costs that the marginal vessel imposes on all the other loaded vessels using the port per unit of time, Equation 13.4).

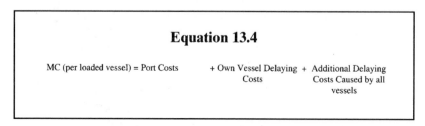

Equation 13.4

MC (per loaded vessel) = Port Costs   + Own Vessel Delaying   +   Additional Delaying
                                                  Costs   Costs Caused by all
                                                                                          vessels

This is shown diagrammatically in Figure 13.9.

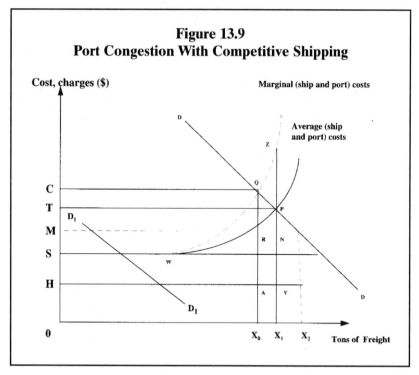

Figure 13.9
Port Congestion With Competitive Shipping

Source: Bennathane E. and Walters A.A., 14

The Y axis measures the cost and revenue from port charges and freight rates. The X axis indicates the total trade (or the traffic flow that is both for exports and imports) in tons. The demand curve represents demand for shipping, including that for port services. At demand level D_1D_1 there is no congestion. It is below point W that congestion begins and, therefore, at demand level DD, there is substantial congestion. Shipowners will have expenses, in addition to freight charges. They therefore surcharge shippers or buyers for the extra time and port charges caused by these delays. OH is the port charges per ton at a constant level, regardless of unused capacity or the presence of congestion. Without the presence of congestion below W (X^2), ships operating costs are HS. Beyond W, they begin to rise through R and P. There is substantial demand present, indicated by DD, and the surcharge is PM per ton . Such surcharges fail to adequately cover the true economic cost of additional tonnage throughput. The true cost is shown as tonnage at level XO. It is the area under MC (that is, WQZ) and above AC (that is, WP). The congestion cost at X, is the shaded area QZP. As argued in the earlier model, congestion increases as the vertical distance between AC and MC increases, MC being the true cost level of all vessels in the port beyond WX2. Should the objective be to limit the extent of the congestion and insist the true cost of using the port would be paid for, a toll of QR (or MC) at QZ would be established.

"This analysis corresponds precisely to the theory of highway congestion. The policy of charging conventional prices for the service of the ports generates the same sort of congestion that arises on urban streets and some intercity highways and, of course, the solution is the same. The port should raise its charges from OH per ton, by RQ per ton, where the RQ per ton represents the congestion's levy of the port. Clearly, if the port's levies are Q per ton, the shipowners will not exact the congestion surcharge PN that they imposed under the congestion conditions at X1 and price P. With traffic at XO tons, shipowners' average cost (excluding the port congestion levy) will be 0M per ton. Competition in the shipping industry will ensure that they charge no more than this for their freight services. By levying the congestion toll of RQ per ton, the port authorities will avoid the waste of providing services at a price less than the cost of producing them. This waste of congestion at X, is shown by the shaded area QPZ." [15]

Here, as with the "sea-gap" example, those controlling the ports wish to limit the extent of queuing and ease congestion to a level indicated by X. This does not aim to completely eradicate congestion, because of the resource costs implications of such a policy.

Congestion occurs when berth capacity is insufficient to deal with the number of vessels wishing to use the port facilities. Queues develop as a result of the congestion, imposing costs on the ships in terms of time, and on the ports in terms of throughput. The models developed show that this problem is alleviated, in part, by the imposition of a port toll.

Summary

Ports perform a crucial function in the maritime industry, being responsible for the transfer of goods between land and sea transport. The efficient operation of the port relies on the reduction of "slack" time, or excess capacity, although some "slack" is necessary to deal with unexpected demand. Two different philosophies influence port operations and investment; the European and the Anglo-Saxon. The former sees the port as a public service, in which the State plays a major role, whereas the latter advocates a commercial approach. These extreme philosophies do not exist in practice, but countries do adopt elements which influence their investment decisions. Port investment levels are necessarily high, affording immediate benefits to the consumer. For the investor, however, the returns are made much later, when income finally exceeds the initial costs, as shown by the "pay-back" approach. Total port costs consist of fixed and variable costs, which can be minimised at a certain level of tonnage throughput. Ports impose a cost on ships, in terms of time spent in the berth and time spent waiting for a berth. Total ship costs are also minimised at a certain level of tonnage throughput, but a lower level than that for the port authorities. Finally, it can be shown that waiting time causes congestion and queuing, which attract their own costs. Port authorities can alleviate this by the imposition of a toll.

Further Reading

Bennathan, E., and Walters A.A., 'Port Pricing and Investment Policies for Developing Countries' Oxford, Oxford University Press 1979.
Jansson J.O., Shneerson D.'Port Economics' Cambridge Massachusetts, MIT Press 1982.
UNCTAD 'Berth Throughput', United Nations, New York, 1975
UNCTAD 'Port Development', United Nations, New York, 1985

---

[1] See Chapter 3
[2] J. O. Jansson & D.Shneerson Port Economics, Massachusetts MIT Press
Cambridge
1982, p10.
[3] UNCTAD Port Pricing, New York, United Nations,1975.
[4] ibid para 37.
[5] European Parliament, European Seaport Policy, Transport Series 7,
1993 p27.
[6] See Chapter I Introduction
[7] op. cit. UNCTAD, 1975.
[8] ibid. p29.
[9] op. cit. Jansson, J. O., and Shneerson, D.
[10] Wohli, M and Hendrikson, C. Transport Investment and Pricing Principles,
Chester. John Wiley and Son. 1984 p.263.
Publishing Company,
[11] H. Mohring 'Transport Economics, Cambridge, Massachusetts, Ballinger
Publishing Company,
1976,pp.16-19.
[12] H. Mohring op. cit. p21.
[13] ibid p19.
[14] Bennathan, E.,and Walters A. A., 'Port Pricing and Investment Policy for
Developing Countries' Oxford, Oxford University Press, 1979, p66.
15 ibid. p68.

BIBLIOGRAPHY

Economic and Transport Economics Books:

Baumol W.J. *'Business Behaviour, Value, Growth'* - Revised Edition New York, Harcourtt Brace and World 1967.

Begg D. Fischer S. and Rudiger D. *'Economics'* 5th Edition, London. McGraw Hill, 1997.

Bonavia M.R. *'The Economics of Transport'*, Cambridge, Cambridge University Press, 1954.

Button K.J. *'Transport Economics'*, 2nd Edition, London, Heineman, 1993.

Garb G., *'Microeconomics: Theory, Applications, Innovations'* London, Macmillan 1981.

Gwilliam K.M. and P.J. Mackie, *'Economics and Transport Policy'*. London, George Allan and Unwin Ltd, 1980.

K.E. Boulding Economic Analysis Vol.1. *'Microeconomics'* First Edition, New York, Harper and Rowe, 1966.

Marshall A., *'Principles of Economics'*, London, Macmillan & Co. Ltd.1890

McConville J. (ed), *'Transport Regulation Matter'*, London, Pinter 1997

Mohring H., *'Transport Economic'* Cambridge, Massachusetts, Ballinger Publishing Company, 1976.

Sloman J. *'Economics'*, London, 3rd Edition, Prentice Hall, 1997

Stubbs P.C., W.J. Tyson and M.O. Dalvi, *'Transport Economics'*, Revised Edition, London, Charles Allen Unwin, 1984

Wohli M. and C. Hendrickson, *'Transportation, Investment and Pricing Principles'*,Chichester, John Wiley and Son, 1984.

Maritime Economics and Bibliographies

Barker J.R. and Brandwein R., *'The United States Merchant Merchant Marine in National Perspective'*, Massachusetts, Lexicon Books, H.H. Chese & Co.1977.

Bennathan E., and Walters A.A., *'Port Pricing and Investment Policies for Developing Countries',* Oxford University Press 1979.

Bennathan E. and Walters A.A., *'The Economics of Ocean Freight Rates'*, London,F.A. Peager Ltd, 1976.

Buxton I.L., *'Engineering Economics and Ship Design'*, Wallsend, The British Shipping Research Association, 1971

Deakin B.M. with Seward T., *'Shipping Conferences': A Study of Their Origins Development and Economic Practices'.* Cambridge, University of Cambridge Press, 1973.

Devanny J.W. *'A Model of the Tanker Charter Market and a Related Dynamic Program'* in Lorange p. *et al* Shipping Management. The Hague, Maritime Economics Research Centre, 1993.

Erikson I.B.E., *'The Demand for Bulk Ship Services'* in E. Hope. Studios in Shipping Economics. Bergen, Norwegian School of Economics and Business, 1982.

Evans J.J. and Marlow P.B., *'Quantative Methods in Maritime Economics'* (2nd Edition), London, Fairplay Publications, 1990

Goodwin E.M. and Kemp J.F. *'Marine Statistics - Theory and Practice'*, London, Stanford Maritime Ltd, 1979.

Gripaious H., *'Tramp Shipping',* London, Thomas Nelson and Son Ltd., 1959.

Hawkings J.E., *'Shipping Subsidies and the Balance of Payments'*, London, Lloyd's of London Press, 1989.

Hope Einar (ed). *'Studies in Shipping Economics: In honour of Professor Arnljot Stromme Svendsen'*. Oslo, Bedriftsokonomens Forlag A/S, 1981.

Jansson J.O. and Shneerson D., *'Port Economics'* Cambridge, Massachusetts, MIT Press 1982.

Jansson J.O. and Shneerson D., *'Liner Shipping Economics'*. London, Chapman and Hall, 1987.

Koopmans T.C., *'Tanker Freight Rates and Tankship Building'*. Netherlands, Garlem, 1939.

Lawrence S.A., *'International Sea Transport'*, Toronto, Lexicon Books, 1972.

McConville J. *'United Kingdom Seafarers: Their Employment Potential. A Monograph'* London, The Marine Society, 1995.

McConville J. and Rickaby G., *'Shipping Business and Maritime Economics'*. Annotated International Bibliography, London, Mansell, 1995.

McConville J., Glen D.R., Dowden J. *'United Kingdom Seafarers Analysis 1997'* London, London Guildhall University 1998.

Metaxas B.N. *'Economics of Tramp Shipping'* London, The Athlone Press, 1971.

Nagatsuka, Seiji. *'The Demand and Supply of Grain in the World and its Impact on Shipping'*. Tokyo, Japan Maritime Research Institute, 1986.

Nagatsuka Seiji., *'Study About the Extension of the Scrapping Age of Tankers: Problems and Measures as Viewed from Shipping and Shipbuilding'*. Tokyo, Japan Maritime Research Institute, 1989.

Norman V.D. *'Market Strategies in Bulk Shipping'* in Hope E. Studies in Shipping Economics, Oslo, Bedriftsokonomens, Forlag A/S, 1981.

O'Loughlin C., *'The Economics of Sea Transport'* Oxford, Pergamon Press, 1967.

Rogers, P., Strange J. and Studd B., *'Coal: Carriage By Sea'*, 2nd Edition, London: Lloyd's of London Press, 1997.

Shimojo T., *'Economic Analysis of Shipping Freights'*.Kobe, Research Institute for Economic and Business Administration, Kobe University, 1979.

Sletmo G.K. and Williams E.W. *'Liner Conferences in the Container Age'*, *US Policy at Sea*, New York, Macmillan, 1981.

Stopford M., *'Maritime Economics'*, 2nd Edition, London, Routledges 1997.

Sturmey S.G., *'British Shipping and World Competition'*. London, Athlone Press, 1962.

Sturmey S.G., *'Shipping Economic Collected Papers'*. London, Macmillan, 1975.

Tinbergen J., *'Selected Papers'* L.H. Klaasen Editor, *et al* Amsterdam, Netherlands, North Holland Publishing Company, 1959.

Thornburn T. *'Supply and Demand of Water Transport'*, Stockholm, FF1 Report, 1960.

Tusiai M., *'The Petroleum Shipping Industry'* (Volume I&II), Oklahoma, Penwell Publishing Co., 1996.

Volk B., *'Shipping Investment in Recession'* Breman, Institute of Shipping Economic, 1984.

Yeats, Alexander J., *'Shipping and Development Policy: An integrated assessment'*. New York, Praeger Publishers, 1981.

Zannetos Z.S., *'The Theory of Oil Tankship Rates'*, Massachusetts, The MIT Press 1966.

Articles and Papers

Alderton P.M., *'When to Lay-Up: The Theory and Practice'*, Transport Discussion Paper PDB, City of London Polytechnic, 1988.

Bronfenbrenner M., *'Notes of the Elasticity of Derived Demand'*. Oxford Economic Papers, Volume 13, 1961.

Dabrowski K., *'Comments on the Mechanisms of the World Shipping Market'* Maritime Policy and Management, Vol.8(2), 1981.

Edmond E.D.A. and Maggs R.P., *'Container Ship Turnaround Time at UK Ports'*. Maritime Policy and Management, Vol.4, (1), 1976.

Evans J.J., *'Concerning the Levels of Liner Freight Rates'*, Maritime Policy and Management, Vol.9, (2), 1982.

Glen D.R., *'The Emergence of Differentiation in Oil Tanker Markets'*. 1970-1978.
Maritime Policy and Management, 17, (4) 1990.

Goss R.O., *'Economics and the International Regime for Shipping'*, Maritime Policy and Management, 11(2), 1984.

Heaver T.D., *'A Theory of Shipping Conference Pricing and Policies'*, Maritime Studies and Management, Vol.1, (1) 1973.

Kalindaga Y.C., *'Estimation of Capacity Utilization in World Shipping'* Maritime Policy and Management, 17(1), 1990.

Kendall P.M.K, *'A Theory of Optimum Ship Size'*, Journal of Transport Economics and Policy, Vol.6 (2) 1972.

Laing E.T., *'Shipping Freight Rates For Developing Countries: Who Ultimately Pays?'*. Journal of Transport Economics and Policy X1(3), 1977.

Metaxas B.N., *'The Future of the Tramp Shipping Industry'*, Journal of Transport Economics & Policy, V1(3) 1972.

Svendsen A.S., *'Factors Determining Lay-Up Of Ships'*. The Institute of Economics, Norwegian School of Economics and Business Administration, Bergen, Norway, December 1957, paper No.7.

Zerby J.A. and Conlon R.M. *'An Analysis of Capacity Utilisation in Liner Shipping'* Journal of Transport Economics and Policy XII (1), 1978

Government and Official Reports

Committee of Inquiry into Shipping, May 1970. Chaired by the Viscount Rochdale (The Rochdale Inquiry), London H.M.S.O., CMMD 4337.

'European Parliament, European Seaport Policy', Transport Series 7, 1973.

Transport Committee of the House of Commons (1986-87). *'Decline in the UK Registered Merchant Fleet'*, London, HMSO

Transport Committee of the House of Commons (1987-88) *'Decline in the UK Registered Merchant Fleet'*, London, HMSO

United Nations *'Freight Markets and The Level and Structure of Freight Rates'*, New York, UNCTAD 1969

UNCTAD *'Liner Conferences System'* New York, United Nations, 1970.

UNCTAD *'Berth Throughput'*, New York, United Nations, 1975.

UNCTAD *'Bulking of Cargoes'* New York, United Nations, 1975.

Journals and Annual Report

Lloyds Shipping Economist (LSE) (Monthly).

Maritime Policy and Management. An International Journal of Shipping and Port Research. Taylor and Francis (Quarterly).

Maritime Transport, OECD (Annual).

UNTAD 'Review of Maritime Transport' (Annual).

Institute of Shipping Economic and Logistics (ISL) Bremen. (Monthly).

GLOSSARY

Absolute advantage:
An individual has an absolute advantage in the production of two goods if, by using the same quantities of inputs, that person can produce more of both goods than another individual. A country capable of producing specific goods or services using fewer resources (per unit of output and times) than other countries.

Alongside:
When a vessel standing at the quay or jetty, the cargo is moved from ship direct to surface of quay (or in opposite direction).

Arc elasticity of demand:
The value of elasticity of demand
between two points calculated on the basis of the average price method.

Average total cost (ATC):
Total cost divided by the quantity of a good or service produced in a given time period.

Ballast:
Materials, solid or liquid, carried solely for purposes of stability or to immerse the propeller sufficiently. A ship is said to be 'in ballast' when she is carrying ballast but no cargo.

Barriers to entry:
Impediments protecting a firm from competition from new entrants. They are obstacles that make it difficult or impossible for would be producers to enter a market.

Berth:
Section of quay (pier, wharf, or jetty) notionally designed to accommodate one vessel and including a section of the surface over which labour, equipment, and cargo move to and from the vessel.

Break-bulk Cargo:
Cargo packed in separate packages (lots or consignments) or individual pieces of cargo, loaded, stowed, and unloaded individually.

Bulk Carriers:
A single deck dry cargo ship designed to carry bulk, usually non-liquid cargo.

Cabotage:
Coastal trade.

Capital:
A factor of production, being a stock of resources which have been produced in the past, or involve a sacrifice of present consumption , to enhance productivity and in so doing increase utility. The word in economics means 'real capital', physical goods, ships, bridges, ports, roads etc.

Cartel:
A group of firms that act as if they were a 'single seller'. By entering into a collusive agreement to control or restrict output so as to increase profit, or price.

Ceteris paribus:
Other things being equal. The assumption of nothing else changing, all other relevant things remaining the same.

Channel:
Passage of water leading to the port that is normally dredged and policed by the port authority.

Charter:
A person who hires a ship.

Charter Rate:
Payment by charterer (such as cargo owner) to shipowner for the charter of the vessel. It is determined by market conditions and terms of charter.

Chemical tanker:
Vessel constructed and arranged for carrying hazardous cargoes in special tanks.

Cost + insurance + freight (c.i.f.):
Terms of sale where the price quoted by the vendor includes the cost of delivering the goods to destination. He or she is responsible for arranging their transport and insurance during transit.

Comparative advantage:
A country has a comparative advantage in an activity if that country can perform the activity at a lower opportunity cost than other countries. The ability of a country to produce a particular good or service at a lower opportunity cost than other trading countries.

Competitive market:
A market in which no buyer or seller has market power. They are all "Price Takers".

Conference (liner conference):
Any type of formal or informal agreement between shipowners which restricts competition. A combination (technically, a cartel) of shipping companies (or owners) which sets common liner freight rates on a particular route and which regulates the provision of services.

Container Ship (Full Container):
A ship designed or adapted for the carriage of containers in cellular holds. That is a vessel fitted throughout with fixed or portable cell guides for the carriage of containers above and below the weather deck.

Contract of affreightment:
Commonly used, to cover a contract between the shipper and ship operator under which the latter undertakes to carry specified quantities of a bulk commodity on a particular route or routes over a given period of time, using ships of his or her own choice which are not necessarily specified in the contract.

Cross trades:
Business undertaken by the ships of a nationality (flag) other than those of the countries at either end of the trading voyage.

Dead weight ton (dwt):
Unit of measurement of a ship's size. The deadweight tonnage of a ship is the weight, in long tons, of cargo, fuel, stores etc., which it is able to carry at the applicable loadline. The weight in long tons that a vessel can carry when full laden.

Deep sea trades:
All trades entailing voyages outside coastal and short sea trading areas.

Deferred rebate system:
An arrangement agreed between members of a conference for a rebate to be paid in arrears to a shipper provided that he or she has continued to use, exclusively, the services of the lines which are members of the conference.

Demand:
A willingness and ability to pay for some amount of a good or service. The quantities of an economic good or services that buyers will be prepared to purchase, within a specific time, at various freight rate (price).

Depreciation:
The decrease in the value of capital stock or of a durable factor that results from wear and tear, obsolescence and the passage of time.

Derived demand:
Demand for an item not for its own sake but for use in the production of goods and services. Demand which arises from the wish to satisfy the demand for another commodity or service. The demand for a factor of production that depends on the demand for another good or service. The greater the demand for the final product, the greater the demand for the factor of

production. Simply, no one wants capital goods, such as ship for its own sake, but for the final consumer good they help to produce. (The demand for a tanker is the demand oil and its products).

Dry cargo:
Merchandise other than liquid carried in bulk.

Dry cargo ship:
A vessel which carries all cargoes in bulk, excluding liquid cargoes.

Duopoly:
A market structure which contains exactly two firms or producers of a good or service.

Dual rate contact system:
An arrangement agreed between members of a conference for an immediate rebate to be given to a shipper (by making a deduction from the freight account) if he or she contracts to use exclusively the services of members of that conference for all his or her goods passing on the route it covers.

Economic cost:
The value of all resources used to produce a good or service.

Economic model:
An analysis of certain aspects of the economic world that includes only those features of the world that are required for the purpose at hand.

Economics of scale:
They are said to exist when expansion of the scale of productive capacity of a firm or industry causes total production costs to increase less than proportionately with output. It causes the average cost of production to decline as output increases. Diseconomies of scale exist when the average cost rises with increased output.

Elasticity:
The responsiveness of a change in one variable to another. For example, the responsiveness of quantity demanded (or supplied) to a change in a given variable (such as own price, the price of another good or individual income).

Elastic of demand:
Where a small percentage change in price results in a proportionately larger change in the quantity demanded. (elasticity greater than one)

Elasticity of supply:
The responsiveness of the quantity supplied of a good or service to a change in its price. The percentage change in quantity supplied divided by the percentage change in price that brought it about.

Entrepreneur (or Enterprise)
These terms are sometimes interchangeable. It is the name given in theory to organisation and management of production.

Equilibrium:
A situation in which the forces, say of demand and supply, making for changes in opposing directions are in balance. A state in which there is no net tendency to change.

Equilibrium price:
The price at which the quantity of a good or service demanded in a given time period equals the quantity supplied.

Exports:
Goods and services a country sells to foreign buyers.

Factors of production:
Human and non human resources used in the production of economic goods and services. Traditionally classified as Land, Labour, Capital and Enterprise with some disagreement concerning the latter's inclusion. An economy's productive resources.

Feeder (Service):
Transport of containers which are first carried by the main line container vessel to a port of transhipment, unloaded, and then loaded on a (smaller) vessel for feeding to a further port. Feeder service implies transhipment.

Fixed cost (F.C):
The cost of a fixed input; a cost that is independent of any level of output. Costs that do not change when the rate of output is altered.

Fixed exchange rate:
A system in which the value of a country's currency is pegged by the country's central bank.

Flag of registration:
Flag of the country in which a ship is registered.

Free on Board (f.o.b.):
Terms of sale where the price quoted by the vendor includes all expenses up too and including the cost of loading the goods on to a vessel of the purchaser' choice. In the case of ocean carriage it means the value of the goods (including the value of packing) when placed on board the vessel. It includes such charges as the shipper had to pay to the port but excludes cargo insurance and freight and corresponds only approximately to market value in the exporting country.

Freight tons:
A heterogeneous unit for counting cargo or traffic in liner shipping. It is based on the rules by which freight rates are assessed. For cargo paid for by weight tons, the weight tone (long, short, or metric) is a freight ton. For cargo paid for by measurement tons (for example, 40 cubic feet), the measurement ton is the freight ton.

General Cargo:
Cargo, not homogeneous in bulk, which consist of individual units or packages (parcels)

General Cargo Ship:
Single or multi-deck general dry cargo vessel with facilities for loading/discharging cargo.

Gross registered ton (grt):
Gross registered tonnage. A measure of the total space of a vessel in terms of 100 cubic feet (equivalent tons) including mid-deck, between deck, and the closed-in spaces above the upper deck, less certain exemptions. The GRT of most of the world's ships is recorded in Lloyds Register.

Indifference curve map :
A map of an individual's utility function showing a consumer is indifferent, between any collection of the two goods represented by point on a single curve. With any point on a higher curve being preferred to any point on a lower curve.

Labour:
One of the primary factors of production. It embodies all human economic effort, both physical and mental contributing to the production of wealth, in the creation of utility.

Land:
A factor of production embracing all natural recourses. Free and useful gifts of nature including all minerals. It is original new materials for economic production.

Law of demand:
The quantity of a good or service demanded in a given time period increases (decreases) as its price falls (rises).

Law of Diminishing Returns: (Law of Variable Proportions - Law of Proportionate Returns)
The hypothesis is that if successive increments of one factor of production are employed in conjunction with a constant amount of all factors, these increments will, after a point yield successively smaller and smaller additions to total output. A law stating that the marginal physical product of a variable input declines as more of it is employed with a given quantity of other fixed inputs

Law of supply:
The quantity of a good or service supplied in a given time period increases (decreases) as its price increase (decreases).

Lay-up:
The temporary withdrawal of tonnage (laid up) by shipowners from freight earning activity. This occurs during periods of depressed freight rates when trading is no longer commercially viable.

Liner:
A ship engaged in providing a regular service for passengers and/or cargo on given routes.

Liquid gas tanker:
Vessel constructed and arranged for the carriage of liquefied gases either in integral tanks or independent tanks under pressure or refrigerated.

Long-run:
A period of time long enough for all inputs to be varied, there are no fixed costs. A firm can vary the quantity of all its productive resources.

Management Company:
A company, which provides specialised services for the management of ships which it does not own itself.

Marginal:
The additional unit produced and consumed. It is the margin, a unitary change increase or decrease in an economic aggregate.

Marginal cost (MC)
The additional cost increased (decreased) producing (or not) one more unit of output of a good or service. It is the increase in total cost divided by the increase in output.

Marginal Revenue (MR):
The additional revenue obtained by a firm when it is able to sell one more unit of output, be it goods or services.

Net Register Ton(NRT):

A traditional unit of measurement of a ship's size which is little used now. It is derived from the gross tonnage by deducting spaces for crew accommodation, propelling machinery and fuel. Net registering tonnage, the **GRT** minus the spaces that are non-earning, machinery, permanent bunkers, water ballast, and crew quarters. Over the range 0 - 6,000 **NRT** there is a reasonably good correlation between **NRT** and **DWT: DWT = 2.5 NRT.**

Opportunity or Alternative cost doctrine:

The cost of using productive resources for a certain purpose, measured by the benefit given up by not using them in their best alternative use. It is the cost of other goods which must be sacrificed to gain more of a particular good.

Ore carrier (Bulk carrier):

Dry cargo vessel, one deck, strengthening for ore.

Ore/Bulk/Oil Carrier (OBO):

A multi purpose ship developed in recent years which is capable of carrying full cargoes of either ore, other bulked dry cargo or oil. That is a combination bulk carrier arranged for the carriage of either bulk dry cargoes or liquid cargoes often in the same cargo spaces but not simultaneously.

Passenger:

Vessel which carries more than 12 fare paying passengers whether berthed or unberthed.

Port dues:

A charge levied by certain ports on the vessel or cargo.

Production Possibilities Curve: (Transformation Curve)

A curve showing all the alternative quantities of output which can be produced with fixed amounts of productive factors. A curve indicating how the production of one good 'A', can by reducing the output of 'A' and transferring the resources used in the production of 'B'.

Reefer:
Specialised dry cargo vessel with 80% or more insulated cargo space.

RoRo Cargo/RoRo Passenger:
Vessel arranged for Roll-on Roll-off loading/discharging of vehicles (road and/or rail) as cargo and /or passenger conveyances. Cargo carried in wheeled containers or wheeled trailers aboard and moving on to the ship and off it on wheels, usually over ramps.

Ship broker:
A person engaged in buying or selling ships, or as intermediary either between seller and purchaser of ships or between consignors of cargo and shipowners. An intermediary in the charting of ships. A ship's agent.

Short-run industry supply curve:
A curve that shows how the relative quantity supplied by the industry varies as the market price varies assuming the plant size of each firm and the number of firms in the industry remain the same. In perfect competition it is the horizontal sum of marginal cost curves (MC) above the level of average variable costs (AVC) of all firms in an industry.

Specialised Carrier (Special Ship):
A cargo vessel specially designed for the carriage of particular cargoes.

Stevedore:
Labour employed to load and unload cargo and, by transference, the organiser of this work. In may ports, stevedores only work aboard ships for the account of vessel or cargo-owners, and work ashore is done by the port's labour.

Substitute:
Any good or service that can be used in place of another good or service.

Substitution effect:
The effect of a change in quantity demanded of a good or service resulting from a change in the commodity's relative price, eliminating the effect of the price change on real income.

Supply curve:
A graphical representation showing the relationship between the quantity of a good supplied and the price of a good, *ceteris paribus.*

Tanker:
Single-deck vessel constructed and arranged for the carriage of liquid cargoes in tanks mainly crude oil or non-hazardous refined products. Tankers are sometimes used to carry grain.

Tariff:
A tax duty on an import imposed by the government of the importing country

Terms of trade:
The rate at which goods are exchanged. It is the ratio of the average price of a country's exports to the average price of its imports.

TEU:
Twenty-foot equivalent unit. Standard unit for counting (equivalent) containers of various dimensions: 20 x8 x 8 feet; in other words, a 20- foot equivalent container.

Through transport system:
An integrated door-to door system for moving cargo from producer to customer.

Total cost (TC):
The market value of all resources used to produce a good or service. Usually divided into fixed and variable costs.

Total fixed costs (TFC):
Are the total of a firm's costs that do not vary with output in the short-run.

Total revenue (TR):
The value of a firm's sales of its product. It is calculated as the price of the good multiplied by the quantity sold in a given time period.

Total variable costs (TVC):
The total of those of the firm's costs that do vary in the short-run the cost of variable resources.

Total utility:
The total satisfaction or benefit that a person derived from consuming some amount of a good or service.

Ton miles:
A measure of a unit of transport service, calculated by dividing the cargo tonnage over distance covered. For example three tons of cargo conveyed 75 nautical miles will produce 225 ton miles.

Trade deficit:
The amount by which the value of a country of import exceeds the value of its exports, in a given time period.

Trade surplus:
The amount by which the value of a country's exports exceeds the value of imports, in a given time period.

Tramp Ship:
A dry cargo ship which is not being used for the provision of a regular services and usually finds employment in the carriage of homogeneous dry cargoes in bulk. The two main sub-divisions are general purpose tramps (usually multi-deck) and bulk carriers. They are non -scheduled, nonconference vessels.

'Tween deck:
The first continuous deck below the main deck of the ship A ship with more than three decks has an upper and lower 'tween deck. The gap between the 'tween deck and the main deck above is known as the 'tween deck

Uncertainty:
A situation in which more than one individual event might occur but it is not known which of them will occur.

Utility:
The ability of a good or service to satisfy a want. The satisfaction that an individual or household receives from consumption.

Variable cost (VC):
Cost of production that will vary with the output level. It is the cost of a variable input.

INDEX

415

419